EVEN ME
EVEN YOU

A believer's walk out of darkness back into the Light

KEN BURKHALTER

Scrolls of Zebulon, LLC
Mobile, Alabama

Scrolls of Zebulon, LLC
P.O. Box 190309
Mobile, Alabama, USA
ScrollsOfZebulon.com
For inquiries, contact info@scrollsofzebulon.com

Cover and Interior Design by Sarah Smith
Edited by Layne Prince

All Scripture quotations are from the New American Standard (NASB) translation unless otherwise noted.

Scripture quotations taken from the (NASB®) New American Standard Bible®, Copyright © 1960, 1971, 1977, 1995, 2020 by The Lockman Foundation. Used by permission. All rights reserved. www.lockman.org

Scripture quotations marked KJV are from the Holy Bible, King James Version (Authorized Version). First published in 1611. Quoted from the KJV Classic Reference Bible, Copyright © 1983 by The Zondervan Corporation.

Scripture quotations marked (NLT) are taken from the Holy Bible, New Living Translation, copyright ©1996, 2004, 2015 by Tyndale House Foundation. Used by permission of Tyndale House Publishers, Carol Stream, Illinois 60188. All rights reserved.

Scripture quotations marked (NIV) are taken from the Holy Bible, New International Version®, NIV®. Copyright © 1973, 1978, 1984, 2011 by Biblica, Inc.® Used by permission of Zondervan. All rights reserved worldwide. www.zondervan.com The "NIV" and "New International Version" are trademarks registered in the United States Patent and Trademark Office by Biblica, Inc.®

Scripture quotations marked (ESV) are from the ESV® Bible (The Holy Bible, English Standard Version®), Copyright © 2001 by Crossway, a publishing ministry of Good News Publishers. Used by permission. All rights reserved.

Scripture quotations marked (AMP) are from The Amplified Bible, Old Testament copyright © 1965, 1987 by the Zondervan Corporation. The Amplified Bible, New Testament copyright © 1954, 1958, 1987 by The Lockman Foundation. Used by permission. All rights reserved. www.Lockman.org.

Scripture quotations taken from the Amplified® Bible (AMPC), Copyright © 1954, 1958, 1962, 1964, 1965, 1987 by The Lockman Foundation. Used by permission. www.Lockman.org.

Scripture quotations marked (MSG) are taken from The Message. Copyright © 1993, 1994, 1995, 1996, 2000, 2001, 2002, 2003 by Eugene H. Peterson. Used by permission of NavPress Publishing Group. www.messagebible.com.

Scripture quotations marked (AHLB) are taken from the Ancient Hebrew Lexicon Bible. Copyright © 2018 by Jeff Brenner.

Scripture quotations marked (WT) are taken from The New Testament: An Expanded Translation. Copyright © 1961 by Kenneth S. Wuest.

Scripture quotations marked (JBP) are taken from The New Testament in Modern English, J.B. Phillips, 1962 edition, published by HarperCollins.

Scripture quotations marked (NKJV) are taken from the New King James Version®. Copyright © 1982 by Thomas Nelson. Used by permission. All rights reserved.

Scripture quotations marked (TV) are taken from The Voice™. Copyright © 2012 by Ecclesia Bible Society. Used by permission. All rights reserved.

Scripture quotations marked (SEAET) are taken from The Artscroll English Tanach: Stone Edition. Copyright © 2011 by Rabbi Nosson Scherman, Mesorah Publications.

Scripture quotations marked (TLV) are taken from the Tree of Life Version. Copyright © 2015 by The Messianic Jewish Family Bible Society.

Scripture quotations marked (TPT) are from The Passion Translation®. Copyright © 2017, 2018 by Passion & Fire Ministries, Inc. Used by permission. All rights reserved. ThePassionTranslation.com.

ISBN: 978-1-7346430-9-1
LCCN: 2022905335
For Worldwide Distribution

Printed in the USA

To Ruthie, who was faithful to God's calling to fight for me
despite my sin, and who saw a future I could not imagine.
To James and Bill, who found it in their hearts to forgive a
father who failed them.
Their faith in a love I could not fathom saved me
from a fate I could not endure. In them I see God's grace,
and in their love, His mercy.

Darrell and Connie,

I thank Father for your understanding and forgiving hearts. While the news Ruthie and I shared is difficult, your grace to both of us was another measure of God's mercy. This is what He does for overcomers, those who choose to walk out of darkness no matter the cost. I pray this mercy and grace will be in you as well, and His peace your constant companion.

Ken

Table of Contents

EDITORIAL NOTE

The reader will note that there are instances where the rules of capitalization have been suspended. This is on purpose. Virtue words which refer to a power such as Truth, Mercy, or Grace are capitalized when used as a noun. The intent in these cases is to magnify God's glory, power, and character.

ACKNOWLEDGMENTS

I can divide my adolescence and adulthood into two spheres: wandering lost in the desert of sin and drinking in the sweet wine of redemption and restoration. There are numerous people who invested themselves in my life, many of whom I desire to look in the eye and thank in person but who are now gone. I know with assurance that they hear my prayers of thanks. Then there are those who in recent years played a willing and active role in my journey. These fall into three groups.

The first group is comprised of a small body of believers in Southern California's High Desert. Here I experienced my first meaningful exposure to studying the Word of God through Hebrew language and thought. This small group of faithful people humbled me, accepted me as I was, and believed in me when I refused to acknowledge what I was and bow in surrender. It was here that I found deliverance and freedom. Ruthie and I have since moved on, but these saints will always be in my heart.

Pastor Mike opened my heart and mind to the real Word of God, laying out the power of the ancient language to describe the depth of God's love for us. He also challenged me to stand against the evil in my life through his unbending truth. I knew that he knew, and it was he whom God used as the instrument of my deliverance. I am forever thankful.

Will and Syl were the young couple who mentored us at the most critical point of our marriage with their insight and understanding, teaching and encouragement, and boldness in confronting me, all of which brought the point of decision. They are the ones who opened the door; without them, I may never have taken the step that changes everything.

Georgia, who was and is a faithful encourager and friend, knew what I was before I confessed and loved me anyway. She was a stalwart support for Ruthie through the hardest of times. A prophet and dear friend, she never gave up on us and never accused me. All she did was love us with the love God put in her heart, and it is a big love.

Toni is another of the High Desert saints. It was Toni who sent me a text message late one evening just before Christmas. It was a message straight from God, and it put the fear of God into my heart. She is another who counseled and supported Ruthie when she did not believe there was hope for our marriage. Toni is a valiant warrior for people trapped in and coming out of horrible circumstances, and yet another with the heart of God. I am thankful for her love and for reading the second draft and contributing her encouragement and wisdom.

And what can I say about Steve? I saw in him a man who had overcome great evil in his life and who paid a heavy price, yet his joy in the Lord is all he cares to talk about. This humble giant has a big voice and a bigger heart. His faith uplifts me. One night, I got out of my seat and joined him in worshiping our Lord without concern for how proper I appeared and discovered the indescribable joy of complete abandonment to God.

The second group includes others who contributed, most of whom I did not know when my journey started.

Lynette is a good friend whom I met after my deliverance when I was beginning to work through things in my life. A veteran of her own journey, she was a good sounding board, advice giver, and friend to both Ruthie and me. And she agreed to proofread the drafts as I worked my way through the book. Her insight, wisdom, prayer, and friendship contributed much to this book, and I am thankful for her partnership in it.

Denny and Carol saw immediately and understood exactly what I was hiding yet loved me without judging me. Their counseling, support, and friendship are some of my most treasured possessions. Their ministry, Eliyahu Praise,[1] focuses on creating a pathway for intimate encounter with Yahweh, and the reclamation and restoration of devastated lives lost in deep darkness. They have touched many who are free today because of their faithfulness to God's way. I am one of them.

---

1   https://www.eliyahupraise.com/

Brian provided a wisely insightful review of the final version and offered compelling confirmation just when I needed it most. He is a rock of faith, a good friend, and one I count as a mentor.

Finally, there is my good friend Mark, whom I have known for twenty years. A pastor and mentor to men, he is one who knew the me I presented to the world. When I revealed the truth to him, he responded with love and compassion. He is another who added to this book by reading drafts and contributing what God put on his heart.

The third group is comprised of ministry leaders who are changing the world through God's provision. They operate as individual ministries, but many also operate in cooperation with each other. Each has touched my life in ways I cannot adequately express.

Ian Clayton (Son of Thunder Ministries[2]) is a true forerunner, searching out the hidden mysteries and secrets of the Almighty. He is different, and it is a good different. His passion, strength, transparency, and integrity are like supercharged magnets.

Grant and Samantha Mahoney (Ohel-Moed Ministry[3]) are also stepping into the future and bringing others along with them. Their teachings on cleaning up the junk of our lives, generational freedom, and what we are being called into are helping people reclaim the truth of their destiny. In addition to all of that, Sam offered to walk the journey of this book with me, reviewing each chapter as I wrote it and providing critical commentary and encouragement.

Marios Ellinas[4] is a pastor, speaker, writer, consultant, and so much more. Ruthie and I asked him to meet us for breakfast one morning so I could ask him about tips for writing and publishing a book. Instead, he offered to be my coach through the entire process. I cannot adequately express how his encouragement, coaching, and counsel have contributed to this work and my life.

---

2   https://www.sonofthunder.org/
3   https://www.moed-ministries.com/
4   https://www.mariosellinas.com/

These friends of the aforementioned third group collaborate through The Foundation Nest[5] to help believers mature into the fullness of who God intends them to be, and through Origin Gate,[6] another platform they use to reach a world-wide audience of believers and searchers. I thank them especially for allowing me to include elements of their teachings which have been so important to me in my walk back into the Light.

Justin Paul Abraham (Company of Burning Hearts[7]) is a true mystic, one who seeks and finds God in ways most will never think of or attempt. He once looked deep into my soul and saw its dark stain. He did not judge me or condemn me; he simply loved me. I sat in the pew one evening in a small church in Venice, CA and listened as he described and sketched the condition of man's heart. I thank him for allowing me to include that teaching and its impact on my life as a part of this book.

Lastly, there are two others without whom this book could never have been. Layne Prince is a freelance editor who agreed to take on a mountain of a project, working with a rookie author. Her patience, encouragement, and wisdom cannot be overstated, especially her patience, I might add, as we worked through technical challenges and multiple revisions. Another professional who came to my rescue is Sarah Smith of Scrolls of Zebulon.[8] She is the creative talent behind the graphics, and it was she who formatted and shepherded the book through the production process with its myriad details. I never would have gotten to the finish line without the talent and energy of Layne and Sarah, and I thank them beyond measure.

To all who have been part of this process, who encouraged, counseled, cajoled, and advised, I say thank you from the depths of my heart. To the God who redeemed me out of the dungeon and restored my life I say, to You be the glory forever!

---

5   https://www.thefoundationnest.com/
6   https://www.origingate.com/
7   https://www.companyofburninghearts.com/
8   https://www.scrollsofzebulon.com/

"*Great sins do draw out great grace; and where guilt is most terrible and fierce, there the mercy of God in Christ, when showed to the soul, appears most high and mighty.*"

John Bunyan, *Grace Abounding*

INTRODUCTION

This is the story of a personal journey from the darkness of great sin back into the light of God's mercy and grace. In it, I trace the missteps of a wayward believer, the bitter fruit of his life, and the divinely illuminated pathway back into God's heart. I know the story well because it is my own. As *painful* as it is to say, every word is true. As *glorious* as it is to say, every word is true. Sadly, my story is not unique. The news too often includes scandalous revelations of the misdeeds of those we hold in great esteem, including ministry leaders and government officials, among others. Not all who fail make headlines; some are our friends, people we work with, those whom we sit next to in church and participate in community life with. They are hiding in plain sight, just as I was. Theirs are stories of failure, ruined relationships, and the havoc that follows, or at least that is what we generally see. Yet, the stories don't have to end in ruin. Those who are willing to humble themselves before God are not dependent upon society for restoration. They have a different source and a different path to follow.

My story is a hard one and the first chapters reflect that truth. I was a believer who had lost his way, knew it, and had come to a place of hopelessness. I had all but given up, but God hadn't. He had a pathway for me to walk if I could find the will. He has one for you or your loved one as well. That is the real point of this book: to remind those who have never encountered and surrendered to God, and those who have but have since lost their way, that when we are at our end and without hope, God leans back on His throne and says, "Now, I've got something I can work with!" His plan for you is different from mine, but His mercy and power displayed in my experience is a message to all. No matter who you are, what you have done, or how bleak life looks, God has a plan specifically for you, to rescue, restore, and renew your life. I know this because I lived it myself, and I am certain He is waiting to do the same for you.

I grew up being taught and believing that knowing and pleasing God meant knowing His Word and living a good life. In failing to do either, I learned that what God wants is our heart. He desires the kind of intimacy with us that is hard to comprehend yet breathtaking when we experience it. What God has done for me He is waiting to do for you and those you love, if only you will take that first step. That is my prayer, that you will take the step that changes everything.

This book is about the journey from believing whom I *thought* God to be to understanding who He *really* is. It is written in three parts. "Part One - A Lost Life" describes my early life and descent into the depths of sin, complete with its bitter fruit. It includes my early and long-term fascination with pornography, which dulled me to its realities and paved the road ahead. That road eventually led me into online chat rooms and relationships and the discovery and adoption of a perverted lifestyle, one that would become an obsession, even my self-identity. As a result, I went deeper and deeper, embracing demonic spirits as I pursued pleasure. At times this included recognizing these spirits in others, which drew me into relationships with people who were as lost and deceived as I was. Conflicted on every level, I lived a double life of one who said he loved and served God while secretly living a life that ridiculed God's love. On the inside, I knew that what I had become was evil and hated myself because of it. Depression, unworthiness, multiple personalities, and thoughts of suicide followed. I was consumed by fear, guilt, and shame. I was at rock bottom, and I knew it.

"Part Two - Discovery, Deliverance, Freedom" tells the story of how God confronted me, used others to minister to me, and eventually redeemed me. Here, I share my awakening to the depravity of my life, my desire to fix it on my own, and how profoundly I failed. At the same time, others were beginning to see and speak into my life. In one case, a close friend at church sent me a late-night text that shook me to my very core, telling me that God was running out of patience and that my clock was running out of time. On another occasion, someone I had never met before looked into my eyes as we faced each other, and I knew instantly that he knew. He would become a close friend and the shepherd of my early journey back into the light of God's grace. I was under conviction which soon enough led to confession and repentance, the step that changes everything. I admitted everything to Ruthie, my wife, praying that God would somehow restore our marriage. A period of prolonged intense questioning and revealing ensued, a time I came to call The Inquisitions, during which the process of detailing my life was brutally honest and blunt, and the outcome uncertain. One evening several weeks into the process, I got my answer. God was faithful and Ruthie was forgiving, but there was hard work to do. We started to rebuild our marriage one breath, one day at a time. Two months after my confession we met with our pastor. This deliverance session was nothing like I expected, but I knew it had been effective. Not long after, I had a spiritual encounter with Jesus, and for the first time in over fifty years I was completely free. There was still hard work in front of us, but I knew that God had forgiven me. As we continued to work the process God laid out before us, we learned about how God sees our heart, how His anger is righteous, and how He can turn from his anger to forgive and embrace us again. In the last two chapters of this section, I explain what I learned about the miracle of forgiveness, including how we can and must forgive ourselves, and share the process that God brought to us, teaching us how to forgive and start the healing of deep wounds.

In "Part Three - A New Life," I describe the protocols God introduced me to and what is required to rebuild life. Taken together, these sections tell the story of how God led me out of the wilderness. He could lead, but I had to do the walking, just as we all do. Each of us is different; our circumstances, beliefs, and conditions are not the same. I do not suggest that the path we must walk will be the same. However, God does have a path for each of us. Our task is to discover His way for us and to walk it in faith.

Along the way, you will learn how to discover what God intended for your life and how to reconnect with that purpose. In walking this journey, many who have lost hope will discover that promises long abandoned are still there waiting to be rediscovered and will be encouraged by the good news of Truth, Power, Mercy, Grace, and Love.

The journey required me to test and sometimes reject beliefs I held since my acceptance of Christ as my Savior as a young boy. We think of doctrine as an intellectual pursuit, in reality it can be the difference between life and death. Knowing truth, however, is just one step of this journey. The knowledge of truth is worthless if not put into action. In my case, for example, I had to lay down misconceptions about the Holy Spirit's role in our lives today, allowing Him to exercise His power like I never had before.

Like one walking a mountain trail, there will be times when we will struggle, times when the trail is obscured, and times when it lies open before us like a neon-lit expressway. Each portion of the walk has its own character, requiring us to be constantly observant and sensitive to where it is taking us, what lies ahead, and what dangers and risks we must navigate on our way to the summit. In the end, it will require us to reach beyond our known limits of trust, faith, belief, perseverance, and endurance. In the end, it will test everything we are, allowing us to discard the chaff and strengthen our faith. In the end, for those who persevere, it will reveal a beautiful panorama of God's grace. His real grace.

The overcomer must be willing to make the trek, seeking that beautiful vista. In the process, we will discover how strong God's love really is, how to forgive and be forgiven, and how to love ourselves. We will learn new tools and explore five protocols that guide us through emptying ourselves of the hubris of our sinful past and help us feed the intimacy between our heart and God's heart. We will also learn the importance of our generational history and how to resolve it, and how to mature our deliverance into a new life of freedom. We will explore the work of rebuilding trust in our most important relationships. Finally, we will learn about our new identity and hiding place, our life of oneness with Christ, in Christ.

Our God is bigger than our sin. His redemption is more powerful, His restoration more faithful, and His renewal of our lives deeper than we have known. It is time for us to discover Him as He really is and to understand that while He judges evil, He loves us. He is waiting to move us from sin and agony so deep it cannot be described except by lost hope and abandonment to certain death, to sudden and surprising redemption, restoration, and renewal. He is waiting to move us from walking in the world to walking in Heaven, from living in shame to breathing new life with every breath.

The purpose of this book is not just to tell my story but to draw you into yours. Can God's love really overcome the very worst in us? Yes, it can.

Even for me, even for you.

PART ONE

A Lost Life

But each person is tempted when he is lured and enticed by his own desire. Then desire when it has conceived gives birth to sin, and sin when it is fully grown brings forth death.
James 1:14,15 (ESV)

CHAPTER ONE

HIDING IN PLAIN SIGHT

I sat on the sofa in our den and wondered how to answer my friend's question. It was the one I had been hoping no one would ask and praying that someone would. Now someone had.

"Have you committed adultery?"

There it was. My prayers were answered. What would I do now?

Sitting in our den, surrounded by my wife of forty-four years and two dear friends, I felt my response rise from within me with surprising calmness.

"Yes, I have."

It was a few days beyond our forty-fourth wedding anniversary. I had planned a romantic getaway to one of our favorite spots. Ruthie had suggested another option. She had often asked for us to go to marriage counseling, which I denied each time. This time was different, however. I wanted out of my sin and had proved I was incapable of escaping on my own. Yes, I would get counseling with her, which is how I came to be sitting here pondering the question, my response, and the look on Ruthie's face. My simple statement had taken the air out of the room, but there was a knowing look in her eyes. This was not news to her.

Earlier that morning, I stood in front of the mirror, shaving my mustache and goatee off, something I knew she desired. I had no idea at the time how prophetic the act of revealing my true face was. I liked the facial hair and had steadfastly refused to shave it before, but this morning was different. As I shaved, I wondered if it could be that I would escape this three-day visit by our friends, our "marriage counselors," without the secret of my sin being exposed. They were just a couple of hours from departure, and I thought maybe, just maybe, I would avoid the moment I both dreaded and desired so much. That is just how conflicted I was. Minutes later, the question was asked and answered, and just like that, life took a hard turn.

What led to that moment of truth and those that followed is the story of this book. I was not a person you would have thought likely to do such a thing, but you would have been wrong. I was exactly that person. Despite the view from the outside, I lived a life of deceit for virtually all my adult life while engaging in sin so great it caused me to deny what I knew about my God and to lose hope. Yet the God I mocked chose to give me the one last chance I thought would never come. I had promised myself that if it ever did come my way, I would not turn it down, despite what I expected the cost to be. Now it was staring me in the face. I had to decide; this was the decisive moment my life and others would turn on. The God of the universe had just extended His hand of mercy to me. I was going to grab it despite the heavy cost I expected.

This book is a personal story of life lived in darkness, and the universal truth of God's light and grace. There is nothing extraordinary in this life except the love that saved it, both on earth and in Heaven. It is the story of the everyday man or woman, those who go through life wondering why it is the way it is and wishing for something different. It is a story of hope, faith, and overcoming great trial. It is a story of freedom.

Walking and living in two dimensions at the same time is not fiction. For some of your family members, co-workers, and friends, it is their daily dose of reality. I know because I was one of them. I talked with you, laughed with you, prayed with you, and worked side by side with you, all while I was trapped in sin, depravity, depression, and desperation and you never knew.

If you had asked my contemporaries and family who I was, they most likely would have told you I was an average guy. I worked hard, loved my family, was active in church and professional organizations—overall a normal working professional. That would have all been true, but as the classic expression goes, it would not have been the whole truth. There was another side to this coin; reality was much darker and more sinister. While the public and professional faces I presented to the world seemed normal, the private face I lived with every second of every day was far from it. I was, in fact, in complete turmoil. I was ashamed of who I knew I really was, fearful for myself and my family, and unable, despite my many attempts, to stop doing what I knew to be wrong. I woke every morning wondering if it would be the day that my deceit would be revealed and that I would lose everything.

There was nothing in my family history that I knew of to indicate that this state of affairs was likely. I came from solid, middle-class working stock. I literally grew up in and was raised by the church and accepted Christ as my Savior at a young age. I was active in youth ministry, participated on the speech and debate team in high school, and served in the military. By the time I left the military, I was married and had two young sons. In many ways, I had become my parents, and in many ways, I was as unlike them as one can imagine.

How did I go from being a model of normalcy to being "that guy," the guy who leads a double life? I certainly never desired it, until I did; I never planned it, until I did; and I never acted on it, until I did. The truth is that I did do all those things. I desired it, planned it, and did it. I cannot deny my culpability in what transpired. God has a plan for my life just as He has one for yours, and so does evil. Like many, I made my choices one slippery slope step at a time. Evil had a willing partner.

In hindsight, there were clues. I was introverted and an average student at best except for the two or three subjects I had a natural affinity for. I was a late bloomer socially and can still be uncomfortable amid a group of people I do not know. I was a world-class daydreamer, not that being such is bad, but in my case, it opened gateways that should not have been opened. When being truthful with myself, I admit that from the age of six years until my mid-sixties, I had a horrible opinion of myself. The world saw me as a successful businessperson and father. I saw myself as weak, unintelligent, a failure at almost everything I had ever attempted, and worst of all, an adulterous liar who claimed to be a man of faith. I had a loving family, a good job, and was respected in my career and profession, including sitting on the international board of a professional association. On the outside, life looked good. There were just two problems with the view from the outside: Life wasn't good, and I hated myself to the core because I knew it was my own fault.

I grew up being taught and believing that God loves everyone. I believed that there is no one whom He would not rescue if they called out, no matter what they had done. Theft? Murder? Adultery? Abandonment? Racism? Addiction? Abuse? You name it. God has an answer for all of them: Love. But I also believed that I was the exception, that what I had done and what I had become was beyond even His love. I didn't love me, and I thought He didn't, either, and I didn't blame Him.

How Did I Get to This Horrible Place?

What changed me from being a young boy who loved God and gave his life to Him, to a man who lived and walked in two dimensions? How did I go from loving Him to hating me? Remember that part about daydreaming? When we do not like who we are or our circumstances, when reality does not measure up to expectations, it is easy to get lost in what we desire but cannot have. All we must do is imagine that it is true and make it our internal reality. This internal reality may be false, a lie and a deceit, but it can be strong and appealing when we believe that the real reality of our lives is painful and unappealing. That is where I began. For everything that seemed wrong in my life, I created an alternative version that matched what the world calls normal and to which I aspired. For me, this began as an internal and private process that eventually opened doorways, allowing my private fantasies to express themselves. But why did I feel the need? What was so wrong with my life that I abandoned what I knew to be true and put myself and those I love at such risk?

Answering that question requires going back to the beginning.

Born with a cleft lip and palate, I let this minor birth defect become the defining part of my personality. I felt the love of a mother who believed anything was possible for me, but when my father did not express love, I knew why. I was unlovable. I knew this because I saw it every time I looked in a mirror, and I knew everyone else saw it, as well. I knew that I was different and not in a good way. As a young boy I longed for love and acceptance and accepted it freely from my family. But when it came from outside the family circle, I knew what it really was: pity. When it became apparent that I was not a good student, I knew why. It was because I was unintelligent. I heard it every day at school, and soon enough I believed it was true. I couldn't read well, had a speech impediment, and math was beyond me. Feeling that I was both ugly and stupid, I turned inward while maintaining a certain normalcy on the outside. Those around me, the people I shared my life with every day, thought I was shy but generally well-adapted. I lived this double life from my elementary school years through my professional career years, pretending to the world while struggling with what I knew I was on the inside. When a girl I was dating in high school told me she liked me but could never be serious because she did not want deformed children, I understood. It hurt like hell, but I understood why she felt that way because I felt the same. These are painful words and thoughts, painful secrets about oneself that we lock away deep inside. Left there to fester, they mature into real ugliness, and we decide how they will manifest.

There is a progression to our lives. We move from youth and innocence to maturity and the fruit of our actions. What that fruit will be depends as much on our beliefs, choices, and actions as it does the plan and purpose planted inside us by our Creator. The doctrine is known as Free Will; we call our application of the doctrine Life.

In my case, there were many good beliefs, times when I made right choices and examples where I moved in faith and courage. I knew right from wrong and strove to do the right thing, even when it was not easy. I felt I was a good person. I was raised to believe that all men are created equal in God's sight, that there is no basis for racial discrimination, and to look out for the underdog. I was raised with pride and gratitude that I live in a country that gives everyone a chance, where anyone can overcome anything and achieve everything. I saw examples of honesty, hard work, faith, and integrity everywhere I looked in my family and their friends. But they were all normal people, and I knew I was not normal. Escape from abnormality became my goal in life. If I couldn't achieve it in reality, then I would achieve it in fantasy. If the world outside hurt too much, then I would turn to the world inside. Without knowing the word "stoicism," I made it my life goal to escape the pain of rejection by turning inward and living life alone. I might have to feel the pain, but I could hide it, as well. The world could hurt me, but I could deny it the satisfaction of knowing that it had. Not understanding love or how to love, I began looking for it, willing to accept a counterfeit, if that was to be my fate.

Typical of too many boys, my escapism led me to pornography. The magazines were front and center on the racks in the stores, the publishers were acclaimed in the news of the day, and some of the most successful and famous people in the world lent their name and credibility to them. What could be wrong with that? The fact that beautiful women were revealed inside their pages seemed like the icing on the cake. Like most boys of that age, I preferred the icing. That early beginning matured and stayed with me in various and increasingly troublesome forms throughout my life until just a few years ago. Pornography is a damning vehicle for those who become trapped in its enticements. Like everything else, it is a gateway into what lies beyond it.[9] We choose if we will step through the gateway. I knew it was wrong but chose to step in because of the appeal of

---

9   Norman Doidge, M.D., *The Brain That Changes Itself* (New York: Penguin Group, 2007), 93-131 The chapter presents an excellent discussion of how addictions of all kinds change our brains, all in layman's terms. The good news: it is possible through desire, will, and commitment, not to mention the mercy and grace of God, to rewire what has been mis-wired,.

its promised alternate reality. What lay beyond in my case, what I stepped into through that gateway, was all too real and life-destroying. It followed a predictable path: addiction, perversion, destruction.

Pornography led to other gateways, one of which I discovered late one evening at the office. I had been working long hours and was exhausted, and I knew I still had hours ahead of me yet before heading home. But I needed a break, a small diversion to clear my head. Then a simple question ran through my head. I had been hearing about this new thing called a chat room. "What is that all about?" I wondered. I had heard that there are rooms where people talked about sex and developed relationships, others where people played a wide variety of games, and other rooms where the focus was on specific topics of interest such as hobbies. There was an initial twinge of hesitation, a questioning inside me asking if this was a safe or right thing to do. This caution from my inner self was soon overruled by curiosity and a desire to experiment. It did not take long to discover that all I had heard was true. My initial forays were limited to exploring and learning to navigate. I was amazed at the variety of interests one could explore and the numbers of people who were dialoguing with each other. As I observed, I could see that most were strangers who did not really know each other, but there were also many who had developed ongoing relationships. There was a lot of information and banter, and few knew anything about those they were chatting with except what the other person was telling them. It seemed too good to be true. I realized I could tell people anything. People would accept me as I presented myself if I was consistent and knew what I was talking about. No one inside the chat rooms would know my secret; to them I could still be "just another guy."

Initially, I played games, just getting to know how things worked and developing my online persona. It is not true of all who participate in online activity, but it is not uncommon for people to develop alternative personalities that optimize their appeal as they see it or wish it to be. It may be their physical description, likes and dislikes, their profession, or their personalities. Or all the above. In my case, I created a false image of who and what I was for the specific purpose of having people like me. I developed a small circle of friends whom I would regularly play and converse with. Attachments formed, interests piqued, and eventually a line was crossed. My simple "Would you be interested in a different kind of conversation?" question to a lady I knew only as a game-player soon turned into a long-distance, romantic relationship which lasted seven years, eventually resulting in a face-to-face meeting. The seeds of my destruction were truly and well-sown, but I was too blind to see them. Blind even to the disintegration of my marriage and family. In lying to myself, I lied to them. The difference was that they knew I was lying while I pretended everything was okay and that I could control events. How terribly wrong I was.

Diving to the Bottom

What followed was several years of exploration and an increasingly deep dive into depravity. Perhaps the most troubling thought of all is that I found willing partners everywhere I turned. This disease, and that is what it is, has a large population, including some whom we admire for their position, success, influence, families, faith, and wealth. Sin and death do not discriminate. They will accept anyone foolish enough to play their game.

I was not alone. I did find willing partners—and lots of them. Websites and chat rooms specializing in various forms of immorality permeate the Web. In just a few keystrokes, one can join, create an identity, and begin searching for others who want to share in promiscuity or something far more nefarious. The options are as unlimited as the human appetite for hedonistic pleasure and depravity. Chat experiences, phone sessions, long-term relationships, strangers meeting strangers for only one purpose—all of these are real and common occurrences in this murky web. It happens every minute of every day.

Chat sessions were a routine occurrence when I was trapped in depravity. I had different and often multiple online partners many nights, moving from one fantasy experience to the next. I tweaked my persona to fit the stated desires and interests of each, emphasizing areas where we shared similar interests and desires. I was most often honest when asked if I was married, my response determined by my reading of the other person. I learned that many married women prefer liaisons with married men, believing that involvement with someone else who has too much to lose is a safer path. In fact, my most intense and longest-lasting relationships were with married women who loved their families, and several of my partners were professing Christians. I was deceived, and I was not alone. Over the course of twenty years, I developed multiple relationships. A few of these were intensely real. One was an intimate, long-distance relationship with a woman in which our business travels facilitated times together. Another woman was my online and phone lover for years, as well, in a relationship that was real, intense, and emotionally powerful.

Was I in love? Yes, many times, and frequently entangled with more than one woman at the same time. Did I know what I was doing and that it was wrong? Yes. Did that stop me? No, because I was addicted to physical and emotional pleasure, the control that I could exert in these relationships, and the pseudo-reality I was living. I was untethered from my moral compass, although it constantly accused me.

I was not just unfaithful to my wife. I was involved in a perverted lifestyle. This lifestyle provided a place where I could be in control, call the shots, and determine when pain, pleasure, happiness, or tension was on the menu. Bondage, Discipline, and Sado-Masochism (BDSM) is a dark world where lusts, desires, urges, pain, pleasure, manipulation, and control combine with intensity to overwhelm our senses and what we know to be right. It may be private and closely guarded, but it can also be intensely real. It may even sound good as you read this. Beware, it is not. The addiction is as real as alcohol or drugs and just as destructive, sometimes more so. Despite popular opinion, there is no grayness or goodness to it. We fool ourselves when we say that there are no victims, only people of like mind experiencing mutual enjoyment and satisfaction. We ignore the pain in our families and the disintegration of our own personalities, all in the name of pleasure. When you are a living lie, you know it, even if no one else does. You may be saying one thing, but the voices on the inside are incessant in their accusations. Hell is being alone with your own thoughts. It is as simple and horrific as that.

Before moving on, allow me to address the issue of BDSM within marriage, which is something I've seen discussed in various forums. Often, these discussions begin with a question about the propriety of engaging in BDSM in the context of a marriage, even a Christian marriage. Society has largely put its stamp of approval on BDSM. It is prevalent in today's literature, television, and movies. Even Christians rationalize its acceptance in a committed relationship, but it is a rationalization that fails before God. Something grounded in evil cannot be righteous. Intimacy in marriage is a God-given gift with a God-given purpose. Sex is intended as an expression of one's love for another, a love meant to serve, uplift, edify, and encourage. Yes, the pleasure manifests, in part, as a physical sensation, but it emanates from the soul within. The pleasure that BDSM brings is in response to a person's need to dominate or be dominated physically, mentally, and emotionally. It tears one down to elevate the other, even if only in roleplay, and is a counterfeit love. The entire psychology of BDSM is one of emotional domination and surrender, which is far from the nurturing partnership God intends.

BDSM may be glorified in today's sensualist society, but its roots are in ancient darkness. Baal worship's satanic rituals, torture, and human sacrifices[10] as part of depraved sensual cravings precede modern society's captivation. We cannot divorce ourselves from this spiritual legacy even if we do not recognize it specifically, and we cannot pretend we can successfully hold it at bay.

We pervert God's gift when we surrender and co-mingle it with something that has an unholy root and thus cannot be holy, or even benign. Since righteousness and evil cannot coexist peacefully, there must be conflict. We may not always recognize it, but it is at work inside us, nevertheless. Essentially, we must choose which altar we will worship at.

---

10   1 Kings 18:25-29 See also *The Ignorant Fishermen Blog, Baalism's Suicidal Nature Worship and Sexual Decadence (Earth Day)*, https://www.theignorantfishermen.com/2010/12/baalism's-suicidal-nature-and.html

We cannot worship God and evil at the same time. When we rationalize acceptance of sin, we choose our soul's desire over Godly righteousness, wisdom, and understanding, yoking ourselves to its evil legacy and allowing it to be present and operate in our lives. The antidote to this poison is to humble ourselves before God and cling to His plumbline of Truth. I didn't and suffered the consequences as a result.

GOD'S PROMISE

But God had a plan. Circumstances would eventually put me in a position where I must make a life-or-death choice. Many people were faithful and often unknowing participants in this series of events orchestrated by Heaven, which brought me to the point of deciding my life's fate. It was the most difficult time of my life. Finally, however, I was asked the question point-blank and given a chance to grab for the golden ring of freedom. Not knowing what would result but unwilling to pass up the opportunity, I took it.

The time following my confession was raw, emotionally and spiritually. I was overwhelmed by God's grace and mercy and the forgiveness of a wife who loved God so much she could still love me. Yet I had deep feelings of unworthiness. My sin had been so great. How could a righteous God extend mercy to me? I knew that He had done just that, but I still asked how it could be possible. It was the seeking of one who wanted to understand to experience it more deeply, not of one who doubted. I asked this question many times without getting an answer. Sometimes, God waits for us to walk out our faith with perseverance.

Even in the midst of our hidden sins, God sees everything we do and knows every thought. When we struggle, His heart aches for us as a true father's heart, which is why He sometimes interrupts us to bring our attention back to Him. Sometimes we recognize His subtle hints, and sometimes He needs to be more direct or dramatic to get our attention.

On the morning of Good Friday 1994, I was in a situation I did not like. At that point, I had been unemployed for nearly a year because of a recession that hit my career field particularly hard, and there were no options in sight. All our savings were gone and we were down to our last few dollars. It was bleak, and I was demoralized. I trusted God but prayed and wished that He would hurry up with His answer. That morning, I was to have one of my first encounters with the Holy Spirit, and it gave me confidence.

Ruthie and I had joined several church friends at our pastor's home, which had been seriously damaged by an earthquake a few months earlier. The home was a near total loss, and we were there to help prepare it for the start of reconstruction. As the group sat on the front sidewalk eating lunch, I became uncomfortable. These were my friends, but something was pulling me away. Finally, I rose and stepped back into the house, just to distance myself from them and the unsettled feeling that had come over me. Stepping into what was left of the family den, I saw an absolute mess. Broken glass, drywall scraps, and thick dust were everywhere. It looked like how my life felt at the moment. I stood there looking at it all when a feeling of deep compassion swept over me for the family I knew and the countless others I did not know who were enduring this hardship. As I stood there, I prayed that God would be merciful in their lives and situations. Then I had the thought, "Do something practical about it." Do something practical? What in Heaven's name could I do? I was unemployed and broke. I barely had enough gas to get us home and to church on Sunday. What could I do? "Do something practical about it." There it was again! And at that, I saw a broom in the corner and thought, "Well, the least I can do is sweep this mess into a pile, so it is easier to manage." So, I began to sweep the debris into the middle of the room. As I worked, the pile became a large but neat cone and I thought to myself, "This could be an altar." Immediately, I felt the Holy Spirit descend upon me. My metabolism slowed down rapidly, moving from the top of my head to the soles of my feet. In just a second or two, I was in a trance and barely breathing, but fully aware of what was happening to me. Then I heard these exact words in a clearly audible manner: "Do not worry. Everything will be alright. I am taking care of you." At that, my metabolism came back up as I felt energy and life return, moving from the bottom of my feet to the top of my head. I was in a state of humbled awe. God had just spoken. To me! But why? Why did He allow me to encounter Him on that morning?

He did it not just to encourage me in the moment of a trial, but to remind me that He is always present in my life, just as He is always present in yours. No matter what we have done, no matter what we have become, no matter what we may be experiencing, He remembers what He wrote in our scroll and is willing to breathe life back into us. Sometimes, however, He needs us to pick up the broom. He needs us to give Him an anchor that He can grab onto, a tool that He can use to leverage our hearts.

When Jacob fled Beersheba, he encountered this same God, who promised to protect and bless him and his generations.

> *"Behold, I am with you; I will guard you wherever you go, and I will return you to this soil; for I will not forsake you until I have done what I have spoken about you."* Genesis 28:15 (SEAET)

There are three distinct promises that God makes to Jacob in this verse: He will protect him, He will return him to his land, and He will accomplish what He set out as Jacob's assignment. I am certain that Jacob liked what he heard! During his trial, God speaks to him and assures him that He, God, is in control. Notice, however, that Jacob must do his part. He is given land which must be worked to be made fruitful; he must "do something practical" to fulfill God's plan in his life. We might think of it this way: God had the plan, and Jacob had to choose if he would be obedient and diligent in living a life that allowed the promises God made to be realized.

As God had a plan for Jacob, He also has one for you and me. He will respond when we turn our hearts to Him with earnest desire, intent, and humility to ask for His intervention. He loves us so much that He sacrificed His only Son to redeem us from exactly the kinds of sin we get ourselves into. Jesus is not only our Savior, but He is also the one who intercedes for us and acts as our Advocate before the Throne of Grace as God judges our lives. God the Father is perfect, and He expects nothing less from us; He has never compromised on this standard. Jesus as God understands that. Because He came to walk and live in our world, He also knows from His own experience how weak and tempted we are. It is this that allows Him to intercede for us with the Father, and it is His own blood that He offers in trade for our lives. As God, He expects perfection. As our Advocate, He appeals to the Father for mercy. As our Savior, He offers His own life in exchange for ours.

One of the most amazing things to me is that Jesus Himself had to make choices, just as Jacob, you, and I do. Jesus, too, had a scroll written which He could not have fulfilled without obedience and righteousness:

> *Consequently, when Christ came into the world, he said, "Sacrifices and offerings you have not desired, but a body have you prepared for me; in burnt offerings and sin offerings you have taken no pleasure. Then I said, 'Behold, I have come to do your will, O God, as it is written of me in the scroll of the book.'"* Hebrews 10:5-7 (ESV)

Christ volunteered to come and fulfill His scroll, just as we seek to understand and fulfill our own. Four verses later, we are cautioned that God does not want part of us or what we believe will satisfy Him. He wants all of us. God wants our very hearts, nothing less.

> *And every priest stands daily at his service, offering repeatedly the same sacrifices, which can never take away sins. But when Christ had offered for all time a single sacrifice for sins, he sat down at the right hand of God, waiting from that time until his enemies should be made a footstool for his feet.* Hebrews 10:11-13 (ESV)

We are the priests of our lives, and we serve daily. The question is: Who and what are we serving? Just as the priests of Christ's time offered inadequate sacrifices, our own too often fall short of the standard and purpose set by God. Our good intentions, rationalizations, bargaining, and attempts to make up for our sins are worthless and shameful in God's eyes. He desires our total abandonment to Him, resulting in an intimacy that begins in His heart and changes our heart.

He desires only one thing: everything.

I am thankful God is true to His Word and that His faithfulness followed me wherever I chose to go in life. Without God's faithfulness, I would have lost everything I cherish and my future. God is with you in your darkest moments, as well. When you contemplate sin and carry it out, He is there. When you live carelessly and without regard or with casual regard for His desires, He is there. When you bargain with Him with insincere intention, He is there. When you doubt or do not believe, He is there. When you try and fail, He is there. Why? Why does God remain with us as we sin our way through life, doubt Him, or lose hope? He is there because He is waiting. Waiting to see the appeal in our eyes, to hear our cry of surrender, to know that our heart is finally His. He is always with us; He never abandons us. God's Faithfulness, Love, and Mercy never fail.

That is what this book is about: one man's journey from darkness so dark it cannot be imagined into the light of God's forgiveness and grace. I cannot suppose that your experience will be the same as mine, and neither should you. I can promise, however, that the God who created you still loves you and is waiting for you to turn into His embrace. This is no small promise, as you are about to read. Not only is He waiting, but He has prepared for you a pathway to that wonderful place and the peace which inhabits it. What follows is my story: how God used patience, forgiveness, redemption, and restoration to change my destiny. Like most things in life, it is a process, one that must be taken step by step, day by day. First, however, I had to turn away from the pleasures and pursuits of the world and into His arms. And that is where the battle for my soul was joined.

CHAPTER TWO

SIN MATURING INTO DEATH

My journey into the darkness was not quick at first. I had been unfaithful to my wife many times throughout our married life, beginning early in our marriage. As bad as that was, however, it was only a small taste of what was to come. It was not until I was deeply entrenched in sin and wanting to get out that I realized just how deep I had gone, how desperate my situation was, and how helpless I was against it. The full impact of what I had done and what I had become settled on me. I was ashamed and afraid. Between the beginning of my "other life" and my attempts to leave it, I had changed into a person who was trying to fake his way through a normal life. I now know that I had multiple personalities, suffered severe depression and anxiety, and was consumed by fear, guilt, and shame. At one point, I had a plan to put an end to all of these, to end my life if that was what it would take to be free. One cannot reach that point without serious problems, and my list of problems was as long as you might imagine. What began as a slow exploration of tantalizing taboos had become a breakneck spiral into a bottomless pit.

To think that it all began as a young boy just trying to escape to a safe place. Where I ended up was everything but.

FANTASY LIFE

I recall being bored in early elementary-grade classes. My attention and mind frequently wandered far afield. You could accurately say I was often present in form but absent in reality. Where was I? I do not recall this period with detail, but there are several vignettes that remain strong: sitting at my school desk and gazing out a window while imagining grand scenes. I always saved the day. I was always the hero. These types of explorations became more common as I grew. There were many report cards and notes home telling my parents how polite and well-behaved I was, each invariably ending with an appeal to get me to pay attention. My grades suffered, and math was especially challenging. Our pastor's wife was a teacher, and she volunteered to tutor me. My parents did not tell me of this arrangement, and I had no idea what was about to happen when they showed up at our house for dinner one night. At least that's what I thought. There was coffee and small talk, but no meal. Then the questions began. I was surrounded and there was no escape. Trapped and now realizing what was afoot, I began to panic. My pastor's wife began to ask a series of simple math questions that made the real intent of the evening obvious, even to a young boy. I knew what this was, and I knew I was truly and surely had. There was no way out unless I created one, and I did. To say that I put on quite a show would do my imagination and young acting abilities great injustice. My fantasy play was totally out of character, but it worked. I paid a price for it, but I also avoided what I feared most. I considered it a fair trade. As it turned out, it was a trade I would make repeatedly in life.

In high school, my fantasies revolved around sports and girls. That's normal for that age. Shyness aside, I was doing better in school while avoiding subjects I lacked the confidence to attempt. I attempted one year of foreign language only because I had to. My dismal performance there proved to me again that I just wasn't very smart. The interesting thing in retrospect is that there were areas in which I did well and even some where I excelled. I graded at the top of my class in Civics and Architecture, and near the top in Art and History. I had largely overcome my speech impediment, thanks to the good work of speech therapists, and took Speech in my junior year to build my confidence. I found I enjoyed it and was good at it. When I was asked to consider joining the Speech and Debate Team for my senior year, I jumped at the chance, especially since it offered one of the few options to avoid English Literature, a class I viewed as a drudgery and certain poor grade. I enjoyed debate, oral interpretation, and impromptu speech. I participated in competitions around the state and fared well, sometimes better than that. On the whole, that doesn't sound so bad. But when I talked to myself, it was always the failures that took top billing. Under no pressure from home to excel, nothing I did well seemed enough to balance my failures in my own mind. I was not happy with who I was, and fantasy once again became an easy retreat from reality.

As I matured into adult life, the escapes fantasy offered never left me. Over time, different themes emerged. Great exploits of heroism and glory were just a blink of an eye away whenever I desired them. My imagination could create grand scenes and schemes, and I would live them out in my mind. As things progressed, the link between fantasy and my ongoing relationship with pornography grew strong—so strong that, at times, it challenged reality for primacy in my psyche.

Scripture tells us that what our eye hooks into will become our reality. In other words, we will become what we look at:

> "Do not store up for yourselves [material] treasures on earth, where moth and rust destroy, and where thieves break in and steal. But store up for yourselves treasures in heaven, where neither moth nor rust destroys, and where thieves do not break in and steal; for where your treasure is, there your heart [your wishes, desires; that on which your life centers] will be also.
> "The eye is the lamp of the body; so if your eye is clear [spiritually perceptive], your whole body will be full of light [benefiting from God's precepts]. But if your eye is bad [spiritually blind], your

whole body will be full of darkness [devoid of God's precepts].
So if the [very] light inside you [your inner self, your heart, your
conscience] is darkness, how great and terrible is that darkness!
"No one can serve two masters; for either he will hate the one and
love the other, or he will be devoted to the one and despise the
other. You cannot serve God and mammon [money, possessions,
fame, status, or whatever is valued more than the Lord]."
Matthew 6:19-24 (AMP)

How great and terrible is that darkness, indeed. My life proved the
Word to be true. We cannot serve God and anything else, which is exactly what I had been trying to do. I was confident that my conversion,
although at a young age, was true. I knew I had accepted Jesus as my
Savior but had not yet made Him Lord and King of my life. Jesus was in
me, but He wasn't alone. My demons were there, as well. My addiction to
pornography became an obsession. I spent hours at a time collecting and
cataloging images, and I did this over a period of years. My eye gates were
wide open to the filth of the world, and I eagerly took it in, making the
images and videos the basis of my own fantasies. Then I began to desire
them in reality, and then I began to engage them. This is truth: What your
eyes hook into will become your reality. The eyes are not the only gates we
need to guard, but they are critically important. What we allow our eyes
to settle on will become the desires of our heart, and it is the desires of our
heart that we pursue above all else.

Later, when I became immersed in fantasy chat experiences, the ability to create alternative realities became a staple. A word or phrase would
cross the screen, or a thought cross my mind, and instantly, visions would
form. I could see the entire experience as if watching a movie. I could hear
the words and sounds, and feel the emotions, sometimes so deeply that
they would overwhelm me. The acceptance and pleasure they brought
were an elixir as euphoric as a narcotic. As I engaged with others, I learned
that I was alone in neither the desire nor ability to create alternative realities.

Familiar Spirits

I was surprised at how drawn I was to others who had similar abilities, and how drawn they were to me. This was a common occurrence when chatting on one of the sites dedicated to lifestyle pleasures. It led to a handful of virtual long-term relationships and occasional one-time encounters with several women. I did not try to understand this phenomenon, simply accepting it as a pleasant surprise. The reality, however, is that these "familiar spirits" were neither unique to me nor unusual. In fact, they are often the temptation of choice when evil wishes to take us further down the death spiral of sin.

It is important at this point to draw distinctions between different types of familiar spirits. I place them in two broad categories while understanding that there is a great deal of crossover and interconnection between them. When the Bible speaks of familiar spirits, it is usually in reference to sorcerers, mediums, and necromancers. Most biblical references are found in the Old Testament, typically when someone inquires of a medium or sorcerer for guidance or information from the dead. Saul was held accountable for doing this, forfeiting his life as the penalty.[11] This practice is not specific to the Old Testament, however. Acts 8 and 16 make mention of sorcery, as do other New Testament passages. The scale of the practice of sorcery in New Testament times may surprise you. Acts 19 includes the account of the high priests' sons, who were casting out spirits without proper authority. This resulted in a spirit rebuffing and then attacking them, which put fear into the local populace. So much fear, in fact, that many believers confessed their own practices.

When we hear the term "spirits" in our day, we often think of supernatural spirits. These fill our culture today in the movies we watch and the books we read. We've become comfortable with them as a concept; some of us are comfortable with them as a reality. Such is the acceptance of the notion that supernatural spirits are around us and interact with us. We are not the first to arrive at this state.

---

11 1 Chronicles 10:13

And a number of those who had practiced magic arts brought their books together and burned them in the sight of all. And they counted the value of them and found it came to fifty thousand pieces of silver. Acts 19:19 (ESV)

Fifty thousand pieces of silver in that day is an amount equal to several million dollars in our day. All of that from just the professing believers in the region of Ephesus alone. Imagine what the total scale of sorcery and witchcraft at the time must have been!

There is another type of spirit: ones that we are familiar with, and which are active in our own lives today. It is this type of spirit which tempts us and prods us along our sinful ways. In many ways, they are our seducers, accusers, taunters, and trail guides into our own darkness. We must depend upon the Holy Spirit and the blood of Christ as our defense against these powerful beings, and we should not give them too much credit. Once we know what they are, we can see their vulnerabilities. So, what do we know about them?

I know that they knew me personally and intimately, knowing even my deepest secrets. The voices in my head knew me very well indeed, and sometimes they sounded like my own. Every failure was cause for them to gloat, every temptation a platform for their encouragement, every concern a bugle call to fear, and every sin a taunt of guilt and shame. Oh yes, they knew me well. And that is the point. Familiar spirits dwell in us and are well-acquainted with our thoughts and desires. Over time, we become comfortable with them, allowing them to be intimate with our thoughts and our most hidden secrets. When this happens, we are, in fact, in relationship with them. For some of us, these spirits may even be our best friends. They know our most private thoughts, greatest fears, and strongest desires. This allows them to attach themselves to us in deep and hidden ways, making exposing and evicting them even harder.

From my own experience, I can tell you they are great communicators. All those little whispers about what you could or should do and that no one will ever know, all of the hidden thoughts that you would never voice to anyone—those are the voices of familiar spirits. They are our dirtiest secret. Hidden from everyone else, they are our constant companions, goading and taunting us every step of the way as they push us on, our every obedience to them a sacrifice offering to their altar. I do not mean that figuratively. We make a decision with each sin, and those decisions are sacrifices to the sin altars of these demon spirits in the spiritual realm. We offer up our souls and our bodies and pollute our spirits with the vilest things, all in the name of hedonistic pleasure, power, lust, and greed. We surrender our power and will to them so they can live their desires out through us, allowing them to manipulate us to do things we know are wrong. The temptations and manipulations may come from them, but we own the decisions when we choose to act them out. We are accountable for our actions before God.

Have you ever asked how it is that we are attracted to specific individuals? What is it about a person that makes them so appealing to us? In many cases, it is a spirit-to-spirit recognition, a spirit that is familiar with us in our own life recognizing itself or a related spirit in another, and the natural drawing together of those spirits. We all carry baggage, some of it heavy with issues that affect our lives. Those who have been abandoned are often attracted to others who have had the same experience, for example. The same may be said of an untold number of spirits. Why do people who have been abused enter relationships with people who are abusive? Why is someone with a family history of alcoholism attracted to someone who is or will become an alcoholic? How are adulterers attracted to each other to form new alliances? On the surface, we may see other attributes that interest us: appearance, intelligence, position, and the like. We see all these things in many people, however. There is another force at work when this initial attraction begins to exert a pull on us, a spiritual attraction that occurs when spirits recognize spirits in others that they desire relationship with. In positive cases, this attraction is based in a desire to love, nurture, and respect its opposite. In negative cases, the desire is to share in the same misery or addiction, or to dominate and abuse the other.

We can recognize familiar spirits at work in us by examining ourselves and testing our motivations, thoughts, and behavior. Do we act the same way and with the same values in person as we do in private? Would we be ashamed if our private thoughts and desires became known, even to our most intimate relationships? Are we hiding the things we do or concealing relationships? Do we lie habitually? The answers to these and other questions are clues of great importance, but getting truthful answers from even ourselves requires a desire and intent to be free. If we are not willing to do the hard work of being honest with ourselves and facing our demons head on, then we may as well not start. Any attempt to work our way to a partial freedom will be a futile exercise. It will only further demoralize us, and we will still be imprisoned in a personal hell of our own making.

I am naturally an introspective and thoughtful person, and most often quiet around people I do not know. That was not the case, however, when I was in search of someone to partner with while pursuing my alternate life. I was forward in approaching people, bolder in how I spoke, and I tended to take the lead in the early part of getting acquainted and developing relationships. In other words, I was not myself. I claimed to be a man of faith, but my hidden lusts and desires were as far from godly as one can imagine. My behavior led first to attempting and then realizing the fulfillment of these lusts. I could say again that I was not myself, but the reality is that I was what I had become. The spirits inside of me were living out their desires through me, and I was their willing accomplice.

All the information I needed to identify my condition and its cause was available to me. I recognized the great conflicts that churned inside of me and knew they were the source of my inner distress. I was conflicted over what I believed about God's desire for us to live righteous lives centered on Him compared to the great sin of my life, including adultery, fornication, putting my own pleasure above the welfare of my family, and the constant lying to cover it all up. Reconciling what I believed with what I was doing was simply not possible. The hardest question was the obvious one: What was I going to do about it?

Fear

In time, I came to understand that the short-term pleasure I sold out to came at the price of long-term agony, and that was merely the price of admission to a personal hell. As my secret became more precarious and burdensome, my fantasies turned on me. No longer the hero in these mind plays, I was now almost exclusively the victim. Multiple scenarios played out in my imagination, most of them ending with me critically injured or dead. They played over and over in my mind, day and night. My mind and psyche had turned on me. I was in trouble, and I knew it.

Fear began to grow as I realized just how deeply I was trapped and how difficult, if not impossible, escape and redemption would be. Once fear had a beachhead in my soul, it quickly became a full-fledged invasion. I could almost see echelons of landing craft headed my way, each filled with battle-ready fear troops intent on attacking every area of my life. I feared discovery, and I feared what would become of me if I wasn't discovered. I feared for our marriage and the effects on our children and grandchildren. I feared exposure in my professional life, what that would mean for employment and our financial future. I feared losing all my relationships and being left alone, unlovable to my family and mocked and abandoned by the world. Every day became a back-and-forth battle as I shifted between the lusts and addictions of depravity and the worry, fear, anxiety, and shame that now consumed me.

The further I spiraled into these hellish dungeons, the further my unworthiness separated me from God. That was another conflict in the war being waged between my spirit and soul. I knew right from wrong but felt I had chosen wrong so often that I was unworthy of rescue. But I fought. My spirit, that small flickering flame somewhere deep inside, would not give in. There was a part of me that would not give up on me. I clung to it in desperation even as fear continued to grow.

Fear is a damning thing to live with, and it has implications and impacts on our lives that exceed our appreciation of its character. In my case, I've learned that it is the root of a long association with lying. We don't lie about things we are happy about or proud of; we lie about our failures and shortcomings. Fear causes us to want to conceal what is really going on in our lives, both to ourselves and others. It is this desire to hide from truth that motivates us to lie. The problem is that we know we've lied, so the very act of lying becomes another accusation in the battle between our soul and spirit. We lie to avoid facing the truth because it is uncomfortable or shameful, and in the process, we heap more scorn on ourselves because we are aware of what we've done and are ashamed of ourselves for doing it. Fear and desire to have the things we lust after lead us into sin; guilt and shame for having sinned and lying about it then convict us; and, just like Adam and Eve in the garden, we withdraw from God and separate ourselves from those who love us most. This is no way to live a healthy and vibrant life, and those trapped in fear and lying don't. We may try to project such to the world outside, but on the inside, we know. And guess what? The world outside knows, as well. Our personal radars are well-tuned to the frequencies of deceit. You know when someone is not being truthful and genuine with you, and the world knows when you are not, as well. When lying becomes normal to you, it becomes part of who you are. Your personality and persona change when you accept lying as a way of coping. Lying manifests itself in our personality, self-talk, and in our physical body. All three of these dimensions change as a result of our actions, and sometimes they are the motivation behind our lies. We think of fear, guilt, and shame as conditions resulting from our behavior, and they are—in part. Before they are a result, however, they are a cause. It helps to think of them as agents of evil, sent on assignment to cause us to fail. That is exactly what they are. Evil tempts us, and we rationalize our agreement based on our impure desires and motives. Then the three agents of deception convict us and lead us into greater sin. So begins a cycle of lying to maintain false realities we have established through our previous lies. What begins as imaginary escapism leads to sin, which then becomes a pattern, which in turn becomes our "new reality." And we wonder why we become dissatisfied with our lives and why our personalities begin to fracture.

The first step in overcoming fear, guilt, shame, and lying is to recognize where they exist in our lives and to commit to the truth. If we lie to ourselves by denying the issues in our life, then we only feed the demons and spirits that control us. They will have even more reason to mock us, not to fear us and our faith. So, we begin by asking what is at work in us that causes us to fear or heaps shame and guilt on us. Is it something we've done ourselves, or are they wounds we carry because of what has been done to us? In my case, this was a long list: Inferiority and unworthiness, failure, lust, coveted-ness, not knowing how to love or be loved—all of these and more opened the doors to my captivity. I lied to make myself seem better than I thought I was. I became addicted to pornography and sex and committed adultery to find the world's version of love, emotionally abandoning my wife and children in the process. That is just a part of the list, and I lied to myself and others to cover it all up. But the question for this moment is to you. What truths are you denying in your life? Is it adultery? Theft? Abortion? Have you murdered someone? Do you ridicule others to make yourself look better? Are you a bully? Feeling like you do not measure up to the standards you are supposed to model? Did you abandon your family, or were you a victim of abandonment? Are you addicted to pornography and sex like I was? Or maybe your addiction is gambling, alcohol, drugs, or wealth. What about physical abuse or satanic worship? Are these your burdens and hidden secrets? No matter what your addictions or wounds are, I have good news for you. Jesus Christ sacrificed His blood for your life, and His blood speaks freedom, restoration, and renewal into our lives when we call out to Him. Even for me, even for you.

[The Father] has delivered and drawn us to Himself out of the control and the dominion of darkness and has transferred us into the kingdom of the Son of His love, In Whom we have our redemption through His blood, [which means] the forgiveness of our sins. Colossians 1:13,14 (AMPC)

Easy to say, you say? True enough, but also true indeed. So where do we start? With three simple yet powerful steps:

First, confess and repent your sin and weakness to God your Heavenly Father. If you do not already know Jesus as the Savior of your life, then start there. Ask Him to come into your life as Lord, the One you love and trust. Tell Him that you believe He died on the cross for your sin, was buried to bury your sin, and was raised to new life in victory over your sin and death. Give your heart to Him and hold nothing back. He created you, loves you, and is waiting for your heart to reach out to His. Then lay everything down before Him: every sin, every burden, every pain, every shame. Lay it all down at the foot of the cross and ask Him to take it from you. Do not hold back, and do not judge His mercy. There is nothing that is too small or too big. Lay it all down, and feel it lift from you as He takes all your sin, worry, and pain.

Next, make a commitment to be honest and transparent with yourself and God. It helps to start a list or journal to record all the things that separate you from God: every thought, sin, unbelief, lust, or failure. Write them down and ask the Holy Spirit to reveal others to you that you are not remembering in the moment, or which may be blocked from your conscious mind. When He does, write them down immediately before they can be forgotten. As you write them down, give them to Jesus and thank Him for covering them with His blood. Do not expect this to be a one-session exercise; it is likely to continue for years. Be faithful to it and experience the joy of new freedom that each release brings.

Finally, have faith in Jesus' faith. One of the mistakes we make is believing that we can do it ourselves, without Jesus. Another is that our faith is not strong enough, especially if our sin is heavy or we have failed in previous attempts. What we fail to realize is that our power and faith will never be enough. Jesus, however, has perfect power and faith. When we have faith in His power and faith the shortcomings of our own are made irrelevant by His perfection. How can we know that His power and faith are perfect? By understanding its source, His position as one facet of God. Being a part of God, having been present at the creation and having created us, He perfectly knows His plan for our life. As God, He is fully confident in His power because He is God. Is your faith weak? No problem, because God's faith is perfect. Why? Because He knows He is God, and being God, He knows the beginning and the end and everything in between.

This simple process of confession, repentance, and faith is a lifelong pattern of diligence and accountability. It is not easy, requiring consistent perseverance, obedience, and endurance. Simple. Not easy. Vital.

This is hard work, and it will test your commitment and endurance, but the reward that awaits you is sweet indeed. There is more to be done, however, as we must also understand the effect of our sin on our life. I was about to learn things about myself that I did not understand even when I knew I was lost in depraved sin. I refer to these as the fruit of my sin. In hindsight, the signposts were all there; I just sped by them so fast that I did not see or recognize them. That oversight did not mean that the hazards did not exist, only that I was blind to them. That would change as God revealed to me just how broken I was. It would turn out to be a humbling and harrowing experience.

CHAPTER THREE

BITTER FRUIT

The world is full of beautiful trees that bear fruit, fruit that tastes sweet and which nourishes our bodies. I like most kinds of fresh fruit, and I love fruit pies, especially deep-dish apple, peach, and blackberry. I come by that love honestly, having been raised in a family that came from Oklahoma and Texas and specialized in Southern cooking. I remember fondly the smell of the house when Mom fixed one of her pies, an aroma that tantalized my taste buds to the point where I would sneak a first taste when no one was looking because I just couldn't wait until dinner time. When a tree is healthy, it produces tasty fruit indeed, and it is both enjoyable and good for us. But when a tree is unhealthy, its fruit can be shriveled, bitter, and poisonous—even deadly. My life was full of such fruit, the product of a life of deceit, sin, guilt, and shame. You could say my tree was all but dead, and you would be correct. Still, however, it existed in a day-to-day pattern filled with the logical results of my sin, barely alive, hanging on, and praying for a refreshing rain that would bring it back to life. My bitter fruit had names you may be familiar with: anxiety, depression, multiple personalities, unworthiness, and suicide.

ANXIETY

When one lives in fear and lacks confidence, the spirit of anxiety is a frequent and taunting companion, like a sarcastic and accusing friend we wish we didn't have. Like many maladies, anxiety can come in different forms. When we are apprehensive, uneasy, nervous, or anticipating some calamity, then we are anxious. This anxiety can manifest itself physically, as in sweat or a weakened voice, and in other ways, such as doubt about our ability to cope and fear of what will result.

Anxiety was one of the most frequent fruits of my experience. Many were the nights I lay in bed unable to sleep, taunted by failures large and small. Every shortcoming, whether in my work life, personal and family life, or spiritual life, was a poison-tipped spear into my soul. A budget overrun on a project, a problem at home, the accusation of my sin—all of these were examples of things that would torment me, causing me to ridicule myself and fear the worst possible outcomes. Trying to live life through my own strength, I was defenseless against the demons hounding me.

In essence, I had abandoned my only possible hope, the Hope of Christ. I thought myself unworthy of His mercy and so took the full load of my sinful life and all its travail onto my own weak shoulders. Trying to do it on my own while knowing that I was unqualified for the task only heaped more disdain and anxiety onto my spirit. Christ Himself tells us that behaving this way is folly:

> *"And which of you by being anxious can add a single hour to your life? If then you are not able to do as small a thing as that, why are you anxious about the rest?"* Luke 12:25,26 (ESV)

Christ says that adding time to our lifespan is a small thing and instructs us that everything else is even smaller. In understanding this, we see that His perspective is much different than our own, and that perspective matters. When we elevate the small troubles of our lives to be tall mountains, we place obstacles before ourselves that were never intended. We create our own worries, then worry about not being able to overcome them. Our worry causes us and those around us to suffer needlessly, all because we do not understand and are unwilling to surrender to God's way or think ourselves unworthy of His love and care.

By refusing to accept God's provenance in our lives, we deny the truth of His Word when He says that He is our protector:

> *But now thus says the LORD, he who created you, O Jacob, he who formed you, O Israel: "Fear not, for I have redeemed you; I have called you by name, you are mine. When you pass through the waters, I will be with you; and through the rivers, they shall not overwhelm you; when you walk through fire you shall not be burned, and the flame shall not consume you. For I am the LORD your God, the Holy One of Israel, your Savior ..."*
> Isaiah 43:1-3a (ESV)

Our provider:
> *Even though I walk through the valley of the shadow of death, I will fear no evil, for you are with me; your rod and your staff, they comfort me. You prepare a table before me in the presence of my enemies; you anoint my head with oil; my cup overflows. Surely goodness and mercy shall follow me all the days of my life, and I shall dwell in the house of the LORD forever.*
> Psalm 23:4-6 (ESV)

Our peace:
> *Do not be anxious about anything, but in everything by prayer and supplication with thanksgiving let your requests be made known to God. And the peace of God, which surpasses all understanding, will guard your hearts and your minds in Christ Jesus.*
> Philippians 4:6,7 (ESV)

Who would you rather depend upon: yourself with your limitations and weaknesses, or the God of the universe with His unlimited abundance and ability? The answer is obvious, isn't it? If it is so obvious, why do we continue to live as if our lives depended only on ourselves, as if we are free to do as we please without consequence or as if there is no hope? If you are a Christian, the answer is either that you've lost your way, or you were not as secure in your conversion as you thought you were. Or possibly you are like I was, knowing the sin you are living but unwilling to surrender it and feeling unworthy of God's mercy. If you do not know Christ, then you have no basis for hope other than your own inadequate self. These conditions are merely different paths to the same waypoint in life. You have fallen for the great lies of the world and become trapped in the never-ending toil of trying to do everything right in your own power and wisdom, which cannot be done. The good news is that the path away from this waypoint is the same for all: Turn into the cross and surrender your sin, worries, failures, and lost hope to Jesus. Let His blood redeem you; let Him carry your load. He has the strength; you do not. Surrender it and let the "peace of God, which surpasses all understanding" manifest in and through your life.

Depression

Anxiety and depression are close kin; where you find one, you will frequently find the other. Their relationship is bi-directional, with an episode of either one likely to trigger the other. I found this to be true in my own experience, not realizing until I was past deliverance and on the road to peace that for much of my adult life I suffered from depression. I was often in a sad or hopeless state, earmarked by listlessness, inability to concentrate, overeating, and a general "What's the use?" attitude. When we feel dejected and hopeless, there is no reason to try.

Had I ever recognized and admitted to the state I was in and sought help, a diagnosis of clinical depression would have been a likely result. That did not happen, however. As difficult as it may have been to experience, it would have been infinitely better than the decades of pain and abandonment that occurred in its place, for loved ones and for me. I suffered from the classic dynamics of one facing this condition, not understanding what I was experiencing in the medical/psychological sense, fearing finding out, and using denial as a shield.

Any failure, perceived slight, unfair comment, or rejection would send me into a funk that might take days or weeks to climb out of. The Great Liar would be on his soapbox playing to an enthusiastic audience, every demon inside me cheering him on, agreeing with every taunt and accusation. This is what depression does. It lies to us. It magnifies everything negative in our lives, puts the blame on us, and then taunts us with our inability to do anything about it.

The lies that depression tells are as vicious as they are insidious. I already thought I was so broken as to be beyond repair, that was one lie I had already taken as truth. There were others, however. When paralyzed by depression and without motivation or energy to do even the things I cared most about, my inner voice told me that I was lazy and worthless. When I could not focus or think clearly, it was a lack of intellect that was the problem. When I could not come up with a workable solution to a problem, it didn't really matter, because nothing was ever going to work. When I withdrew into my own world, abandoning even those I loved the most, it was because I wasn't worthy of their love and knew that being alone was my destiny. I would be safer in this solitary world of mine, I thought, insulated from the pain of failing in life.

Like many diseases, depression is not something that you can simply work your way through. A pep talk may help for a few minutes, if that. Refocused effort and concentration are likely to be short-lived. When a person under depression has failed, they will recognize it. The failed attempt will quickly become another overwhelming weight, causing them to sink deeper into the quicksand of lost hope. Attempts to work it out on one's own will inevitably be defeated by the strongman who battles against us.

Low self-esteem and lack of self-love can even turn into self-hatred. When one is convinced that they are broken beyond repair or that there is no hope, they are like a person running from danger who finds themselves trapped in a dead-end alley. Believing that there is no way out or rejecting the notion of backtracking their way out as simply too hard, they give up. The thought process goes something like this: "I couldn't keep myself from getting into this mess even when I wasn't this far gone. What makes me think I can help myself out now? It's hopeless. Why try?" Rejection by one's family, friends, and peers is one thing; rejection from within your own being, however, is devastating. If you don't believe in yourself, then you can't blame others who don't believe in you. From that point, withdrawal is a natural progression, separating us from those who want to help and from those who can help.

UNWORTHINESS

Unworthiness is a natural companion of anxiety and depression. When one believes they are a failure, especially on a large scale or stage, then it is easy to heap scorn on oneself. Easy, because it seems justified, as if it is the only rational response. One might know intellectually that it is not rational, but that knowledge can be overwhelmed by failure and despair in the moment. We all have incidents in our lives when we've done something foolish or unkind, or failed miserably at something we should have succeeded in. When our inner voice begins to replay those incidents and taunt us with our failure, we can be sure it is the spirit of unworthiness at work.

I believe there are two primary reasons we sometimes feel unworthy: We measure ourselves against invalid standards, and we judge the quality of our lives based on our feelings. The first is incorrect by definition; the second, by its lack of foundation.

When one feels unworthy, it is because they are comparing themselves to a standard they have failed to meet. Often, people obsess over what they must do, how they must improve, and what must change for them to meet the standard they judge themselves against. The better question to first ask is how the standard compares to reality. We see it in our lives every day, this judging oneself or others poorly because they do not measure up. But what are they not measuring up to? Is the standard realistic or unrealistic? Is it valid or invalid?

If you happen to question this point, I will simply refer you to pop culture. Television shows, for instance, are filled with predominately beautiful people, most of whom seem to live in the sunshine, wear designer clothes, and drive expensive cars. No one has a yard with weeds or a kid who needs braces. Bosses are all sympathetic, unassailable, or comedians. I could go on, but I think you get the point. When we do not measure up to what is portrayed as normal, we experience feelings of failure and unworthiness. The standards we set for ourselves, or allow to be set for us, are often unrealistic. What we too seldom realize is that feelings of unworthiness caused by failing to meet a false standard are also unrealistic.

Feelings of unworthiness or self-hatred are powerful exactly because they are feelings. Emotion is one of the most powerful forces we know. Emotion causes us to love, to sacrifice, to experience indescribable joy and the depths of agony. Our emotions can steer us into life's greatest accomplishments, or into its deepest pits. Being in control of our emotions—in the sense that we understand which are valid or invalid, their source, and their trajectory—is important because understanding allows us to judge emotions correctly. Yes, we are capable of judging our emotions. In fact, it is one of the most important things we do, since our emotions often act as the rudder of our ship, steering us either into calm seas or onto the rocks.

Unworthiness is an emotion and is thus subject to change. Feelings are temporal; they change based on the conditions around us and our evaluation of our role and place. I've heard it said, and largely agree, that one of our biggest problems is that we live our lives based on our feelings instead of our values and core beliefs. We seek to align ourselves with what society says is right, only to be left flailing in the wind when social norms change. We are in a good place, then suddenly we are not. What changed? Did we change, or did the standard change? We too often become a prisoner of false standards. They cause us to reject ourselves, and in doing so, we place our own determination ahead of God's.

Who then would dare to accuse those whom God has chosen in love to be his? God himself is the judge who has issued his final verdict over them — "Not guilty!" Who then is left to condemn us? Certainly not Jesus, the Anointed One! For he gave his life for us, and even more than that, he has conquered death and is now risen, exalted, and enthroned by God at his right hand. So how could he possibly condemn us since he is continually praying for our triumph? Who could ever separate us from the endless love of God's Anointed One? Absolutely no one! For nothing in the universe has the power to diminish his love toward us. Troubles, pressures, and problems are unable to come between us and heaven's love. What about persecutions, deprivations, dangers, and death threats? No, for they are all impotent to hinder omnipotent love ... Romans 8:33-35 (TPT)

If God loves us despite our greatest shortcomings, failures, and sins, then how are we justified in not loving ourselves? Do we have greater knowledge, understanding, or more accurate emotions than the God of the universe who created all things and knows all things? I think not. When we recognize this, we have a pathway back to level ground. Walking that path requires effort, diligence, and perseverance. It requires obedience.

Dissociative Personality Disorder

Dissociative Personality Disorder is comprised of three major types.[12] Dissociative Amnesia is a severe form of memory loss that is not related to a medical condition, and which is more severe than normal forms of memory loss. It can affect memory related to specific traumatic events, and in rare cases can result in complete loss of memory of one's own life. Dissociative Identity Disorder (previously called Multiple Personality

---

12 https://www.mayoclinic.org/diseases-conditions/dissociative-disorders/symptoms-causes/syc-20355215

Disorder) includes having multiple identities with one taking precedence over others depending on what stressors or other conditions are being encountered. Symptoms include hearing voices of others talking inside your head, having different personality traits, personal histories, voices, and manners, each affiliated with one of the alternate personalities. The last major form, Depersonalization-Derealization Disorder, results in one feeling detached from themselves. Symptoms include observing yourself from an outside perspective, as if watching yourself in a movie, for example. Some with this disorder also sense time speeding up and slowing down, or see the world around them in a fog-like state.

While I experienced all of these, it is the second, Dissociative Identity Disorder, that was most prevalent. When searching the Internet, I would be driven by moods and desires that would overtake me, depending on the spirit at work. It may have been a search for images portraying the lust of the moment, or a quest to find a chat partner for sexual role play. Whatever the motivation, realization would usually come in moments as a new connection was made. The vast majority of these were one-time encounters, some lasting minutes, and others longer. A small handful became repetitive encounters, and a very limited number became long-term relationships. This last category involved deep emotional connection and affection which muddied my emotional, relational, and attitudinal persona. Each relationship was nuanced to fit the particular role, scene, personality, and partner that had been established. Each required a different me to be successful. I became very good at keeping my different personalities sorted, or so I thought. The reality is that the spirits at work in me determined which lust would play out at any given time and would direct my thought and emotional patterns and which "me" would be activated. There were periods when multiple personalities would compete for primacy, leading to conflicting emotions, thought patterns, and behavior. The inevitable outcome was most problematic: when my "others" began to manifest themselves in daily life, outside of the fantasy world I had constructed to contain them. There were no extreme manifestations that I recall, but there were thought patterns that I recognized and a rare slip of the tongue which I was able to cover quickly. I don't believe that anyone else picked up on these occurrences, but I did, and it scared the hell out of me.

My journey into the world of multiple personalities began during elementary school years but was innocuous enough until my exploration of pornography became an obsession. Each image or movie presented a role I would play in my mind, each role requiring a different set of characteristics, actions, and personality. Later, the advent of the Internet and its plethora of opportunities opened my gates even wider. They were busy gates, too, as I stood in them welcoming each new perversion that rushed in. I was always a quiet, shy, introverted person and would never have been bold enough to attempt in real life what I fantasized about. The "safe" option of doing so discreetly with online partners, however, was too appealing to pass up. I could be whomever and whatever I wanted to be at any given time. Far from safe, it resulted in the fracturing of my personality, the betrayal of all that I thought I held to be true and pure, the greatest of all sins against my beautiful wife, emotional abandonment of my family, and loss of hope. In the end, it would lead to contemplating and making basic preparations for suicide.

Suicide

In my darkest days, I did contemplate suicide. I had a plan; I knew how, where, and when, and I had prepared for my family's security after I was gone. My work commute took me along many miles of coastal road, curvy and dangerous at places. I normally left in the early morning long before sunrise when the road was often deserted. I had a fast car and loved to press its limits and was known for my heavy foot. Once or twice every year, someone died on this road, going off at speed to the rocks and ocean below. It wouldn't be an unusual occurrence. A simple morning commute accident. Speeding on the coast highway in the dark, missing a curve. No one would know. The agony would end. That was my plan.

In the period just before my confession, I was at the lowest point. I had tried to end the last of my adulterous relationships and failed miserably. Knowing I had been "that close" and unable to break the bonds of sin was demoralizing. It was another failure to add to the list, but it felt much heavier than that. In my mind, I had just proved that escape was impossible. That left one other option.

I knew that suicide is a sin and that it would devastate my family, and I could not bear the thought of causing even more pain. But I had the thoughts, and I listened to the lies of darkness. I was living a secret life of sin and surely bound for Hell. Why not go now and end the agony? Ruthie and my sons would hurt but only for a little while, and then they would be better off without me. She could be rid of me and make a better life; she would have financial security; her pain would eventually evaporate, and mine would end. Just jerk the wheel on the approach to the curve—that's all it would take.

As I sped along the dark coast road on my way to work one morning, I thought about it. I knew that all it would take was an instantaneous action that could not be reversed, but I couldn't do it. I had planned it out and made all the basic preparations, but now that the moment was upon me, I did not have it in me to follow through. I decided to tempt the demons inside me, thinking maybe they would do it for me. I pressed down on the accelerator and the car surged ahead, moving at nearly 100 mph on this dark and curvy road. Falling rocks, animals, and objects laying in the road were not uncommon here. Maybe fate or the demons would use one of them to end my misery. I screamed at them, trying to taunt them into doing the dirty work for me. Silence, then an overwhelming sense of weakness and failure as the taunting began and the voices in my head ridiculed me. I couldn't even do this. Giving in to them, I slowed down and went on my way, anticipating another day of searching for answers that never seemed to come.

Suicide. How could I even contemplate the act? The Devil is a cunning adversary and sometimes even when he loses, he wins. I did not act on my plan but even thinking about it brought more shame, fear, and guilt. Who was I to end what God began? How could I be so weak as to even visit the notion? What was wrong with me? How could I distrust God in such a way? Why couldn't I believe? Why wasn't I worthy of His mercy? As bad as the pain of my shame and hopelessness was, the agony of wondering how I could have messed up my life to arrive at this place was worse. Most troubling, there were no good answers to these questions. All the voices in my head were giving me lots of input, none of it healthy. The demons in me were roaring again, chastising and goading me toward an end.

There was a point where I was hanging on by a thread, and I knew it. I pleaded with God to release me, even asking Him to take me Himself. Still, I heard nothing. Dead silence. Do you know what it is like to cry out to God again and again and hear nothing in return? How empty and doomed that makes one feel? To believe and want to believe and get nothing in return? Then the thoughts begin to come: I am so far gone that even the God of Love has no time or concern for me. I am nothing to Him. He must abhor who I am and what I've become, and He is right to feel as He does. I will never escape this hell; I should just leave now and get it over with. No one will miss me, not for long. I should finally do something right for once and set my family free.

Lies, all lies.

I cannot say why God chooses to respond or not respond, or how He chooses His timing. Possibly it is a test, or maybe it is part of taking us all the way down. But I know that He is listening, watching, and waiting for us to give Him an opportunity. Simply asking may not be enough. Often, God waits for us to do something, to take the first step, to demonstrate our desire for life. He waits for us to give Him a reason to reach His hand out to us. For some, it may be a last-minute decision not to take the life He created; for others, it may be surrender of our facade and pride to appeal for earthly help. Whatever the case may be, I know this: He is a God of love. There is nothing we can do to merit His mercy and love in our lives on our own, and there is nothing we can do to negate it—except steal what is rightfully His.

I am not suggesting that God forgives everything. He does not. Nor does He forgive every person, only those who surrender to Him and abandon everything they have put above Him. We must act. We must give Him a reason to forgive. We must repent from our heart and abandon ourselves to His will and power, leaving behind our hatred of ourselves. If He can still love us despite what we have become, then we have a reason to love ourselves.

Thank God my feeble attempt failed. Even when life was torment and agony, there was a place hidden deep inside where I never gave up on the possibility of a miracle. Hidden in a small corner of my heart was a barely flickering flame kept alive by faint hope, waiting for a fresh breeze of God's breath to bring it to life. Suicide, I knew, would rob from God the chance to work a miracle of redemption. I did not think it likely but knew it was possible, and it was the only chance I had. In my heart of hearts, I could not give up on God. I could not rob Him of the chance to save me.

Satan is the Great Liar. Recognize that, understand it, and do not listen to him. Just as God was sitting with me in the car each time I listened to Satan's lies and contemplated a quick end, He is sitting with you in the midst of your life. There is a flame inside of you, a flame of God's love. It may be small and barely flickering, but it is there. Do not extinguish it before He can breathe new life into it.

Surrounded by family and friends, I was alone, emotionally isolated from those who loved me, pretending to be someone I was not, and accusing myself from every imaginable perspective. It was not what I intended, not what I wanted, but it was where I found myself. There seemed nothing I could do about any of it, and there wasn't. My multiple failures at trying to escape on my own had proved that. It would require intervention by a higher power, something I had been crying out for but had not yet experienced. Deep down inside I loved God. I wanted to believe that there was still hope for even me, but the silence in response to my prayers was deafening. Where had God gone? If He never gives up on anyone, why wasn't I hearing from Him? Convinced again that I was the case that disproved the law of grace, I resigned myself to the life I had, complete with its fear and shame. The best I could hope for is that my great sin would remain undiscovered, and my personal hell would remain mine alone to bear. I would do my best to normalize my life and carry on. I had come to the end. I would live the rest of my life as a charade, normal on the outside, broken on the inside. I could accept that as long as no one else knew and no one else had to bear the pain of my sin.

God had a different plan. Everything I was trying to avoid would soon be required of me and those I loved. That would be the price of freedom. He had already set the wheels in motion; I just didn't know it. That was about to change.

PART TWO

DISCOVERY, DELIVERANCE, FREEDOM

Then they cried to the LORD in their trouble, and he delivered them from their distress. He brought them out of darkness and the shadow of death, and burst their bonds apart.
Psalm 107:13,14 (ESV)

CHAPTER FOUR

FINALLY, SOMEONE SEES

Once again, Ruthie and I were with a group of church friends, helping a couple we loved move into a new home. They needed the
help, and all of us were there doing what friends do. It was a long day of
moving and unpacking, assembling furniture, putting things in order. At
the end of it everyone was tired, but before we headed home, someone
suggested we pray. Instead of the entire group praying together we broke
into small groups. Ruthie and I were paired with a young man whom
we spoke with every Sunday but barely knew. The three of us gathered
in one area of the living room and quickly went through the usual small
talk. As we began to pray, the young man said he felt moved to pray for
us, to pray for our marriage. His assumption as he felt this unction was to
pray for our ministry. That quickly changed as the Spirit moved in him
almost immediately after he began. He stopped abruptly, and I opened
my eyes to see what was wrong. His eyes were shut tight and anguish
filled his face. He was holding our hands tightly, and then he said: "God
is showing me the inside of your house. It's a nice house, and everything
looks to be in perfect order, but it's not. The two of you are in different
rooms of the house. You never talk, and there is only pain, no love. You

appear to be a perfect couple, but you are broken, and so is God's heart. He is weeping for you."

By the time he finished his prayer, he was sobbing. That made three of us.

Driving to work the next morning, I wondered if this was the first crack. There had been several close calls, but no one had ever seen through the facade like this before. Every time we would meet a new prophet or visit with friends in ministry, I would wonder if they would be the one to finally see the real me. I thought surely one of them would, but no one had. This seemed different. The revelation had come quickly to this young man, and his words were straight from God. It had been a difficult ride home and an even more difficult evening, but this was a new day. As I drove along the beach road, I asked myself if this would be another false alarm, or if it would be the beginning of my undoing.

DENNY SEES INSIDE MY SPIRIT AND SOUL

Soon after, our church was visited by a guest speaker. He was known to be a man who operated through the Spirit, one who saw things, who could read people. He and his wife were late arriving, and the service was already beginning, but I knew he was on his way. His cousin, a good friend of ours, sat just in front of us with two empty seats at her side. I waited for his arrival with great anticipation. Would he be the one? Then my heart palpitated, and I felt his presence before I saw him; without looking, I knew he was approaching down the aisle. Then he was moving into his seat, and as he turned to set his things down, our eyes met. I knew instantly that he knew. He held my look with intensity for a brief eternity, his dark eyes penetrating deep into my soul, then he smiled gently and said, "We'll talk after the service." To say that I did not hear much of what the pastor said for the next few hours would be an understatement. My entire thought process was focused on the man sitting with his back to me, the man whom I knew with certainty knew my secret.

He spoke during the service, and then ministered to nearly everyone in attendance afterward. It took a long time, but I waited until I was the last and the room had cleared. Ruthie and I stepped up to him, and he took my hands and proceeded to gently speak out the ugly truth of my life, naming my every heartache and many of my sins. He saw the big one but did not speak it out, saying instead that it was between me and my wife. It took a long time, and at one point, his cousin and wife were struggling to hold me up as he ministered to me, keeping me upright until he finished. As he spoke to me, I felt as if I were in a trance, completely subsumed in love and peace. There was no fear, no anxiety, no attempt to deny or deflect. There was only love from the throne of Heaven, and gratitude from a broken heart and soul. Later as I lay on the floor, I could barely hear them speaking in soft tones as my spirit lost itself in a sea of never-ending love, each swell a new euphoria of peace.

This encounter did not end until minutes before one o'clock in the morning. All of us were exhausted, physically and emotionally. As we were finally preparing to leave, his wife looked at me with a questioning look and asked, "Were you surprised by this?"

"I came expecting and hoping," I said. She considered that for a moment and shook her head in wonder, then simply smiled and told me they loved me. This was the moment I had ached for, and it had finally happened. A point had been reached and a corner turned, and I could see a small point of light at the end of my long and dark tunnel. It wasn't big and it wasn't bright, but it was there.

A MESSAGE FROM A FRIEND

I believe that there were people who saw a little of what I was hiding before these two incidents, but they just saw glimpses, shadows of my sin. A friend in ministry, one who deals primarily in restoration, is one of those I believe saw something. We were ending a short visit with them, and as he prayed for me before we departed, he prayed against lust.

A beloved aunt once stopped short in the middle of a conversation and said, "God will not be mocked." It was a direct accusation without any sense of knowing what my sin was.

The pastor of the church we were currently attending could be direct and, at times, sarcastic. He would often refer to me as "the man of God," and I knew it was not intended as a compliment. He did not know what my sin was, but he did know that I was separated from God, regardless of my facade. Others I am sure felt something was amiss but couldn't quite put their finger on it.

There was a lady in the church with whom we had become close. She herself had gone through many trials in life before surrendering completely to God. She knew how hard her journey had been, and she could see it in others. For months, she was an encourager for both Ruthie and me, never confronting or challenging, always uplifting with God's love. She was someone we were familiar with and trusted, but I was surprised to receive a text from her late on the evening of December 23, 2013, just as I was lying down in bed:

> *"Ken, you are at a crucial point in your life and it is about life or death right now for you. Something you are not doing is bringing the spirit of death to you. You were created for this time right now, Ken, and the Father's not given up on you, but he does give you a choice if you want to fulfill it or not? This isn't about anyone but you and the Father. I'm just here to help be his voice for you, Ken. Everyone has to walk out his or her own relationship in Father, and yours is very special in Him. Don't ever think he doesn't remember or he forgot about you. That's the farthest from the truth! You have value and the value is in Him! It doesn't matter about the past of one second ago or two days ago. What matters right now is Him. Love you brother, and I am praying for you."*

This message followed an earlier text I had received the previous week from Denny, the visiting minister who saw my brokenness and spoke it out, in which he said that something I was doing was putting me in immediate danger. The message from our friend, however, referenced something I was not doing. I knew exactly what I was doing that was putting me in immediate danger, but what was I not doing that was endangering me?

Sleep did not come for many hours after reading her text and then only through exhaustion. *It is about life or death right now for you.* Those words kept repeating over and over in my mind. I lay there praying, crying out to God to save me, wondering as I prayed if I would live through the night. Fear drove me to plead with God for my salvation and safety. In those hours, I promised Him I would change if only He would save me and spare Ruthie the anguish of knowing the truth. Then I begged for mercy, and finally I gave it all to Him. I didn't want to die, but my fear was of facing my wife and God's judgment.

Notice the evolution of my prayers for mercy. First, I promised to change, but it was a conditional promise. I wanted something from God in exchange; I wanted Him to shield Ruthie from the pain of knowing my sin. Unstated in my prayer but present in my heart was the desire to avoid having to face her anger and pain myself. Finally realizing that God would not honor a request that allowed me to avoid full confession and transparency, I tried begging for mercy, telling God I knew I was unworthy of His consideration but calling on His love simply because that is His nature. That did not work, either, because we cannot manipulate God. It was not until I had spent hours in these prayers that I surrendered it all to Him and finally fell into a short and exhausted sleep.

God does not negotiate.

The Crux of the Matter

My prayers and God's response were not unique. Many have come to this point, and many more will in the future. We try to reason, rationalize, and negotiate with God. Oftentimes, as in my case, we surrender only when every other approach we can think of has failed. It is a wonder that God puts up with us as long as He does. He may not negotiate, but His love and patience are signs of His mercy despite our sin.

Sadly, my life story is not as rare as you might imagine. Even many who do not live such defiled lives; however, put themselves at the same risk. Saying and pretending we believe God while living secret lives that betray these beliefs is sin. It may not be adultery or addiction to sexual immorality as was true in my case, but in God's mind, sin is sin. We rationalize our behaviors in all sorts of ways, building false defenses for our actions. We think and talk in nuance, one sin being greater or lesser than another. Sometimes, we justify our behavior by circumstances, e.g., "I must cheat, or I will lose this deal," promotion, or whatever the issue of the moment may be. We can create all kinds of scenarios in which sin, even a large one, is a "necessary evil" to get to a good result. There is no such thing in God's eyes. We define sin as anything that breaks our personal moral code, with great allowance for leeway where we perceive the result to be desirable. God, however, has a different definition, and it is the only one that matters. Sin is anything that misses the mark of perfection, anything that displeases Him. We think in degrees of sin; God thinks only of perfection. Is that unfair or unreasonable? It is not. In fact, it is the only perspective that can result in a harmonized creation. In this perspective, there is one arbiter of what is right: the One whose heart is perfect and whose will is just. Any other answer must allow for individual preference and bias, and those must at some point conflict with others who supposedly hold the same rights. Our God is all about harmony and oneness. He is not a god of anarchy.

We must come to grips with this divide between perfection and our sin nature on a personal level. Not resolving this divide can only result in a conflicted life, assuming one is not amoral. Such a conflicted life represents a divided mindset, or conflicting values and desires. The Apostle Paul, as great a man of faith as there has ever been, was first a well-educated and widely respected man of his times and a sinner of great proportion, having persecuted the early church with unrivaled zeal. Then he had his Damascus Road encounter with Jesus and his life was instantly changed. Still, however, he found it necessary to come to grips with the divide between his sinful nature and his commitment to God. He articulates the battle well:

> *We know that the Law is spiritual, but I am a creature of the flesh [worldly, self-reliant--carnal and unspiritual], sold into slavery to sin [and serving under its control]. For I do not understand my own actions [I am baffled and bewildered by them]. I do not practice what I want to do, but I am doing the very thing I hate [and yielding to my human nature, my worldliness--my sinful capacity]. Now if I habitually do what I do not want to do, [that means] I agree with the Law, confessing that it is good (morally excellent). So now [if that is the case, then] it is no longer I who do it [the disobedient thing which I despise], but the sin [nature] which lives in me.* Romans 7:14-17 (AMPC)

Paul did not write these words about his life before his conversion experience, but his life after it. He had a life-changing encounter with Christ yet was forced to make righteous decisions as he walked out his new life in Christ each day. Sound familiar?

This is the crux of the matter. What will we do with our lives? Will we continue trying to rationalize sinful behavior, or will we instead nail ourselves to the cross with Jesus, dying to our sin and allowing Him to resurrect our lives? That is our choice. There is no negotiating, no middle ground. It is a choice between Heaven and Hell.

DESIRE AND INTENT

And how will you make that choice? What will you do when it happens, when someone sees and approaches you? Will you turn away from truth and choose the temporary pleasures and vices of this world, or will you choose to please God and thus reap the joy of His pleasure over you? You can wait a long time for someone to finally see and call you out, or you can call yourself out. Either way, it's decision time.

It begins and ends in the heart. If one does not desire to be free with the intent to do whatever is required to achieve freedom, then one is simply lying to himself or herself when they say they want to be free. We can know that we need to change, we can want to change, and we can try to change through willpower or even seek help from others. Willpower is good, getting help is good, but they are doomed to fail if the heart is not invested. It is the deep, burning desires of our heart that drive us; all the willpower and determination in the world cannot move one to surrender and will eventually falter against your demons unless your heart is invested. The question you should be asking yourself is: What is in my heart?

One must be willing to be honest about themselves and willing to listen to honest, godly counsel. God has gifted those who can help, but one must choose a counselor wisely. A counselor's standing in God, ministering from a place of godly wisdom and truth and with His heart, is paramount. A counselor who is not ministering from God's heart and truth cannot help you; they cannot build a bridge to a place they have never been themselves or lead you to ground yourself in beliefs they do not hold. The problem is the broken relationship between you and God. Worldly wisdom cannot fix it. God must be the answer. When we are sinful, He is our judge. When we turn to Him in genuine confession and repentance, He is our merciful Father.

> *Who is a God like You, who forgives wickedness and passes over the rebellious acts of the remnant of His possession? He does not retain His anger forever, Because He [constantly] delights in mercy and lovingkindness. He shall again have compassion on us; He will subdue and tread underfoot our wickedness [destroying sin's power]. Yes, You will cast all our sins Into the depths of the sea.* Micah 7:18-19 (AMPC)

We will discuss the topic in greater detail later, but for now let it suffice to say that confession and repentance are the key. They require the kind of transparency that is unusual in our world: One must be willing to be totally vulnerable. That means taking down your entire set of defense and concealment mechanisms and letting those you love see you as you really are. This is not your battle alone; they have been with you every step of the way. You owe them the whole truth. How can you possibly do that when you know how high the stakes are and how unsure the outcome is? You can do it because your heart is driving you, because the desire to be free has reached the tipping point, and you are ready to pay any price to experience freedom. That is what it takes. It will be hard, and you may lose some whom you care deeply about, but that is their choice. Your choice is to secure your own freedom and ask others to forgive. Maybe not everyone will, but you will be surprised by how many will welcome your openness and embrace you in love. Confession, repentance, forgiveness—these are the weapons God will use to set you free.

WHY BEING SEEN IS A GOOD THING

When one is trapped in sin, they generally know it. Usually, they most definitely know it. If they know right from wrong, then chances are they know if they are doing wrong. With the knowledge of our sin comes the burden of concealing it and carrying it. Placing that load upon ourselves often leads to being critical of ourselves. Not to excuse sin, but sometimes we need to give ourselves a bit of grace. We are not, after all, the first sinner the world has seen. Again, this is not to excuse or condone sin. Rather, it is to point out that we aren't the first and won't be the last. Others before us have sinned and been redeemed, and we can take hope in that, the truth of redemption.

Having your sin exposed, especially when someone else calls it out, is painful but also a good thing. Having it out in the open means that you must no longer spend your energy concealing it, with all the emotional capital that requires, and can begin dealing with it. It means that hope exists. When I reached this point, I experienced two things: an immediate reduction in my overall stress level, and the recognition that I had just been given a huge opportunity, one I could never have created myself. You heard correctly: My stress level went down! Oh, there was still plenty of stress in my life, but it had a different source. It was the stress of going through the confession, repentance, and healing process, which is a process of love, not the stress of lying and hiding, which is a process of deceit. My new stress was based in opportunity. Finally, I had a chance to leave my sin behind, to lay it down and walk away, a chance for a different, better future. I knew that I had to walk it out and that doing so would be difficult at times, but I also knew that peace was waiting at the other end. This was the opportunity of a lifetime, to trade chaos and desperation for peace. That opportunity is available to you, as well. All it requires is that you lay everything down, surrender it all, and trust Jesus to be for you the One He came to be for all.

Your sin is not unique to man or God; both have seen it all before. You do not have to bear it; that is why Jesus came. You are not alone. Those who truly love you will support you, and Jesus will never abandon you. All you need to do is trust in Him.

At this point, I knew I was engaged in a process set in motion by Heaven. Before that process began, before people started to see and speak out my condition, I had been trying to do it on my own. In the aftermath of the initial breakthrough when people began to see, I was in an in-between zone, having decided to end the relationships and obsession with pornography but not yet willing to admit my sin openly; however, I could sense that God was moving and knew the moment of decision could come at any time. I wanted out and, at least for the time being, was still hoping to avoid full disclosure, if possible. My plan was to live up to my values, to exercise my will power, and regain control of my behavior and life. Trying to do it alone, without God leading the way, was a predictably hit-and-miss proposition.

CHAPTER FIVE

FAILING UPWARD

Before that morning in our den when Ruthie and I came face to face with our future, I had decided to make one more attempt to extricate myself without revealing my secret life to those I loved. Over the course of several months, I ended all but one relationship. It took some time, but eventually I ended the last, or so I thought. The attempts to sever this relationship led to a struggle inside as the spirits in me and the emotional entanglement fought to retain their last remaining holds on my life. I was intent on laying it all down, thinking that if I could stop sinning, I would once again be worthy of God's grace and forgiveness. All I had to do was exercise strength of will and end what I knew to be wrong. All I had to do was stop.

A DOOMED ATTEMPT

I was in the office early one morning, hours before others would arrive. Sitting at my desk and debating with myself, I decided that the time had come. I made the call. At the beginning, I was determined; by the end of the call, I had agreed to see her one last time, just to say goodbye face to face. Before the phone was back in its holder, I knew I had failed. Our last meeting was a renewal of everything I was trying to escape.

I wanted so badly to leave my life of sin behind yet was unable to deny its hold on me. Why? The reason I could not leave my sin behind in my own power is the same reason you cannot leave yours behind in your own power. It is not possible. Those of us who attempt to walk away from our sin on our own forget two things: We did not and cannot pay the sacrificial price for our freedom, and we cannot repatriate our past. Our sin and lack of authority disqualify us from both. We are caught in the classic condition of sinful man articulated so well by Paul:

> *For we know that the law is spiritual, but I am carnal, sold under sin. For what I am doing, I do not understand. For what I will to do, that I do not practice; but what I hate, that I do.* Romans 7:14,15 (NKJV)

To put it in plain language, it simply is not in us to save or redeem ourselves. As much as we celebrate human willpower and its ability to accomplish great things, it cannot save us. We can try all we like, and along the way we may even discover things about our generations and ourselves that disturb us, but knowing them and deciding to change cannot redeem us or change the past. As Paul states, it is a spiritual condition that ails us; our natural, carnal soul lacks the credentials to heal us. Only Jesus, the perfect Son of God who sacrificed His life and then returned to life has the power and authority to accomplish this miracle. Only His blood can speak redemption into our lives. Our willpower is no equal for the power of God's mercy and grace. We, the created, are not the equal of our Creator, and despite what much of modern psychology and even modern Christianity tell us, exercising our willpower to live a sinless life is nothing short of folly. Which would you rather bet your life on: your own ability and power, or the God of the universe's heart that desires to see what He created redeemed and restored?

The failed phone call I made that early morning was not my only failure, not by a long shot. There were many attempts over the last couple of years, and some of them seemed to have taken hold. Then I would fail again, often in sudden, unpremeditated fashion, and wonder why I was incapable of following through on what I had committed to. Sometimes, I would rationalize that chats or viewing pornography was not really adultery; other times, the urges would be so strong that I simply gave in to them. I would break a relationship, then return to it. I would swear off porn, then be drawn to it with overwhelming craving. Each failure seemed to build the case against me until eventually I felt like I was prosecuting myself, which is exactly what I was doing. Each sin was a sacrifice to the altars established against me by my own decisions and actions. In that, I was not alone.

A Real Life Example

This inability to save ourselves is part of human reality. History and our own lives are filled with experiences that prove this truth. In Matthew 14, we find the account of Herod's decision to murder John the Baptist. It was not a decision he wanted to make, not an event he wanted to occur, and he did not agree with it. He ordered the execution anyway. Why?

> ...for Herod, having seized John, bound him and put him away in prison for the sake of Herodias, the wife of Philip his brother, for John had been saying to him, It is not lawful for you to have her. And though desiring to put him to death, he feared the people, because they were holding him to be a prophet. Now, Herod's birthday having come, the daughter of Herodias performed a rapid-motion, leaping, lewd dance in their midst and pleased Herod, because of which he put himself under oath, and acknowledging the obligation he incurred thereby, promised to give her whatever she would ask. And she, having been previously high-pressured to action by her mother, says, Give me

at once, right here, on the spot, upon a dish, the head of John the Baptizer. And though having been put to grief, the king, yet because of the oaths under which he had put himself and because of those who were reclining at the banquet table with him, issued the order for it to be given. Matthew 14:3-9 (WT)

Herod never had a chance. His political calculation not to kill John the Baptist was no match for the seduction that tricked him into making an oath, which he was unwilling to deny because of his lusts and concern that he would appear weak before his guests. The fix was in before Herodia's daughter stepped onto the dance floor, set in place by evil's plot to maneuver him without his knowing. Tricked into a position where he must choose between honoring his own desire to keep John the Baptist alive, at least for the time being, or honoring his oath to his seducer and protecting his image, he chose the latter. As a result, he did exactly the thing he did not want to do, even though it grieved him.

You may be able to think of similar occurrences in your own life. You have probably never caused anyone to be put to death, but I am certain you have done things and made decisions even while knowing they were not right that you would like to have back. Undoubtedly, there have been times when you were deceived by your desires or made a calculated choice that went against what you knew to be right. We've all been there.

Understanding the Sin Cycle

Why do we sin even when we do not want to? The answer to that question lies within us and results from our lack of authority over our sin outside of our relationship with Jesus, our Savior. When we establish a pattern of sin in our life, that sin then has a legal right to exist and to continue to insert itself into our thoughts, actions, and words. This is one reason that our willpower and good intentions are not enough. They cannot invalidate the legal right of access that our sin has established. Each act of sin strengthens the altar we have built to it, and we become trapped in the pattern that we ourselves create through our active agreement and engagement. We may be giving in to our sin nature and sinful desires, but we cannot point the finger at them. They are part of us, and we bear full accountability for their existence and the consequences of being complicit in the realization of their desires. Each decision to sin is a weight we alone must bear, until we choose to surrender it to our Savior.

God allows us to make our own choices, and He honors them even when they violate His commandments and plan for our lives. He lets us live the life we choose. We see this even in Jesus' life. Our Lord had to choose to remain sinless when tempted, and He had to choose to submit to God's plan for our salvation, even when He knew the cost would be His physical life. He did not sweat blood as He prayed because He was joyful; He did so because of the travail in His heart over the decision only He could make. In the end, He agreed to what was required of Him, the only One who could save humankind. We are just as powerful to make our decisions as He is to make His, and God the Father respects our power just as He respected our Lord's. Here is the thing: God will give us the desires of our heart no matter what they are, and that is both a blessing and a curse.

It comes down to the desires and intents of our heart. These determine what we pursue, watch, listen to, strive for, and realize. My own life illustrates this cycle perfectly. I desired the pleasures of pornography, set the intent to make them real, took the actions required for that to happen, and finally, I experienced exactly what I had been lusting after. If I were a mathematician, I might express it this way:

$$(\text{Desire} + \text{Intent}) \times \text{Action} = \text{Result}$$

The formula works, regardless of what the desires and intents are. That is the blessing and the curse.

Why do we hang on to our sin when we know it is wrong and want to leave it behind? I am sure there are many answers to this question. For me, there were three main factors that inhibited my path to freedom: I was addicted to the pleasures, afraid of what would happen to myself and my family if I came forward, and wanting to avoid the pain and disgrace that would follow revelation of my sin. Why do we keep on sinning? Possibly because we have not reached the point of wanting to stop, possibly because we do not know how to stop, or possibly because we are afraid to stop. These conditions point to the same reality: We have not yet reached the point where our sin has become too big to bear and we are willing to lay it down, regardless of the cost of doing so.

If that is the case, we might ask how one keeps going when they keep failing. It is a logical question that perhaps is not asked often enough. I say this because many endure repeated failure with resignation to future defeat. Each failure is a defeat, and each defeat gets its own celebration. We accuse ourselves of every possible weakness in our circumstance, belittle ourselves, and set off again, hoping only that we can avoid the failure a bit longer before succumbing to it again next time. We repeat the cycle over and over, moving from sinful desire to sin, remorse, resignation, and a new attempt to clean up our act. And this we call rational.

When Hearts Are Entangled

Breaking our sin cycle is especially difficult when there is a real relationship that must be broken. In today's world, that can mean real as in face to face, or as in an online relationship. Any time hearts are connected it is real, regardless of how they are connected. When we have a relationship with someone with whom we share history, emotions, and commitments, and we care about them, it is natural not to want to hurt them. The truth is that if the relationship is really felt on both sides, then pain cannot be avoided. Affairs that entangle our hearts are hard to face and deal with, but there is no freedom without facing them. In my case, I did not want to hurt those I was involved with even though I knew the relationships were wrong. I cared for them deeply and wanted to avoid causing them pain. The truth, however, is that this is simply not possible. If we are to be successful in our quest for freedom, we must cut the ties that bind us to captivity, including unrighteous relationships.

We must come to a point where we realize that right is right and wrong is wrong, and that right cannot accept or condone wrong. If we do not come to this point, then we are trapped in the sin cycle by our failure to honor what is right. Freedom will not be possible. Not wanting to hurt someone is understandable, but sometimes it is unavoidable. If we do not come to the point of choosing right over wrong regardless of the pain it will cause, then we extend the sin cycle out of a false sense of obligation. Doing this only prolongs our misery and puts us in the position of being dishonest.

It's complicated, it's messy, and it's difficult. We must make hard choices and be resolute in acting on them, and trust that those we have been entangled with will have the maturity and strength to find their own way to freedom.

CREATING A DIFFERENT CYCLE

There is a better way: Create a different cycle. When we choose to engage with hope and not desperation then there is something to hope for. We can hope for hope. Start by recognizing and owning your sin. God knows. You're not going to fool Him with your rationalizations and denials. Don't try to fool yourself, either. You might succeed, and that would be tragic.

By not giving up on our dream of freedom, we establish a beachhead of hope. It may be a small beachhead, but it is there, nonetheless. That little spot deep inside of us, where we refuse to surrender completely even in our darkest days, is important. It gives us a reason to try one more time, regardless of how many "one more time"s have preceded it. Not giving in is the start of everything. It gives us a reason to change, and change brings a new path to walk. Instead of feeding unworthiness with self-recrimination, we can feed hope by believing it is real. Yes, we may have failed again, but that was then, and this is now. Not giving up means being willing to get up and start again. That small beachhead is a gateway to a better future, but you must occupy it, secure it, and move forward from it.

Confess to God and those you have been offending. This one will be hard—believe me I know. But it, like the steps that follow, is non-negotiable. Not confessing means that you must keep the secrets secret, which in turn means you must continue lying to those you love the most and who love you, and to yourself. Those truths on their own will cause your attempt at finding freedom to fail. You cannot achieve a life of truth, integrity, love, peace, and harmony while knowingly and purposefully practicing deceit. Pretty obvious, isn't it? Despite that, people live this way every day. The opposite of continuing to hide our secrets is exposing them, not out of coercion or fear but from a desire to be free and experience the life we've always dreamed of. It takes courage, like taking that beachhead. With confession comes the relief of not having to lie, not having to conceal, and an urgency to take the next step.

Repent and ask for forgiveness. Repenting does not just mean saying you are sorry. True repentance requires action, not words. By "action," I mean changing your behavior. Words sound nice and may give a momentary feeling of relief, but they are meaningless and harmful if not confirmed by actions that prove your sincerity. If your confession is sincere, let your repentance be just as sincere. Prove it by turning yourself around and walking a new path into truth and accountability. The thing about repentance is that you must own it completely. There are no excuses, no contributing causes, no mitigating factors or circumstances that forced you into your sin. There were only choices, and you made each one of them. Own up to them. I cannot tell you why or how, but I know from my own experience that these two acts, confessing and repenting, begin a chain reaction. You will hear more about that part of my story in later chapters, but I will tell you now that this process works when you persevere with it. And if you fail in the middle of it, start again. Do not give up on Hope. Repent, and then act on it.

Forgive yourself and others. For me, forgiving others was easy, but forgiving myself was another matter. After confessing and repenting, a great weight lifted off me. It was an amazing feeling, but soon, deep pangs of guilt began to settle over me, and it took work for me to forgive myself.

I knew it was the right thing to do, but my sin had been so great I even felt guilty about the thought of forgiving myself, as if that was a ludicrous and blasphemous notion. Eventually realizing that this guilt was a new attack meant to rob me of my victory, I was able, with God's grace and love, to forgive myself at the heart level. It was hard, but when it became real, when it wasn't just words anymore, it opened a gateway to greater healing.

Restore. Be intentional about grasping the opportunity you've been given. Work on strengthening your most important relationships. Be purposeful about creating new memories and shared experiences. Most of all, spend time with your Creator. He loves you; show Him you love Him back. Be expecting a new freshness in that most important relationship and feed it with everything you have in you. Let Him restore your spirit and be willing to act on it. Your relationship with God and Jesus is the foundation of everything that will follow. Everything. As He begins to change you, take note. My guess is that He will be at work in others, as well. They will notice the changes in you and will begin to treat you differently. It's a good thing. When they do, be thankful and praiseful. Give God room to work in your heart and notice how it is changing, how your thoughts, speech, and beliefs are changing. You are a work in progress, so keep making progress.

Experience and participate in your renewal. You may be surprised by renewal's power and reach as it touches virtually every area of your life, including your most intimate relationships. The best word I can find to describe what I experienced in this phase is "exhilaration." Everything was exhilarating. I had a new focus and energy, a new attitude and new expectations, a new joy. Things that bothered me and depressed me before were not given a second thought. I started to smile and laugh (that one really made people sit up and notice), and my relationships began to change. Ruthie and I were overwhelmed by God's grace in our relationship. There were many tough conversations and tears, but there was more love, tenderness, and affection than we had experienced in many years. I started caring about people, really caring. One of the things that surprised me most was how quickly God moved me from sitting on the sidelines to being active in personal ministry. Don't get me wrong, I was still a work in progress, but part of that progress was ministering to others who were trapped. A new, unabashed approach to ministering to people took me by surprise. That was not something I had ever done, yet there I was, ministering to folks I barely knew in impromptu fashion as God brought hope, healing, and encouragement to my lips. And my personal relationship with God and Jesus took off like a rocket. I began to crave being in His presence and worshiping Him. Instead of sitting stoically in my seat during worship, I was up at the edge of the stage, jumping and singing, just like the guy I had never been before. This was more than renewal; this was a whole new me!

There it is, your new and better cycle, the process for escaping the bonds of sin that shackle our lives. Confess, repent, forgive, restore, renew. Where does it all begin? With hope. Hope is the match that will start the fire in your heart that moves you to take the first step. What does hope require? Faith. Faith that there is a God and that He cares about you and is waiting to gather you back into His arms.

When we come to the point of being willing to own our sin it makes everything else we must do easier, jump starting the healing process. Making that decision may be the hardest part, but once it is made, what follows is simply doing what we must to honor the decision. The choke holds are broken. It will not be easy, but you will be on your way. In one sense, you can say that this process is a contact sport. You must have faith to believe in God and those who love you. You must be brutally honest and transparent, and that will mean you have to take your lumps. You will have to fight for every relationship and victory. Do it. Whatever your hesitation or doubt, just do it. Do not let your fears rob you of the victory, and God of the glory.

Why, you ask, is this section about confession, repentance, forgiveness, restoration, and renewal in a chapter about continuing to fail even after we've made the choice to change our lives? Because most, if not all, will fail many times before they succeed. If you know of someone who has been successful on their very first attempt without any relapses, I would like to meet them. They will be rare, indeed. Most will fail their way to success, which must mean getting up and starting again. This process will lead to success, but you must work it until it does. Linger too long at any point in this new cycle and you risk being stymied. So, keep going. Take that beachhead. Move forward. Create your new life.

From the moment I began sinning I knew it was wrong, but a series of rationalizations coupled with increasing cravings and the perversion of my heart and mind led me to continue going deeper and deeper until there was no light to be seen. The door to my restoration was shut tight. I knew the choices were mine and mine alone, that I had been weak, and that I could not save myself. I was lost and near hopeless. Then I made a promise to myself and God. I did not know if it would ever happen, but if God in His mercy could ever see His way to offer me a chance at freedom, I would not let it pass. I promised that there was nothing I would not surrender in exchange for freedom and restoration in God's heart. I came to the hard place of knowing it would probably mean the loss of my family and cause them great pain, but I promised myself and God that, should that chance ever come, I would surrender everything to it. It did not come immediately, not for over two years, and there were many failures in the interim. Finally, however, I saw a crack in the door. A few people had seen and were faithful to speak God's love to me. Ruthie had abandoned me to God but was praying from her heart that I would turn back to His love and hers. There was an ache in my heart for the love of God to be restored. The door was ajar, there was a sliver of light, and I was hoping against hope that it was real. What happened next blew the door off its hinges, and I was suddenly in a fight for everything I had been praying for, even for my family and future. God was moving. Would I move with Him?

CHAPTER SIX

THE STEP THAT CHANGES EVERYTHING

In the moments after my confession in the den that April morning, a gentle calm began to settle. It was a quiet brought on by the realization in everyone that what I had just revealed was only the beginning. I had admitted to adultery, but I had not yet admitted to the full scope of the life I had been living. Still, there was a silent recognition that I had taken a first step. There would be trying times ahead and the outcome would not always be certain, but there would be victories, as well—and hope. Always hope. Just a little over an hour after my revelation, our friends departed, and Ruthie and I were left alone. It was not a comfortable feeling, but we were both, in our own ways and thoughts, trusting God. A threshold had been crossed. Now the hard work would begin. We would go on from that point to examine each area of life, each time period, and over time, the full story would finally come out. It was gut wrenching for both of us, but God was doing something, and even at this early stage, we could feel it. We did not know exactly what it was or what the result would be, but we knew that He was in control, and that gave us the strength and confidence to go on.

THE INQUISITIONS

We developed a pattern almost immediately. I would come home from work and we would sit in the den, Ruthie with her yellow legal pads, and me with my prayer that this night's session would be easier than the last and that her pain would begin to ease. It was an unrealistic expectation. For weeks, these sessions were intense and went deep into the night. Then I would get up and go to bed, get up and go to work, then come home and start the process over again. The first three weeks were the toughest; that was when the questions were hardest and the emotions rawest. We did not miss a single night. It was excruciating, having to relive my sin over and over and watch her struggle with my revelations. Still, we went on. There was no let-up. I came to believe that Ruthie had missed her calling in life. She should have been a detective or prosecuting attorney. Her questions were pointed and penetrating, and her diligence in cross-checking every detail of every story was unrelenting. I began calling this period The Inquisitions. I would leave the office and think about it during my long drive home, wondering where the discovery would take us that night. We covered incidents over and over, sometimes weeks apart. Every comment I made was tested and checked against her notes of previous conversations, and holes in the narrative were filled in. We covered our entire history together. She learned of my addiction to pornography, my first wanderings while I was in Southeast Asia, the escorts while I was on business travel, the strip clubs I went to, how I discovered online chat rooms, my rapid descent into the depths of BDSM perversion, and my most intimate relationships. She had every right to be wounded and angry, and she was. There was nothing I could or should have said to temper the story. It was time to get it all out and let the chips fall. It was horrible and painful, but it had to happen. Then she surprised me. In one of our sessions, after I had laid it all out again, she turned to me with a stern look and a hardness in her voice and spoke the most beautiful words I've ever heard: "I will not give you a divorce." I was stunned and elated on the inside. The thing I had been fearing the most, not being able to be with her and our family, was off the table. I knew she could change her mind and might still, but those words rang in my heart for days and gave me one more reason to hope.

One night near the end of the third week we were sitting there, she in her chair and me on the sofa, going through what was now our set routine. She would ask a question and I would answer. She asked me a question that evening, exactly what I do not recall. I paused, formulating my response, then started to speak. As I spoke, the full impact of my sin began to well up inside of me with a fury and suddenness I had not experienced before. I broke. I broke completely. I didn't just cry—I wailed, and I wailed non-stop for over an hour, pouring out my agony at what I had done to God, Ruthie, and my family. I asked God to forgive me, again. I asked Ruthie to forgive me, again. And then I wailed some more. It was not pretty, but at the end I felt like something had left me. I was done in, but I also felt clean on the inside, for the first time in a long time.

THE LAST DOMINO FALLS

Most nights, the questions did not end when we went to bed. I would lie there and wait for what I knew was coming. More questions. She would ask; I would answer. Then she would ask how I could have done this, and we would start over again. Some nights I got little to no sleep, and neither did she. We would lie there after the talking had finished, each consumed by our own thoughts, sometimes dozing briefly and sometimes not. Middle-of-the night wake-ups to answer another question were not uncommon. When morning finally came we were both exhausted and ragged, both fighting for our marriage against all the odds. On one of those nights the last domino fell, and the only part of my story that I was still holding back came out.

Several years before, there had been an incident. Ruthie had gone away to visit a family member, and I had taken advantage of her absence to arrange to meet a woman who traveled from afar. We had been in an online relationship for two years; this would be our first meeting.

When Ruthie returned home earlier than planned and I was nowhere to be found, alarm bells went off. She called my mobile phone and got no answer. My assistant told her that I had planned the week off and was headed to San Diego. Planned the week off? What was she talking about? Why didn't I tell her? What was going on? After repeated attempts to call me with no answer she became frantic, fearing that I had done something dreadful.

Ruthie had come home early because God spoke to her and told her that I was in trouble and thinking of suicide. I wasn't thinking about it—yet. That came later as I drove home after receiving the voice messages and speaking with her. In our den that afternoon, after I finally returned home, our conversation was very hard. She was relieved that I was home safely, and livid at what I had done, all at the same time. She had been worried sick as she drove home after receiving God's message, not knowing where I was, why I had left, and fearing I had committed, or was about to commit, suicide. Now we were together, and I had no good way to explain why I had done what I had, and she was far from believing my explanation. All the emotions were on full display. She was distraught and angry, and I was trying to fake my way through it. In a word, it was horrible.

The interesting thing is that God warned and positioned her beforehand. God knew what was going to happen before it did and interceded to cause her to come home early. His intervention and her obedience set the scene for our confrontation. God was giving me an opportunity to admit my sin years before I finally would. If only I had. Years of desperation and sin could have been avoided if only I had been willing to face reality when the opportunity came. I wasn't, and we both suffered through years of added misery because of it.

I still do not know why her calls did not get through to my phone, but they didn't until I was back in our area and on the way to take the woman I had spent the week with to the airport. Minutes before dropping her off, my phone went wild. Phone messages from Ruthie, my sons, and even my ex-boss poured in. When I realized what had happened, I was aghast, and my gut was ripped out. I could hear the fear and anguish in her voice in the messages, and I knew she was deeply wounded, and I was afraid that I was on the verge of being discovered. I called to tell her I had just received all her messages and was on my way home. I had an hour to figure out what I would say to her.

What could I say? There were two choices: the truth or a lie. I lied. I told her I just needed to get away and have some space for a while, and I thought doing it while she was away would be a good time. I hadn't told her because I didn't want her to worry about me. It was all a lie. The truth is that I used her planned absence to arrange meeting the other woman. I had never told Ruthie the truth in the years between then and my confession, even though the question often came up. I always denied anything other than my original lie.

I cannot explain why I held this truth back while admitting to everything else. It makes no sense. I had already admitted to everything else, but there was something inside me that just would not let this one go, that refused to admit this event and the lie. I do know that there was a bitterness attached to it, not against Ruthie, but against admitting that I had been lying all those years, over and over again. Reflecting back, I think a part of it was how terrible our conversation had been when I returned home that afternoon. She was so profoundly hurt and afraid, her pain so deep, and I knew telling the truth now would bring it all back again. She had been afraid that I had committed suicide and was beside herself. How was I going to now admit the truth?

Lying there in bed listening to her bitterness, and emotionally strung out myself, I gave up. I finally told her the truth, which opened the floodgates. I surrendered this last bit to God, and then I surrendered it to her. When she started asking what else I was still hiding, I did something I had never thought of doing—it just happened. I told her about every crush, infatuation, experience, puppy love, real love, and all my romantic relationships from my first discovery of girls up until the time I started chatting with women online. It all came pouring out. Then an amazing thing happened. She did the same. I learned about her sexual journey from the time she was a young girl with school crushes through her time of sexual awakening and discovery, the difficulties it caused with her parents, and her near escapes with boys who were too aggressive and one whom she could not escape from. Here I was, forty-four years into our marriage and learning for the first time that she had been raped as a young woman. Neither of us got any sleep that night, but somehow, when the sun came up, we were in a better place. We had a long, long way to go, but there had been some sort of cleansing in the process. Hope was burning a little stronger in both of our hearts.

God Loves a Broken Spirit

With my breaking and this last reveal, I had finally laid everything down. Both came from deep inside without warning. I had not planned either, had not expected either, yet they came with urgency and power. On each occasion I still had to make a choice to either yield to this force or resist it. In each case I yielded immediately, consequences be damned. Why? How did that happen? I believe it is because my spirit was broken and my heart contrite, and that these were genuine travails, not devices being used to manipulate the moment. As such, they were acceptable to God.

> *My [only] sacrifice [acceptable] to God is a broken spirit; A broken and contrite heart [broken with sorrow for sin, thoroughly penitent], such, O God, You will not despise.*
> Psalm 51:17 (AMP)

Jesus is our Redeemer, of course, but He is not in the business of redeeming the unrepentant. Our soul must be crushed by the weight of our sin to the point that we reject its authority over our lives and submit to His authority in total abdication. Nothing less will do. When one's guilt (broken spirit) and mortification (contrite heart) reach this point, they have passed another crucible. God is watching, ready to respond.

For thus says the One who is high and lifted up, who inhabits
eternity, whose name is Holy: "I dwell in the high and holy place,
and also with him who is of a contrite and lowly spirit, to revive
the spirit of the lowly, and to revive the heart of the contrite."
Isaiah 57:15 (ESV)

It is, however, possible to be broken and contrite in a manner that opens the door to persecution and not redemption. The heart must be tested and purged of fear. Fear is a fierce taskmaster and the opposite of faith, and it will freeze us in place, not allowing trust to bring forth the actions that will open the doors of freedom.[13] The antidote for fear is love. We fear the repercussions of our sin and try to deny it, hide it, or bluster our way past it. What we really need to do, the only cure that works against fear, is to give ourselves over to the perfect love of God. We fear God because we do not know Him, and thus deny ourselves His love.

As in so many things, the choice is between God's way and man's way, as Paul instructs the Corinthians:

For godly grief produces a repentance that leads to salvation
without regret, whereas worldly grief produces death.
2 Corinthians 7:10 (ESV)

Repentance that leads to salvation comes from a broken spirit, one that recognizes the gulf between it and its Creator caused by its own callousness and disregard for the Creator's way. Turning to look across the gulf, the broken spirit sees what it has lost, feels the weight of its sin, and desires above all else the communion with its Creator that will restore its purpose and position. Leaving the world behind and abandoning all the temporal things righteousness has been sacrificed for, all the things desired so much in previous days to attain the pleasure and glory of man, brings no regret. Living for the world, however, abandoning righteousness

---

13   Robert Henderson, The Prophetic Promise of the Seventh Day (Shippensburg, PA, Destiny Image Publishers, Inc., 2010), 70

to please man and self, will inevitably lead to death of the spirit and all that it gave itself for. The grieving of our spirit is a call to righteousness which requires us to respond or turn away. We must choose.

EVERYTHING WE HAVE LOST IS HIDDEN IN GOD

It is not easy to face our demons. It takes desire and courage and a willingness to pay the price required to find what we seek. And just what is it that we seek? I suppose there are many answers, but I suspect those who are seeking a way out of great sin and its bitter fruit seek many of the same things. I know that I was desperately seeking peace, a place where I did not have to wrestle with my sins, failures, and their many effects on my life and family. I wanted to find a place where I could rest securely, heal, be restored, and experience the intimacy I so desired with God and my wife. It was more than wanting to be forgiven, it was a desire to experience the joy of the love I had abandoned. I desired also to discover a renewed sense of self-worth, to feel like I mattered, like what I thought mattered, and to know that my sin had not robbed me of being worthy of love. I wanted most of all to live a life loving and honoring God, my wife, and my family like I had never done before. I wanted the emptiness inside me to be replaced by the fullness of joy that comes from knowing I am living a life of truth and integrity, one filled with love and acceptance. I wanted a new life, one that was diametrically opposed to my old life in every fashion. I knew what I was searching for, but there was one big question I had to answer: Where would I find this new life, this new me?

In my renewed faith, I found clues that would lead me to the place I sought. I believe that God is the Creator of all things that exist. I believe He chooses to live in us, including when we sin, and that He allows us to live in Him. This belief led me to understand that He was present each time I sinned. When I thought no one would ever know, the One who matters most was present and knew everything, even my secret thoughts. Recognizing this truth, confessing, and repenting to God that I was aware of His presence and sinned anyway was a sobering experience. When I compared who and what the God is that lives inside me to the ugly life of selfishness, greed, deceit, and immorality I had lived for most of my life, I was shattered. I had to recognize, admit, and repent for living a life that was so out of order from what God expected of me that there could be no rationalization. It forced me to see my arrogance in an even darker light. It did not, however, diminish my desire for complete freedom and peace—it made it stronger.

Then I had an epiphany of sorts. Not a new revelation, but a gut-level understanding of something I had known to be true all along but had not recognized. As God was in me throughout my life of sin, I was in Him. If I was in Him, then what was in me was in Him, and so was everything I had lost. Everything I had abandoned and lost was no longer in me, but it was in Him! All the love, all the righteousness, all the peace, all the worthiness, all the forgiveness, all of ... everything! It was all in Him![14]

Suddenly, I knew exactly what I had to do to regain everything. I knew exactly where it was, and I knew how to get it all back. Of all the relationships I needed to restore, only one could unlock and release back into my life everything I had thrown away. Only God could do that, only He had that power, and only He held the key to that storeroom. Only my sincerest love and desire to know and please Him could restore and renew my life. I knew that I had not lived righteously as had Job, but I trusted that the same love that motivated God to restore Job's life could motivate Him to restore mine.

And the LORD restored the fortunes of Job, when he had prayed for his friends. ... And the LORD gave Job twice as much as he had before. And the LORD blessed the latter days of Job more than his beginning ... Job 42:10,12a (ESV)

Could God do the same for me? Yes! Would He? The jury was still out on that, but I knew where I had to start. I had to start with my relationship with God, and I knew I could not manipulate or fool Him.

---

14   Adonijal O. Ogbonnaya, Christos Soma (Venice, CA, AACETEV* Ministries International, 2016), 148

He would know instantly if my desire to have a new relationship with Him was because I truly loved and desired Him, or if I simply saw it as a way to get everything else I desired. If there was anything I had learned, it was that I could not fool God. Thankfully, I also knew that, in my case, this potential barrier was not an issue. My heart was truly broken and contrite. I desired the restoration of my relationship with Father God first and foremost, because I loved Him and could not stand to be separated from Him anymore. As much as I longed for reconciliation with Ruthie, my strongest desire was to be reconciled to my Father in Heaven. That was the most compelling factor in my decision to risk everything to gain everything.

I became focused on that most important relationship and on Ruthie. I started spending time with both, lots of time. I worked hard on being transparent, and I held myself to His standard and not the world's. I walked away from things that were important to me because they were taking time and energy from my primary goal: the full and complete restoration of my two most important relationships. I devoted myself to studying the God I had known about all my life without having ever really experiencing Him. I didn't want more head knowledge; I wanted to experience Him, to hear and see Him, to feel His Spirit moving in me, to worship Him as I never had, to let Him lead my life as He chose, to take me into places I could never have gone before.

New Intimacy

As I dove headlong into my new relationship with God, life began to change. Some of this was me working out how I would approach Him; some of it was God responding and encouraging. First, I made it a point to spend time in His Word and in prayer each morning. I had a long commute and was usually in the office by 6:00 a.m. That didn't matter. Getting up at 3:00 a.m. each morning to spend time with Father God was one of the first patterns I changed. I had grown apart from Him in part because I never made time with Him a priority. I had intellectual knowledge of Him, but I didn't have a relationship with Him. Now that relationship was my highest priority. I couldn't change the hours I worked, but I could change when I got up each day. As I prayed, I asked God to reveal the secrets hidden in His Word, to let me experience Him, and to change my heart. I began to pursue Him with all my desire and intent, not just in the early morning hours but throughout the day, anytime I had a few moments. Even a pause between meetings or phone calls was enough time to tell Him I loved Him, desired Him, and wanted Him to love me as a friend, even as a son.

Things began to happen. Not big things necessarily, but things that let me know God was listening, watching, and responding. I began to dream again, have the occasional vision, and people I trusted would sometimes give me words for my life that they had received from God. In the early stages, these were almost always meant to encourage me in my new walk. I frequently heard things like, "You don't know who you really are, what God has prepared for you. You are going to be amazed," or "God loves you so much. He is so proud of you, and He wants you to know that He is holding you in His heart." For someone coming out of the depths of sin I had been living in, it was still hard to accept that God could love me this much. I struggled with unworthiness, still. But His grace was never-ending. One Saturday morning, Ruthie and I were sitting in our kitchen talking through how our relationship was changing when suddenly she stopped and said God was giving her a download, a word meant for me. Then she began talking, speaking out His vision for my life. Twenty-five minutes later, she stopped. I was speechless. The scale and scope of what she had spoken challenged me to believe it could be possible. Could God do that? Could He use me that way? Would He? Of course, He could and would, if only I would allow Him to. I purposed in my heart that there was nothing I would deny Him.

One of the most demonstrable changes was in my prayer and worship life. In private prayer time I was often burdened to the point of tears, crying out for God to move in the lives of loved ones, friends, and acquaintances. I didn't know everything about their situations and lives, but I knew enough to know they needed Him in ways they didn't understand. Unlike in my previous prayer life, God was now revealing things to me, and those became prayer petitions. I began to praise Him in my private worship, getting lost in simply describing His character, calling out His name, rejoicing in Him, and giving Him glory. Public worship during praise time in our church was another radical change for me. As I mentioned in an earlier chapter, I used to sit in my seat, praying stoically as the music played and others released their joy and praise. I would watch them, sometimes envious and always filled with reasons why that was for them but not me. I was too shy, I couldn't sing, and I sure wasn't going to dance around. There was a man who always stood at the edge of the stage, banging his hands hard on the wooden stage floor, bouncing up and down, yelling out his praises to God. I didn't think I could ever be like him. Then one day as I stood in the aisle at my seat, I was overcome by the need to let out my love for God. I couldn't get to the stage fast enough and found myself standing at his side and doing the exact same thing. I even sang out loud, and loudly at that! I was full of praise and emotion, overflowing with joy and happiness I had never known. All the boundaries were gone. The room was filled with people, but as far as I knew, it was just me and God. I was in Heaven, and I loved it.

This new intimacy with God and the Holy Spirit was not the only renewal. Because of my sin and its effects in my emotional life, Ruthie and I had experienced very little intimacy—emotional, physical, or otherwise over the course of many years. She was deeply wounded, and I was just numb. We had been navigating a dry desert landscape, both of us thirsting for true love in all its dimensions.

The night of my admission was the end of a long day and the beginning of The Inquisitions. Our friends had departed just before noon, and we had been at it since the front door closed behind them. It was late and there was work the next day. We were both exhausted and our emotions were raw, but we knew we had to get some sleep. We called a halt to the questions and began to prepare for bed. There was just one problem: I didn't know where to go. I did not think she wanted me anywhere near her, and I was having a serious bout of unworthiness and guilt. At that point, I thought the likelihood of us remaining together as a couple was less than a 50/50 proposition. How could she possibly still love me? How could we ever have a life together after what I had done? In fact, I was running through short-term living options as I stood there, quickly realizing that my most likely sleeping location in the future would be in the car parked somewhere along the beach road. All our friends were church friends, and I was confident that I knew what their reaction would be. But what about tonight? Which room should I go to? I was paralyzed by the question, literally paralyzed and unable to move. Minutes later Ruthie found me, standing in the hallway between bedrooms. She looked at me and said, "What's wrong? Are you okay?" to which I haltingly replied, "I don't know which room to go to."

As I drove to work the next morning, I was in a bit of shock. It turns out that God's grace extends to areas I had not anticipated. We had held each other in our arms and talked about our early love and how we could not stand to be away from each other. We did not talk that night of what had driven us apart but proved to ourselves that God's love for us extends to our love for each other. It would take a while, but as my cleansing and healing progressed, we would eventually experience a new honeymoon phase.

God is Waiting

> *"Now everyone in Israel can know for certain that **Jesus, whom you crucified**, is the one God has made both Lord and the Messiah." When they heard this **they were crushed and realized what they had done** to Jesus. Deeply moved, they said to Peter and the other apostles, "What do we need to do, brothers?" Peter replied, "**Repent and return to God**, and each one of you must be baptized in the name of Jesus, the Anointed One, to **have your sins removed**. Then you may **take hold of the gift of the Holy Spirit**. For **God's promise of the Holy Spirit is for you**

and your families, for those yet to be born and for everyone whom the Lord our God calls to Himself." Peter preached to them and warned them with these words: *"Be rescued from the wayward and perverse culture of this world."* Acts 2:36-40 (TPT, emphasis added in bold)

In my own experience, guilt and shame convinced me that I was beyond redemption. Yet God redeemed and blessed even those who crucified our Lord by their words and deeds. If He can forgive those who murdered His only Son, redeem and restore them to a blessed and fruitful life, then there is nothing that can separate us from His love except our own hardened hearts. It takes a special kind of arrogance to convince ourselves that we are unredeemable when our Creator stands waiting for us to confess, repent, and ask.

It all begins with the step that changes everything: the confession and repentance of a genuine heart. That is the key that unlocks the door to a world of riches, a world we cannot imagine when standing in the dark. Not only does He forgive us, but He also restores us. Imagine, the very ones who screamed out for Jesus' crucifixion are not only forgiven but also given full and free access to the Holy Spirit, a promise that not only attends to them but to their families and future generations as well. Other than Christ's obedience in going to the cross, the breaking of the curse of generational sin is the greatest example of love I can imagine. Not only does our Creator forgive and restore us, but He also in effect says, "I forgive your sin and raise you all of your family generations."

If I had been presented the option of condemning myself to eternal Hell in exchange for the freedom of my children, grandchildren, and future generations, I would have taken it in a heartbeat. But that is not the option I was presented. He offered me instead forgiveness, life, love, peace, and fruitfulness—and these in abundance.

This is not to suggest that eternal salvation is a given for anyone. We must all walk it out for ourselves. But as Jesus paid a price for us, we pay a price for others. He is the only gateway to the Father, but our redemption is a path that others can choose to walk to find Him in their own lives. Our example and God's mercy reveal the lie of the world and the truth of God's redemptive power.

What is holding you back from letting go of your sin and giving it to the One who stands waiting to take it? Is it Pride? Guilt? Fear? Shame? Are you going to believe in them or believe in the power of God's everlasting love? Earlier, I said that I reached the point of being willing to risk everything to gain everything. Have you reached that point yet? Is God calling you to kneel and surrender? God is standing next to you as you read this, as close to you as the air you breathe, waiting to hear your heart and lips say:

Father God, forgive me. I confess every sin (name them) and, Father, I repent for and renounce each one. I lay my life down on Your altar and give it to You. I've made a mess of it. Clean me, Father. Change me. Rescue me.

CHAPTER SEVEN

OUT OF THE DUNGEON, INTO THE LIGHT

At this point I was encouraged while also realizing there was still much to be done. I had a chance at a new future and a redeemed destiny, but walking that out would be a matter of courage, perseverance, and faith. I had made a beginning, but it was only a beginning. I had confessed, repented, and renounced everything, and was seeking God in ways I never had before, with a heart that never hungered for Him like it did now. God was meeting my approach with encouragement, and I could feel Him inside me, His love capturing me.

Ruthie was experiencing her own set of conflicting emotions. She loved me on one level but hated what I had done to her, and her resentment would sometimes take front stage. We would give each other time and space, and then come back together to pick up the pieces and put them back together again. It was a cycle that repeated itself many times, and there were times I wondered if we could really survive as a couple. If not, I knew that it would have to be her call, not mine. I realized she might still make that decision at some point, but I prayed that she would not. Her pain was evident every day. Her heart was broken, but her faith and strength were not.

The Serious Work of Healing

The period after my initial admission was a challenging time. We were both on edge, trying to work through things without upsetting the fragile peace between us. We worked through a forgiveness process that our friends taught and coached us through (more on that in a later chapter) more times than either of us can remember. No issue was too small or too large. Suffice it to say, we spent a lot of time with this process. Then Ruthie decided rather suddenly to attend a seminar in another state. She had heard of a counselor who worked with people coming out of situations like ours and wanted to hear him. She traveled with a friend and spent several days there. When she returned, I heard the story, and it gave me hope.

Dr. Henry W. Wright and his wife, Donna, lead Be in Health,[15] a ministry devoted to physical and spiritual healing. Their work and story are well-known among folks who work in these areas, but they were new to us. When she returned from the conference, Ruthie was in a different place. It had not been easy, but it had been good. She was still shaken by all she was experiencing but had a different level of hope. The seminar had been good. She felt like there was a chance for us, and she had information.

She related a story that broke my heart. At some point in the conference, they directed people to gather in small groups of three without being in a group that included anyone they knew. In this exercise, they were to tell the group why they were there, what was going on in their life that they felt the need to attend. Ruthie cried when she told me what she had said to the group: "Two weeks ago was my forty-fourth wedding anniversary. Last week my husband confessed he has been unfaithful for almost the entire time we've been married."

You can imagine the shock. Then a gentleman in the group began to cry. When able, he sobbed his admission: "My wife is in another group

---

15 See https://www.beinhealth.com/ to view the Be in Health website and learn more about their ministry. Dr. Wright has since passed on, but his wife and team continue their good work.

in the room here. I was unfaithful to her, and she was so hurt she was unfaithful in revenge. I never knew I hurt her so bad until I saw your agony. I am so sorry for you and your husband, and for us."

She came home with books and CD's, one a twelve-CD set. I did not know if these would help us or not, but she was insistent that I listen to them. It was like taking a graduate-level course in our relationship with Father God, the evil that resides in the world, and how evil tricks us into believing what we do won't matter, and then convinces us we are unworthy after we have sinned and come to grips with the havoc we've wrought. We spent weeks working our way through the material, listening over and over, taking session notes, discussing the teachings at length, digging into our lives and patterns to see where we had fallen into traps without ever recognizing them, and praying for forgiveness and restoration. We did a lot of praying. I learned more about myself and my experience from this set of teachings than I ever would have suspected possible. Character traits that I thought were just the way I was were revealed to be the product of false beliefs and the actions that resulted from them, generational sin, and deception. It all brought to mind the lyrics of a favorite Roberta Flack song, "Killing Me Softly."[16]

As difficult as it was at times to listen to the teachings and learn what had really been going on in my life, it was also a pivotal point in my transition. I had information I never had before and understood things I didn't even know were a "thing" before hearing the teachings. Perhaps most importantly, I understood that I was not unique in my experience. Others had suffered the same and worse and had been restored. There was hope I might make it yet, that we would make it. Hope had another flame.

A Template for Changing One's Destiny

In Acts, Paul describes his experience on the Damascus Road to King Agrippa during his defense of his faith. Reading it through a personal lens

---

16   Roberta Flack, 1973, *"Killing Me Softly,"* Atlantic Recording, Inc.

brings one to understand that, while his sin may have been extreme and overt, ours is no less an assault against Jesus and His sacrifice. At the instant of Christ's intervention, Paul realizes that all his teaching, intellectual knowledge and acumen, and the rules he sought to enforce were no match for the power of the Messiah. The light of the holy presence blinded Paul physically but opened his spiritual eyes and heart. Against that power no teaching of man could stand.

> *"I myself was convinced that I ought to do many things in opposing the name of Jesus of Nazareth. And I did so in Jerusalem. I not only locked up many of the saints in prison after receiving authority from the chief priests, but when they were put to death I cast my vote against them. And I punished them often in all the synagogues and tried to make them blaspheme, and in raging fury against them I persecuted them even to foreign cities.*
>
> *"In this connection I journeyed to Damascus with the authority and commission of the chief priests. At midday, O king, I saw on the way a light from heaven, brighter than the sun, that shone around me and those who journeyed with me. And when we had all fallen to the ground, I heard a voice saying to me in the Hebrew language, 'Saul, Saul, why are you persecuting me? It is hard for you to kick against the goads.' And I said, 'Who are you, Lord?' And the Lord said, 'I am Jesus whom you are persecuting. But rise and stand upon your feet, for I have appeared to you for this purpose, to appoint you as a servant and witness to the things in which you have seen me and to those in which I will appear to you, delivering you from your people and from the Gentiles--to whom I am sending you to open their eyes, so that they may turn from darkness to light and from the power of Satan to God, that they may receive forgiveness of sins and a place among those who are sanctified by faith in me.'*
>
> *"Therefore, O King Agrippa, I was not disobedient to the heavenly vision..."* Acts 26:9-19a (ESV)

Paul's life before his conversion parallels my own life in many ways—and possibly yours, as well. He was empowered by the religious rulers and system of his day to carry out a campaign of persecution against the believers. He acted under the power and commission of the chief priests, whereas I lived under the rule of darkness in which I carried a level of authority. Acting under its commission, I abused and persecuted my own faith. It would be easy to say that mine was an extreme case and excuse lesser sins, but sin is sin. Anything that is unrighteous, whether small or large, is sin.

Note the language Jesus directed to Paul on that stark road. **"Rise and stand upon your feet"** is a call to decide and act. Paul had to decide if he would turn his loyalty from the false understanding he was under and abandon its rule in his life. Having made that decision, he was called to action, to stand and face the Lord. The experience was dramatic and powerful to be sure, but in the end, Paul's heart had to change. Standing to give allegiance to the Lord had to be an act of the heart first and the body second.

"To appoint you as a servant and witness" is a call to not only live a righteous life but also to bear witness to it through our actions and to glorify the source of our strength. The call has a purpose. As Jesus paid the price for our freedom with His blood, our changed lives and witness for Him are partial payment on the debt we owe Him. Unlike servicing the debts we incur in this world, however, serving Christ from a heart of thankfulness is not a burden but a joy, one that gives full meaning to our lives.

"Delivering you from your people and from the Gentiles..." speaks to setting Paul free of unbelief, from captivity in a false system, and for some of us, from ignorance.

"... to whom I am sending you..." Paul's commission to reach the unreached and hitherto unworthy, now made worthy by God's love.

"... so that they may turn from darkness to light and from the power of Satan to God..." The purpose of mercy and grace is to set man free of the weight and chains that have kept him bound in sin and unable to see through the darkness.

"... that they may receive forgiveness of sins and a place among those who are sanctified by faith in me." We are sanctified in Christ by our faith in the power of His blood. Only the blood of Christ has the power to cleanse us and free us; only our faith grants us access.

EVIL MUST BOW TO GOD

As we work our way through the healing and restoration process, we must come to grips with the dichotomy that resides in us. Godliness and ungodliness are not happy neighbors as they express themselves through our lives. There is a constant argument going on across their backyard fence, which is the source of our internal conflict. Harboring both, paying allegiance and honoring both, as one often does, is in fact a living definition of being double-minded. We cannot hold two conflicting truths in what we believe or how we act and expect not to experience their fundamental opposition to each other. Those who live their lives without resolving this conflict doom themselves to missing the rewards of living the life God intended for them. They miss out on true happiness, joy, peace, and the fullness of love.

The basic issue here is a failure to recognize the positional power of righteousness over unrighteousness. We choose to live life trying to serve two masters who are in opposition to each other, and wonder why we are stressed out, frustrated, and failing in our attempts to live a good life, not just on the outside but, most importantly, on the inside. The solution resides in the choices we make. Holiness is in the decisions we make and the way we live our lives; righteousness is the gift of God that grants us access to Him; and Christ is the gateway we must pass through to attain the gift. We must choose, and we must choose Christ.

Paul understood well the positional power of righteousness over unrighteousness and was unwilling to leave the conflict between them unresolved. We see an example of his application of this principle when he and Silas were falsely imprisoned. When the magistrates eventually offered them freedom, Paul rejected it because it was offered without recognition of the false basis of their imprisonment, or their innocence. Paul understood that accepting such would be a false freedom, as their reputation and witness would forever be shadowed by the charges. Full exoneration was in order, and nothing less would do.

> But when it was day, the magistrates sent the police, saying, "Let those men go." And the jailer reported these words to Paul, saying, "The magistrates have sent to let you go. Therefore come out now and go in peace." But Paul said to them, "They have beaten us publicly, uncondemned, men who are Roman citizens, and have thrown us into prison; and do they now throw us out secretly? No! Let them come themselves and take us out." The police reported these words to the magistrates, and they were afraid when they heard that they were Roman citizens. So they came and apologized to them. And they took them out and asked them to leave the city. So they went out of the prison and visited Lydia. And when they had seen the brothers, they encouraged them and departed.
> Acts 16:36-40 (ESV)

Paul's wisdom was in recognizing the core issue, his strength in facing it head on. Instead of leaving quietly as offered, he declared his citizenship and its covering over his life. That positional authority caused fear in the magistrates, who quickly acquiesced. As Paul was a citizen of Rome in the earthly sense, he was a citizen of Heaven in the spiritual sense, as are all who have accepted Christ as their Savior. He appealed on the basis of the higher authority of his true citizenship, which had to be recognized by those who were subservient to it. Un-condemned in the natural, Paul and Silas were sanctified and free in the spiritual. Beaten and imprisoned, they were persecuted, which is the state of the believer who allows sin to cohabit with them, or the unsaved who cannot claim the cleansing power of the sacrificial blood of the Perfect Lamb. The magistrates were afraid and submitted to the higher power of Rome, not because Rome exercised its power but because Paul claimed it, a right that you and I have each time evil tempts or chastises us. In apologizing, the magistrates bowed in recognition of the supreme power over their own and asked Paul and Silas to leave because they recognized they would not be able to coexist with them peacefully.

As sons of God, we are joint heirs with Christ.[17] What attends the throne for Him attends for us as well, but we must be whole and righteous (sanctified) in our own position to exercise the full measure of our status as sons. We must live a freed life, knowing who we are and exercising the authority and dominion given us. Too often we surrender both. We are not strong enough or do not discern evil in its many disguises, and thus forfeit our protections.

Evil will always seek to disguise its true nature and purpose when interacting with us. It is our responsibility to see through its many veils of deceit, to call it what it is, and to demand the rights that are ours as sons of the Most High God. When we do not, then we are vulnerable to evil's approaches, subtlety, seduction, and persecution. But when we declare our position as sons and stand with God's strength, then evil must retreat. It cannot coexist with the Light of Truth that is in us, because its purposes and the purposes of the Light are diametrically opposed. In the presence of Light, evil must bow and leave, separating itself from purity and from us.

That is what should be, who we should be. Why isn't it always that way? Sadly, it is because we allow evil to exist in us in the choices we make and the lives we lead. Many professing Christians live lives that are more closely aligned with evil than God. When we do this the forces of evil have legal right to work their plans for deceit and destruction in our lives. Believe me, I know this to be true from personal experience of the worst kind. Only our genuine confession and repentance will appeal to the courts of Heaven, and only Jesus' blood has the power to cleanse and restore us. Genuine repentance is the key. Without it we are forever lost.

---

17   Romans 8:16,17

With it we are rescued and restored. We can choose to accept the misery and destruction that inhabits our lives, or we can choose to open our hearts to the indwelling of Freedom, Peace, Love, and indescribable Joy. We choose to be prisoners or sons. How? By choosing what we allow to cohabit with us and what we set our heart towards.

When one makes the choice to change, he or she must realize that they cannot do it on their own. I made that mistake and failed many times. Pride and fear will tell you that you must do it on your own to avoid the full consequences of your sin. It is a lie, one meant to trick you. What you must do is trust godly people of integrity who have been gifted by God to help. Thankfully, I had such people in my life. When the time came, I turned to them.

Deliverance

I knew that I needed to take the next step. Having come from a religious background that did not include experiencing the Holy Spirit in outwardly visible expression (or any expression really), including deliverance sessions, healing, and prophecy, the thought of going to my pastor for a deliverance session was foreign to me. I had no idea what to expect and thought I would be intimidated but knew in my heart that this had to happen. When the day arrived, Ruthie, our two friends, and I met with the pastor. It turned out to be a very peaceful, conversational experience. It was everything I hadn't thought it would be.

I sat in the middle of the small room with the others sitting around me against the walls. My spirit was calm and trusting as we talked. The pastor asked questions and listened as I responded. Then he began to pray in a calm manner. He brought us before the Lord and petitioned for my release from the bondage of sin. Then he started calling things out of me, things we had not told him, and every one of them was right on. He named sins, called out generational curses, and spoke healing into my life, Ruthie's life, and our relationship. I was at complete peace throughout, fully cognizant of all that was going on, including what I felt inside as I was set free from spirits, demons, and principalities that had exercised their will in my life for decades.

The most dramatic part occurred at the very end. We had already started wrapping the session up when the pastor said he saw something else, and we re-engaged with the deliverance. He prayed for quite a while as he fought in the spirit realm, calling the thing out of me. As he prayed, he eventually reached behind my head to the back of my neck and without touching me began a pulling motion. His prayer became more fervent until he had finally pulled it completely out of me. Then he said that he had never seen or encountered that principality before and didn't know what it was, but it was extremely powerful. It had been wound tightly around the cervical section of my spine and then spiraled down the full length of my spine, and he said that when he pulled it out it looked like thick, black tar. He could not name it, and neither could I, but I knew for a fact that I had been instantly set free from a physical issue I had suffered with for years. For many years I had been unable to turn my head to either side more than a few degrees because of stiffness and tremendous pain. Suddenly, I had complete unrestricted movement without any pain at all. To say that I became a believer in the Holy Spirit's ability to work through others to achieve supernatural healing would be a large understatement. My body was healed, and my spirit set free! It was a dramatic event, even if it had been understated in style. My next spiritual experience, however, would not be so understated.

In late August, I experienced what I will call the Fire of God. I am not certain that is the correct label from a theological perspective, but it accurately describes the experience. It was Saturday afternoon, when we would normally depart for the two-and-a-half-hour drive to the church for evening services. I was not going this particular day, and Ruthie was taking a friend along. They were in the house getting ready to depart when I began shaking. It began as small tremors in my hands and rapidly escalated to a full-on shaking of my entire body. I could not stop it and continued to shake uncontrollably. The strange thing was that I was bemused by it, not concerned. I had no other symptoms and, somehow,

I just knew that this was God doing something in me. The three of us laughed because I looked so comical. After a quick discussion, Ruthie and our friend decided to go ahead and attend church. Unable to work at my computer or do anything else for that matter, I went into our den and sat on the sofa, intending to listen to soaking music and to pray. Within two or three minutes of sitting down, I began to feel a slight fever. I will admit that, at that point, I started asking what was really going on. I knew of nothing that would express itself with these symptoms, but then I was not and am not a medical professional. My own wisdom brought me no confidence. Still, however, I was at complete peace and not concerned. My spirit knew this was a cleansing from God. I lay down on the sofa and started praying as the fever went higher and higher until I was sweating through all my clothes. I began to feel slightly nauseated and weak. It was then that I moved to the bed.

I couldn't sleep as the shaking and fever continued. Then the chills started. Just as I would pull all the covers up to fight the chills, the fever would return. I felt like my entire body was burning up from the inside out. All I could do was pray, which is what I did between shivers and tremors. Throughout the entire experience, I kept hearing, "Do not worry. I AM taking care of you. Release yourself into My care." What else was there to do, and what better physician could I call? So, I gave myself completely to the experience, asking God to cleanse me, to burn every evil out of me, to purify me and fill me with righteousness. As He did, I prayed non-stop, telling God how much I loved Him and desired Him in my heart.

From the time the first tremor started until I felt the fever begin to leave was slightly more than eight hours. It was nearing midnight and I was done in, but as the tremors, chills, and fever slowly faded away I entered a calm and blissful state. I knew I was in God's hands; I knew that He loved me so much He had done this. My heart was overwhelmed with gratitude and joy. I did not have the strength or voice to sing aloud, but my heart did. My heart sang praise to my Maker, Redeemer, and Sustainer as I cried tears of relief and thankfulness. At about two o'clock in the morning, I fell into a deep peaceful sleep, waking a little after eight o'clock. I was refreshed, energized, and filled with excitement and love for my God who loves me so much He would do all of that for me. Imagine that kind of love, that the very Creator would turn His attention to you in such a way, to clean you and shower you with His love.

Just imagine.

Out of the Dungeon, Into the Light

At the beginning of Second Peter, we find these words:

> *His divine power has granted to us all things that pertain to life and godliness, through the knowledge of him who called us to his own glory and excellence, by which he has granted to us his precious and very great promises, so that through them you may become partakers of the divine nature, having escaped from the corruption that is in the world because of sinful desire.*
> 2 Peter 1:3,4 (ESV)

Early one morning, I had an experience. I say "experience" rather than "dream" or "vision" because it was so crystal clear and intense. It did not feel like a dream or vision. It felt real. Even the physical senses felt real. It signified to me that my escape from the hell I had been living was final. I would no longer fear that I might not be good enough or that freedom could still be stolen from me.

The experience began with me hanging naked in a dungeon cell. I was manacled to the rough stone wall which was cutting through the flesh and muscle of my back. My arms were fully extended, and I was shackled to the wall with my feet off of the ground and my full weight hanging on my wrists. The pain was horrific as I felt my joints separating. I was screaming out, begging my jailers to take me down and put me on a stretching rack, because I knew that pain would be less than what I was then suffering. I cried out in agony for long minutes, screaming as my shoulder muscles, joints, ligaments, and tendons began to give way. I was in agony, I was dying, and I was crying out for mercy.

Suddenly, Jesus appeared in the middle of my small, dark cell. His white robe and body were glowing as He looked on me with eyes full of love. Then, just as suddenly, He and I were standing side by side in a high Alpine meadow. I could see the snow-capped Alps. The sky was a perfectly clear, electric pale blue, the sun was bright, the air cold and crisp as it filled my nostrils and lungs, and the springtime meadow was blanketed in color. I stood there drawing the crisp coldness in with deep breaths of wonder. Then Jesus said the only two words He spoke in the entire experience: "You're free."

And free I am. Instantly, miraculously, eternally free. There is only one explanation for what has happened to Ruthie and me: God's mercy and grace. We are living proof that they are bigger than any sin or pain that His children live with. As hard as it is to say, there are millions of people and couples who are as desperate as we were. We know in our hearts that the same God who saved us is waiting to save them, to save you.

> *And after you have suffered a little while, the God of all grace, who has called you to his eternal glory in Christ, will himself* **restore, confirm, strengthen,** *and* **establish** *you. To him be the dominion forever and ever. Amen.*
> *1 Peter 5:10,11* (ESV, emphasis added in bold)

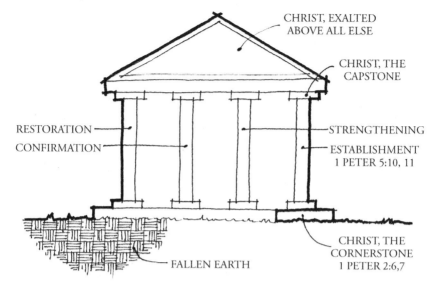

- CHRIST IS THE CORNERSTONE UPON WHICH OUR SALVATION IS BUILT
- OUR OBEDIENCE AND FAITHFULNESS ALLOWS HIM TO BUILD US UP
- WE RISE ABOVE FALLEN NATURE AND GLORY IN HIS DOMINION OVER ALL
- OUR RENEWED LIVES PROCLAIM AND EXALT CHRIST ABOVE ALL ELSE

This image, which I sketched one morning during my devotion time, showcases the four-part process that God has been taking us through: restoring my relationship with Him and our relationship with each other, confirming the truth of His provision, strengthening us, and establishing us for His service. It has not always been easy, but His grace is faithful. Our relationship is strong, new experiences come every day it seems, and we believe God will use our story to heal and restore others. We have dedicated our lives to that purpose, to serve Him by serving others. God's love is a beautiful thing.

I grew up being taught and believing that knowing and pleasing God meant knowing His Word and living a good life. In failing to do either, I learned that what God really wants is our heart. He desires intimacy with us that is hard to comprehend, and breathtaking when we experience it. We are blessed to be in that place—out of the dungeon and in the Light.

Not long after, I read this passage of deliverance, and it resounded through me like a joyous shout. God broke my oppressor and I shout with joy praising the name of my Savior, Rescuer, Redeemer, and Restorer. His name I praise above all others.

When the LORD has given you rest from your pain and turmoil and the hard service with which you were made to serve, you will take up this taunt against the king of Babylon: "How the oppressor has ceased, the insolent fury ceased! The LORD has broken the staff of the wicked, the scepter of rulers, that struck the peoples in wrath with unceasing blows, that ruled the nations in anger with unrelenting persecution. The whole earth is at rest and quiet; they break forth into singing." Isaiah 14:3-7 (ESV)

I was free and beginning to learn about the love I had searched for my entire life, but it was just the beginning. As I had been walking my road of desperation, another had been walking a road of costly love. This road required sacrifice also, the sacrifice of a broken heart that loved so deeply that she could endure the pain of my betrayal as she trusted in the only One who could save us to eventually work His will.

CHAPTER EIGHT

LOVE CONQUERS ALL

This chapter is about love, real love. Love is the single most powerful force in all of creation. I say this with full knowledge, for without Love's intervention, I would have been completely and eternally lost, and probably dead. Can one's love really save life? Without a doubt, of this I am sure.

There is the love of our Heavenly Father, so strong it enables Him to love us through our misdeeds, rejection, and arrogance. Then there is the love of those closest to us who endure so much yet hold us in their hearts even as their own breaks. That is what this chapter is about, the power of Love.

How can an abstract concept have so much power? It can't. Let's start there. When I believed that love is an abstract, a concept, a goal, only something to be desired, my understanding was false and its appeal a lie. Never knowing what real love is, I searched and found many counterfeits, yet I kept on searching. Why is that? It was because I had not found the truth about love. I knew something was missing—I just didn't know what. The "what" turned out to be the missing link. Love is not at all what I believed it to be. The truth is that Love is not an abstract, Love is a fruit of the Spirit, and the Spirit is God.

> *But the fruit produced by the Holy Spirit within you is **divine love in all its varied expressions:** joy that overflows, peace that subdues, patience that endures, kindness in action, a life full of virtue, faith that prevails, gentleness of heart, and strength of spirit. Never set the law above these qualities, for they are meant to be limitless.* Ephesians 5:22,23 (TPT, emphasis added in bold)

I like The Passion Translation's rendering of this verse, in which all the other fruits flow out of love. Without love, there is no joy, peace, patience, kindness, virtue, faith, gentleness, or strength. Every gift of the Spirit flows from the fountain of love.

Love is a fruit of the Holy Spirit, its source found deep in the wellspring of God's heart from whence it derives its position and power. We choose to either submit to it and engage its position and power in our lives, or to accept false and hollow substitutes. One day, I finally made the leap from false understanding to resting in true Love's arms.

THE SECOND GREATEST COMMANDMENT

> Scribe: *Tell me, Teacher. What is the most important thing that God commands in the law?*
> Jesus: *The most important commandment is this: "Hear, O Israel, the Eternal One is our God, and the Eternal One is the only God. You should love the Eternal, your God, with all your heart, with all your soul, with all your mind, and with all your strength." The second great commandment is this: **"Love others in the same way you love yourself."*** Mark 12:28-31 (TVB, emphasis added in bold)

Sometimes you read a scripture passage, one you have read hundreds of times before, and it suddenly hits you like a gut punch, as if it were spoken into existence ages ago for just this time and place to pierce your heart. Has that ever happened to you? It happened to me one morning while meditating on this passage. I struggled with knowing how to love most of my life, and now I know why.

I turned to stoicism early in life to escape the pain of not feeling loved by my earthly father and to buttress myself against the way schoolmates looked at me and taunted me. I knew my father loved me, but I did not feel his love and never felt worthy of his love. I spent much of my life not loving but hating myself. First, I hated the way I looked, then I hated what I was doing, and later I hated what I had become.

Jesus teaches us that the most important commandment is to love God with every fiber of our being. The second is to love our neighbors as we love ourselves. If we do not love ourselves, then true love as God intends us to experience it is out of our reach. All my life I've hungered for love, to know how to love others in a deep, pure way. Finally, I understood why this has been so difficult. I could not love with the passion and heart that I saw in others until I loved myself. I was married to a beautiful, loving woman who sacrificed her life for me. I had two terrific sons of whom I am so proud and was surrounded by a loving and faithful family. I loved them all intensely but could not feel the emotion. It was as if my heart was a rock, and I hated it. Now I understood. I couldn't feel the depth of my love for them because I didn't love myself, and I had to ask how I could possibly overcome my self-hatred given my life and its abundance of bitter fruit.

There was only one way. I knew that I had to forgive myself as God did. I did not have His love, but I could tap into it, asking Him to share His heart for me with me. By seeing myself through His eyes and loving myself from inside His heart, I could experience His love for me. In this way, I learned to love myself, allowing me to experience true, honest, deep, pure love for others. I love Ruthie and our family with all my heart, and my heart's capacity for love is still growing. I pray that God will keep digging my love well and keep filling it to overflowing as He digs it even deeper. Love is life—it is as simple as that.

Love Conquers All

A couple of years after my confession, I decided to write a journal to one of my sons. It was meant to be a love letter to him, not necessarily about my sin, although that was bound to be on my heart at times while writing to him. Sometimes I wrote about the minutiae of life, sometimes about life lessons, our favorite sports teams, family, and sometimes about love. With his permission, I am sharing a few excerpts in the hope that the thoughts of my heart as I wrote to one whom I love and admire so much may also resonate with you. Here is the first:

> May 10th:
>
> Love conquers all. Nothing else comes close.
>
> I am guilty of being one who is often judgmental of other people. I see their lives and situations and am quick to hold them accountable for what I perceive as their mistakes.
>
> Thank God He didn't treat me the way I've treated others.
>
> The problem is that I look at others through worldly eyes, not God's eyes. What I see is the chaos of their sin and condition. I see their refusal or inability to do the right thing, their weaknesses and failures. I see who they are in the world.
>
> That is not how God sees us. Yes, He sees all the chaos, but He also sees something we do not. He sees what He intended for each of us when He created us. That purpose is in each of us because God put it there. Like a good father He never forgets it. He sees our sin, but He also sees what was meant to be and what still can be.
>
> He loves us so much that He is ready to rescue us the instant we turn to Him, no matter what we are turning from. That is how strong His love is.

The key for us is to see humanity through His eyes, not our worldly eyes. I think of your Mom [sic] when I say this. I do not know of anyone else who exhibits God's heart the way she does. Her ministry working with women coming out of brokenness is changing lives. Women who have been abused, who were engaged in deep darkness, trapped in lives of sin ... all of it. I watch her love them as the Father does, mentor and train them, encourage them and hold them accountable. It takes a toll on her, but He is faithful to restore her each time. She discovered her purpose and stepped into it, and it is amazing to see how God is using her.

It is all about love. She does not see what they are or what they were. She sees who God wants them to be. She sees them with His eyes, not her own.

Love conquers all. Nothing else comes close. Ask me how I know!

Dad

WHEAT AND ARROWS

There are enough books written about what true love is to fill libraries many times over. Still, many of us manage to get it wrong even though it is really very simple. Not easy, but simple. We can be very good at overcomplicating things, often because we are trying to manipulate circumstances. That is hard to do when one is dealing with the strongest force in creation. If, however, we simplify the vision of what Love really looks like in our lives, it makes understanding easier. That is what God did for me in a dream one morning a few months after hearing a teaching on the heart.[18] In this dream, I saw the diagram shown here. Let me walk you through it.

AN IMAGE OF GOD'S RELATIONSHIP WITH MAN, AND MAN'S RELATIONSHIP WITH WOMAN

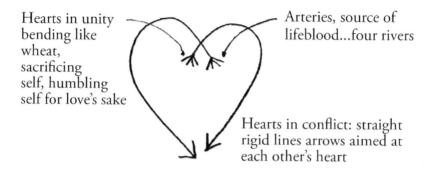

Hearts in unity bending like wheat, sacrificing self, humbling self for love's sake

Arteries, source of lifeblood...four rivers

Hearts in conflict: straight rigid lines arrows aimed at each other's heart

God blows the wind that bends our hearts, humbling us.
The strife between man and God will end.
He will bend our hearts.

The image is of two hearts that have been melded into one through the power of love. That being the case, it has elements of each heart individually and of the two hearts combined. It looks a lot like the universal symbol for the heart, but not exactly, right? Let's see what the symbolism of this image can teach us.

On the top half, we see the two halves of the heart bending towards each other, each with its own arteries. For a minute here, think of the arteries as heads of wheat that are bowing towards each other, representing the sacrifice and compromise that love requires. It depicts the humbling of one's pride in favor of the one we love. Wheat often represents peace and prosperity in God's Word, but these are not achieved easily. The wheat must be nourished, tended to, and separated from the tares before its full blessing can be realized. As the wheat stands in the field, it is subject to the elements. Winter prepares the soil, rain quenches its thirst, and when the winds blow the wheat bows, just as our hearts bow when God's gentle

---

18   Justin Abraham, *Company of Burning Hearts*, February, 2016. Based in Wales, Justin and Rachel Abraham's ministry has a global reach through conferences, books, and their podcast. You can find more info at https://www.companyofburninghearts.wordpress.com/

breath of love blows over us.[19] Under its persuasion, we surrender our hardness to His throne in unison. One can picture a couple bowing before God's throne, their heads bending towards each other in the intimacy of their love for each other and the Father. Not as two individuals now, but as one. It is a different kind of trinity, if you will. Father God, His son, and His daughter become one because of love and grace. As Jesus' death opened the gateway to eternal life, our willingness to die to self releases eternal love in our hearts.

But this is a multi-dimensional view as well, and the arteries must still perform their function of distributing life's blood to the body. Blood, after all, is the essence of life, and we cannot live without it. In yet another dimension, the arteries represent the four rivers of Eden which water the earth.[20] In this sense, our hearts are being watered with Heaven's perfected love, which brings us peace even as we submit to each other.

On the bottom half of the diagram, we see straight and rigid lines like spears with arrowheads moving forcibly towards conflict, the exact opposite of the humility, sacrifice, and love that are depicted in the top of the diagram. There is no bending, no humility, and no love in this part of the image. Instead, we see competition and the intent to force one's will upon another.

Here's the thing: Both elements, the wheat and the arrows, are in each of us all the time. We choose which will rule in our lives through our desires, intents, choices, words, and actions.

The image is a picture of our relationship with Father God, and the relationship between man and woman. Will we bow forward in love and grace toward those that love us, or will we insist on our own way? The answer is a matter of the heart. What does your heart desire? Acceptance, grace, love, and peace, or dominion over the one who loves you? That is the choice we must each make. When we relinquish our desire to control, then God can blow His breath across us, the breath that causes our hearts to bow like wheat before the wind. When we bow with love that sacrifices

19   Meyer, F.B., *Through the Bible Day by Day* (Philadelphia, American Sunday School Union), 1914
20   Genesis 2:10-14

our desires to the benefit of the one we love, there can be no rigid spear and arrowhead, no competition, no strife. There can only be love.

RUTHIE AMAZES ME

Another excerpt from my journal to my son:

> October 19th:
>
> Your mother amazes me. In His wisdom God put the two of us together when I was too innocent and kept us together when I was too lost to know what to do. But God could only do His part, she had to do hers as well. I am eternally thankful that she did.
>
> She is an amazing woman. Strong, loving, sensible, caring, faithful, and at complete peace with who she is. I learn from her every day as I watch her share the love God put in her heart.
>
> There are no strangers to her, and none that are not worthy of her time and love. She touches people and their lives are changed. She sees and knows their darkest secrets. Instead of shunning them she opens her heart. And what do they do? Almost without exception they love her back. She is the richest person I know.
>
> To think that she loves Jesus so much that she can love me is overwhelming. It takes my breath away when I think of it, as I often do. Sometimes, not being able to breathe is pure bliss.
>
> Ours is a different kind of love story to be sure, but it is a powerful one. If ever you need to explain the depth of God's love for us, just tell this story.
>
> Jesus died for me and your Mom [sic] died to herself so that I might have a chance. She gave herself up and asked God

to forgive me, then she told me she will always love me.

I know that you do not always understand or agree with what we say and do. We are not perfect, but the One who lives inside of us is. As He gives us grace we appreciate your grace as well, loving us through it all.

Freedom is awfully good. I've been in bondage and now I am free. I know what both feel like and believe me, freedom is awfully good. Jesus paid a price for me and so did your Mom [sic], and I love them both more than ever before.

Dad

Ruthie is defined by her capacity and willingness to love. She is strong on the inside, the kind of strong that manifests as stubbornness in most. Her greatest strength, however, is that she bows before God and submits to His will over hers. She humbles herself and places herself lower than others so she can magnify His heart. She is a wisdom factory, but it is not her own. What makes her so special is that she is willing to surrender anything at any time when God speaks to her. That willingness to surrender her will to God is a large part of what saved our marriage and my life.

She Let Go to Let God

Ruthie's love for me is beyond human capacity. She can love me despite my terrible sin only because she loves God so much that she bows to Him, allowing her to love me with His love and strength that live inside of her. How did she tap into that? How did she endure all the pain? Put plainly, she loved God more than she hated what I had become.

It wasn't easy. There was a time when we were two completely different people living together, and I mean different. One of us loved God, and one of us loved himself. One of us was safe in the security of God's love, and the other was outside of God and depending upon the world for validation and pleasure. One of us was at peace with who she was even while her marriage was in chaos, and one of us was at war with God, his wife, the world, and himself. No, it was not easy.

There came a point where Ruthie realized she could not go on in her own strength. She had been trying, reaching out to me, asking what was wrong, trying to get me to seek help for myself and our marriage. All to no avail. I was having none of it. There was no way I was about to let go of my sin or to lay it all out on the table for counseling. My pride and arrogance would not let me do it. We were at an impasse and we both knew it, even though we never talked about it. Something had to change, and something did. Ruthie surrendered. Not to me but to God. She reached the point where she had a heart-to-heart with God, telling Him that she could not go on. She told Him that He would have to deal with me, she was taking her hands off. No more pleading, no more begging, no more arguing. No more. In one sense, she washed her hands of me. What happened to our marriage would no longer be her responsibility, nor what happened to me her mission. She let go of me and gave me to God. "He's Yours. I can't deal with this any longer. Please save him, but if You don't, I'll understand."

She had every reason and right to call it quits. She didn't. Instead, she turned me over to God. She would honor God, not man, and let the chips fall where they may. She turned me over to God, His to either redeem or condemn. In doing that, she saved my life and our marriage.

> *I remained on the mountain as on the first days - forty days and forty nights - and HASHEM listened to me this time, as well, and HASHEM did not wish to destroy you. HASHEM said to me, "Arise, go on the journey before the people; let them come and possess the Land that I swore to their forefathers to give them."*
> Deuteronomy 10:10,11 (SEAET)

Ruthie stood before God on my behalf, and He honored her obedience and heart. She prayed and agonized for my redemption, she fasted for the restoration of my love for her and God, and she never stopped believing that God was bigger than my sin. She paid a steep price for decades, walking the path alone to give God something to honor in our marriage. Because of her faith, obedience, and perseverance, God honored her sacrifice. Because of that, I was given another chance to change, to possess the Land of my inheritance. I owe my life and redemption to my lovely wife who bore so much for so long. I cannot change the past, but our present and future are rich with love, affection, and peace. I owe it all to her strength and love, and God's grace.

There is more power in one millisecond of God's love than in all the chaos in the history of creation. As we live in the chaos of our lives, struggling to make sense of it, His power is at complete rest and peace inside His love. Father God does everything from a position of rest, including loving us. To find that peace, that rest, we must enter into Him, abandoning our struggles to find the peace that is at home in the Creator.

For those who love their abusive husband or wife, who agonize at the addictions that imprison the ones they love, and even for those who are on the verge of calling it quits, I beg of you as only one who has been there can: Give love one more chance. If it comes to the point that you simply cannot deal with the agony and pain of the relationship any longer, then consider taking your hands off and turning the one you love over to God completely. Not because it saved Ruthie and me, but because His love is greater, stronger, and more powerful than you can imagine. When you've lost hope, give God's Hope a chance. Let go and let God.

The Truth Will Set You Free

One of the great lies of our culture is that we are in control, that we have the power to change anything and decide everything. We really have power to do only two things: to choose to live holy lives or live lives abandoned to the world, and to choose to have faith in God or ourselves. Both require a choice, a decision, and these are our responsibility alone.

I was a believer living a sinful life, conflicted by my belief in God and lust for worldly pleasure. Longing for freedom and righteousness, I was trapped in the bondage of my sin. I was not alone. I believe there are untold millions in this same position in today's church. Jesus has a word for those living this life:

> *Jesus said to those Jews who believed in him, "When you continue to embrace all that I teach, you prove that you are my true followers. For if you embrace the truth, it will release more freedom into your lives."*
>
> *Surprised by this, they said, "But we're the descendants of Abraham and we're already free. We've never been in bondage to anyone. How could you say that we will be released into more freedom?"*
>
> *"I speak eternal truth," Jesus said. "When you sin you are not free. You've become a slave in bondage to your sin. And slaves have no permanent standing in a family, like a son does, for a son is a part of the family forever. So if the Son sets you free from sin, then become a true son and be unquestionably free!*
>
> *"Even though you are descendants of Abraham, you desire to kill me because the message I bring has not found a home in your hearts. Yet the truths I speak I've seen and received in my Father's presence. But you are doing what you've learned from your father!"* John 8:31-38 (TPT)

Here, Jesus is speaking to those who believed in Him but were not embracing His truth completely, counting themselves as sons of Abraham and not of God. In that, they are like those of us today who believe on one level but deny God's power in our life with our sin, following our fathers and thus turning away from our Father. But there is a way. Embrace God, His Son, and His truth.

The freedom of Jesus' sacrifice is this: freedom to live a life abandoned to His glorious Love, that love through which He obeyed Gethsemane's call to secure our freedom. Embrace that. Do not simply know it and believe it intellectually—embrace it. Plumb the depths of His love to discover its power, not then in a distant time but in your heart now, this instant. There is no stronger power than the love of God. Embrace Him and let the sacrificial blood of Jesus' obedience wash you clean.

As one who was in this condition, believing in God but denying His power in my life by my sin, I can tell you true that His love is life and future changing. I was lost, then redeemed. I was surrounded by hopelessness and pain, and now I am free. My greatest bliss came immediately after my greatest pain. That is the power of Love. God's love, there is nothing like it. Embrace it and abandon yourself to its purity and bliss.

LOVE IS THE SWEETEST OF FRUITS

Life is different when one has a relationship with Love. Note that I said a "relationship with Love," not a "love relationship." It is an important distinction. When I was involved in relationships, I was searching for an idea, the notion of being in love. It is an easy notion to fulfill. Being in love is a "me first" proposition. It is about how being in the relationship makes you feel and is not necessarily concerned with how the other person feels. Loving someone, however, puts them in first position in your heart. Instead of wanting to get something from your relationship with them, your desire is focused on their happiness and joy. While there may be moments like this, morally illegal relationships are grounded in a desire to discover something you have been missing. That is not a good foundation, so it is no surprise that such relationships tend to be empty and sometimes painful. We may rationalize our experience in order to feed our need to be in love, but that is a compromise that will bear bitter fruit.

The love that comes to us from the heart of God, however, bears the sweetest fruit of all. Joy, peace, patience, kindness, virtue, faith, gentleness, and strength—these are the fruits that flow from God's love. This love is ours for the asking, requiring only that we love the One who provides it so graciously, motivated by His love for us. How foolish we are to lust after and accept the counterfeits the world and underworld sell. As if the benefits of God's love listed in Galatians 5:22 are not sweet enough, there is more beneath the surface.

God's love operates from a position inside His heart. Our Father's love is pure and perfect because it emanates from within the heart of the One who is pure and perfect. As we visualize God sitting on His throne, we might also visualize Love sitting on a throne in God's heart. As God rules all of creation from His throne, His motivation and purpose flow directly from His heart. This positioning of God's love in His being is one of honor and power. God could have chosen to give some other virtue the ability to sway His thought. I can predict with some certainty that if left to any of us, other virtues would have been given this seat of honor. Perhaps Might or Wisdom? What about Truth and Righteousness? We could make a strong case for any of these, but God chose Love over all others. Love understands the position it occupies in God's being and honors that position with integrity and grace. We should do the same.

God's love operates with power. Operating from its position in God's heart, Love has the power to change man's heart. I for one praise God for His love and thank Him that His love changed my heart. As I often say, I know where I was, and I know where I am. Thank God that He moved Heaven and earth to redeem and change me. More than changing man's heart, however, God's love has the power to change God's mind, or at least we often think so. The history of the Israelites is filled with examples of God relenting before unleashing their well-deserved discipline. Think of Moses and his petition for the people after they made the golden calf, for just one example. Yes, Moses interceded for the nation, but God was under no mandate to accede to Moses's plea. Love motivated God to take the plea to heart and turn from the destruction He planned. Love made Him do it.

God's love is limitless. Galatians 5:22 is an oft-quoted verse. Sadly, the twenty-third verse is given short breath too often:

> *But the fruit produced by the Holy Spirit within you is divine love in all its varied expressions: joy that overflows, peace that subdues, patience that endures, kindness in action, a life full of virtue, faith that prevails, gentleness of heart, and strength of*

spirit. **Never set the law above these qualities, for they are meant to be limitless.** Galatians 5:22,23 (TPT, emphasis added in bold)

Paul is reminding the Ephesians and us that living by the letter of the law and its rewards is inferior to the fruit of lives lived in intimate relationship with the Father. Striving to perform produces stress, anxiety, jealousy, and all manner of other ills. God's gifts, however, come anxiety-free and have no expiration date on them. God's love is limitless, unbounded by time, distance, or even our failures. The world will accept us if we perform to its standard. God's law will guide us but is not meant to control us. His love is everlasting, even when we do not deserve it. He does not condone our sin, but He remains with us through it as He waits for us to turn back into His arms. One of the struggles I faced was feeling unworthy of God's love. I knew He loved me. He had to, or He would not have delivered me, but it was still hard to accept that He could welcome me back. Eventually, the truth of His love entered in to console me, another turning point as I surrendered my rejection of myself based in my sin to His love for me, which is based in His mercy.

> *"Repentance is allowing your soul to be overcome by Him, not by what you've done."* [21]

The world's temporal performance standard or God's eternal mercy—which is it to be in your life? It doesn't sound like a hard choice, does it? It's not. All you must do is surrender to His love, live as if you mean it, and rejoice in His glory. Believe me, you are not going to miss anything you must leave behind. You can trust me, and God, on that one.

---

21 Karl Whitehead, *Repentance*, Nest Foundation, session 2.120.

CHAPTER NINE

WHEN GOD TURNS FROM HIS ANGER

Why do you keep doing what you're not supposed to do? You will not succeed in your efforts. He will not accompany you, so you're vulnerable on all sides. Because you've rejected the Eternal, you won't have Him in your midst and on your side. When you run into the Amalekites and Canaanites, they will slay you on the spot. Numbers 14:41-43 (TVB)

When I was in sin and unrepentant, God was angry with me, and I received my reward for my stubbornness and arrogance. The punishment? He withdrew from me. For years, I feared that His anger could not be turned and that I was doomed. I knew what the Word said, but believed I was the exception. I was the lost sheep that would be written off. Still, my spirit would not let go, and I longed for the golden ring of redemption. I hoped that it would come around one day but cannot say that I believed it would. I cannot claim that God saw my faith and provided a way out; I can claim that His mercy saw my heart, and in His grace, He put the ring in place. I grabbed for it, not knowing what would happen next. I had made my decision, and now God had to make

His. Would He allow me to approach? Would He reach down to save me, or abandon me to my well-earned hell? That was the question that hung on every breath I took. Before I could know the answer, I would have to face His anger. I wouldn't be the first.

Moses Knew God's Anger

Moses knew firsthand God's anger at the many rebellions of the Israelites. In Psalm 90, he describes this anger and its effects on the people even as he appeals to God for mercy:

> *For Your anger has consumed us, Your wrath has shaken us to the core and left us deeply troubled. You have written our offenses before You - The light of Your presence shines brightly on our secret sins, and we can't run or hide.*
> *Who can truly comprehend the power unleashed by Your anger? Your wrath matches the fear that is due to You.*
> *You have spent many days afflicting us with pain and sorrow; now match those with years of unspent joy. Let Your work of love be on display for all Your servants; let Your children see Your majesty.* Psalm 90:7,8,11,15,16 (TVB)

This was not the only time Moses has cause to fear God, of course. For one, there was the incident at the rock of Horeb,[22] where he offended God and lost the opportunity to see his entire life's work fulfilled. One thing we can be sure of: God sees, He knows, and He remembers. Paul also remembered and used the incident and ancient Scripture to instruct his listeners:

> *For the 40 years they traveled on to the land that I had promised them, that generation broke My heart. Grieving and angry, I said, **"Their hearts are unfaithful; they don't know what I***

---

22 Exodus 17:1-7; Numbers 20:1-13

want from them." That is why I swore in anger they would
never enter salvation's rest.
Brothers and sisters, pay close attention so you won't develop an
evil and unbelieving heart that causes you to abandon the living
God. Hebrews 3:10-12 (TVB, emphasis added in bold)

"Their hearts are unfaithful; they don't know what I want from them." I believe these are some of the most damning of God's words, and the charge against the Israelites stands against us today. His children don't know what He wants and couldn't appear to care less. How broken His heart must be, how He must anguish as He watches our arrogance and immaturity. And yes, how His anger flares when He sees our hearts and deeds. His is a righteous anger, indeed.

Imagine being convicted by a law absent all grace. God's anger caused Him to deny the Israelites forgiveness for their sin, because there was no covering sacrifice at that time. The accountability for their sin rested solely on their own shoulders without recourse to the Savior who stands as the believer's advocate, resulting in their separation from God and denial of His blessings. Jesus' obedience in going to the cross and His victory over death are our covering sacrifice, allowing God to forgive and restore us. How blessed we are!

GOD'S ANGER IS JUSTIFIED

Think back and you will know without a doubt that not one single good thing that the Eternal One, your God, promised you has been left undone. Not a single one.

But in the same way the Eternal One, your True God, has fulfilled
all these blessing, you can be sure that if you turn away from him,
He will fulfill the curses until the Eternal has obliterated you from
this good land He gave you. If you break the commandments that
He has laid upon you and turn from Him to serve and worship

other gods, then his anger will flare white-hot against you, and you will quickly be wiped from the face of this good land He has given you. Joshua 23:15,16 (TVB)

I had certainly given God reason to be angry with me. After all the blessings He poured into my life, I turned my back on Him, worshiping the gods of this world. He had given me everything: believing parents and loving family, a loving wife, two strong sons, and a successful career. But that wasn't enough for me. I wanted everything He said I could not have: material things, pleasure, status, acclaim. I turned my back on God and His commandments to pursue every temptation that came to me. As a very wise man once told me, "Be careful what you wish for." To my detriment, I got what I wished for. It nearly killed me.

My life is not unique, of course. Many have fallen in similar fashion, including some we number among the greats. Take David, for example. David's life had humble beginnings, but his heart for the Lord elevated him to the highest seat in the land. This humble lad grew to be King David, ruler of all he could see and beyond. Victorious in battle and favored before the Lord. And yet, it wasn't enough. He lusted, committed murder and adultery, and saw his reign diminished to the point he feared for his life.

In some ways, I view David's life as a script of my own. Not to say that I am a David, not at all. But as I tossed the blessings of my God to the wind, so did David; and as he prayed for God's rescue, so did I.

I love the Eternal; for not only does he hear my voice, my pleas for mercy,
But He leaned down when I was in trouble and brought His ear close to me.
So as long as I have breath, I will call on Him.
Once I was wound in the wrappings of death;
The terror of dying and the grave had a grip on me;
I could not get away, for I was entombed in distress and sorrow.

Then I called on the name of the Eternal:
"O Eternal One - I am begging You - save me!"
Psalm 116:1-4 (TVB)

And miracle upon miracle, God responded. God chose to save me, not because I deserved it, but because He loves me that much. In that, however, I am far from unique. God loves you that much as well, no matter what your sin is, no matter what depression or lack of hope grips you. I am just one of a multitude of examples of His great love in action. But I had to take the first step of confession, repentance, and asking God to judge me, and you will need to do the same if you are to escape the sin that is in control of your life. I have good news for you! There is another part to this prayer that I, David, and so many thankful others have prayed:

O Eternal One, you know I am Your servant.
I am Your servant, a child of Your maidservant, devoted to You;
You have cut me loose from the chains of death that bind me.
And I come, eager to offer a sacrifice of gratitude
And call on the name of the Eternal. Psalm 116:16 (TVB)

GOD'S ANGER IS RIGHTEOUS

I wonder at times if we realize just how offensive our behavior is to God. Many of us have been taught that God is a God of mercy and grace, and He is indeed. But the notion that His mercy and grace are limitless and available to us through casual intercourse with His Spirit is false. Said another way, we sometimes act like spoiled children, demanding to have it our way even when we've been told our way will lead to pain, then claiming we didn't know and pleading for mercy when our pain arrives. In this, many of our lives mirror the experience of the Israelites as they were establishing their nation. Sometimes they obeyed God; many times they did not. The payment for their disobedience is still coming due, as are the consequences of our own sinful decisions.

The first and second chapters of Judges present a stark description of the Israelite experience and its consequence. First, we are shown an example of godly government:

> *Caleb received the land of Hebron, as Moses had promised many years earlier, and he drove out the three sons of Anak.*
> Joshua 1:20 (TVB)

Here, Caleb dispatches the three sons of Anak, the surviving government of his reign. The Anakim (Anak's descendants) were giants of the Rephiam race, descended from the Nephilim.[23] They were larger, stronger, and more intimidating than the Israelites. Caleb, however, realizes that they are no match for God and goes about driving them out of his inheritance. The fact that there are three sons is significant, three representing government. Caleb has done what we are all called to do: Conquer the giants in our lives through faith in all-powerful God, thus overcoming the illegitimate government that sits in our lives, implementing in its place the righteous government of God. Caleb realized that God would do the fighting if he was faithful, and God fulfilled His part of the covenant in doing so.

Contrast to this the actions of the tribe of Joseph. They were given the city of Bethel, formerly known as Luz. In their quest for intelligence before the battle, they made an accommodation with one of its inhabitants. Why did they make this accommodation? Because they did not trust God to be faithful to His covenant and looked instead to their own wisdom and planning. They were victorious in the battle for Bethel but allowed the man and his family to flee. He then established a new city called Luz, re-establishing its seat of government in a new location. We see this failure to annihilate the enemy repeated time after time in the last verses of Judges chapter one. These failures set up a conflict of epic proportions that continues to this day. Instead of conquering the evil nations through faith in their all-powerful God, they made an accommodation, allowing

---

23   Numbers 13:22,28,33; Deuteronomy 9:2; Joshua 15:13,14; 21:11

the conquered to live in their midst. Eventually, the conquered resented being put into servitude as slaves and servants and rebelled. Predictably, failing to honor God's commands led to disaster. Today, we repeat their failure and endure the consequences.

> *I rescued you out of the land of Egypt and brought you into this land that I had promised to your ancestors. I said, "I will never break My covenant with you. As your part of this bargain, you shall not make a covenant with the inhabitants of this land. You must tear down the altars of their gods." But you did not do as I commanded. Do you realize what you have done? Now I tell you, "I will not drive them out before you. The people of the land will irritate you, and their gods will ensnare you."*
> Judges 2:1-3 (TVB)

Upon issuing this judgment, God's hand is against the Israelites. Instead of fighting for them against overwhelming odds, He uses their enemies as instruments of punishment. The Israelites are in anguish. Still, God has not forgotten or turned completely away from them. He hears their pleas, and His compassion moves Him to offer peace to His chosen ones. He sends godly men to advise them wisely, judge them, and provide the counsel of Heaven. Even these they deny.

> *But the Eternal appointed judges, among them leaders and liberators who rescued the Israelites from their enemies who plundered them. Even then the people of Israel did not listen to their judges, but instead **passionately pursued other gods and bowed down to them.***
> Judges 2:16,17a (TVB, emphasis added in bold)

Instead of accepting God's wisdom and provision, the people stubbornly turn their backs on Him again in pursuit of the pleasures they loved more than God. This, my friend, is a perfect summation of my life before deliverance. I knew better, yet the urges and lusts inside of me overcame what I knew to be right. Why? How is that possible? Because like the Israelites of old, I allowed my earthly desires to rule my heart. The truth is that I loved the pleasures of this world more than God, more than His promises, more than His faithfulness, and more than my future. I sacrificed everything to feed the cravings inside me. God was righteously angry with me, and for good reason. I would suffer the consequences just as the Israelites did.

> *So the Eternal's anger burned hot against the people of Israel. Since these people have violated the covenant I gave as a commandment to their ancestors and no longer listen to My voice, I will no longer drive out from their path any of the nations who still remained in this land when Joshua died. I will put My people to the test to see whether or not they will walk the faithful way of the Eternal as their ancestors did.*
> *So God did as He promised. He left those pagan nations in the land of Canaan. He did not drive them away immediately, nor did He give them into the hands of Joshua and his armies.*
> Judges 3:20-23 (TVB)

Do you have any idea what life is like when God's anger burns hot against you? I pray you do not, but if you do, I can tell you that there is a way back into His good grace. Pass the test. Turn your heart away from what separates you from God and focus on Him alone. He can love you with all His heart, but you must return His love. Without that, without your heart turning to embrace His heart, your future is doomed, because God will give you exactly what you ask for. Fail to conquer the unholy nations that rule you and God will allow them to coexist with you, subdue you, and rule over you. Worst of all, He will withdraw from you.

God Withdraws to Protect Us

> HASHEM *spoke to Moses,* "Go, **ascend from here, you and the people whom you brought up from the land of Egypt,** *to the land about which I swore to Abraham, to Isaac, and to Jacob, saying,* ' **I shall give it to your offspring.**' *I shall send an angel ahead of you, and I shall drive out the* **Canaanite,** *the* **Amorite,** *the* **Hittite,** *the* **Perizzite,** *the* **Hivvite,** *and the* **Jebusite** *- to a land that flows with milk and honey, because* **I shall not ascend among you, for you are a stiff-necked people, lest I annihilate you on the way.**"
>
> Exodus 33:1-3 (SEAET, emphasis added in bold)

In the aftermath of the golden calf incident wherein the Israelites rebelled against God, He instructs Moses to take the Israelites away. God is saying, in effect, "Leave Me, I can't stand to be in your presence." Later, He announces that He is sending them on their way without His presence: "I shall not ascend among you, for you are a stiff-necked people, lest I annihilate you on the way." Yes, God was angry, so angry that He withdrew from the people He predestined to be a blessing to all of mankind. He is also demonstrating His love even in this act. Knowing that His anger is burning hot, God withdraws out of caution, an example of God's anger yielding to His wisdom. His wisdom creates distance between His anger and the offenders, protecting them. God's wisdom gives His mercy a chance to work in His heart and eventually restore the relationship. In the interim, God sends His angel to accompany them.

There is a lot to unpack in this passage. It is not simply about God sending the Israelites away because He is angry with them. He identifies these as "the people whom you brought up from the land of Egypt." In this, God is reminding Moses that these are the same people for whom He has done so much. He heard their cries for mercy and freedom and responded. He sent Moses and Aaron as His personal agents, plagued the Egyptians, and caused them to surrender their wealth to the departing

Israelites. Then He miraculously destroyed the Egyptian army and provided for everything the Israelites needed as they journeyed, and blessed them with laws to guide their lives righteously so they might reap the benefits of a rich relationship with Him, the Creator of all that is. That is what He has already done for them, but He also promises to do more by driving out those who now occupy the land He has promised the Israelites—the Canaanites, Amorites, Hittites, Perizzites, Hivites, and the Jebusites. Who are these peoples, and why is God casting them out and giving their land to the Israelite nation? These nations are spiritually symbolic of the sins of man, the spirits, and demons we struggle with every day. The Canaanites, for example, represent man's lust for power and wealth,[24] which drives us to compromise our faith and position in God. In similar fashion, the Hivites represent a love for life's material comforts, elevating pleasure and enjoyment over our covenant with God and placing us in bondage as slaves to Satan,[25] just as Satan attempted to do when he tempted Jesus.[26] The other nations represent more of the same, meaning beliefs, values, and actions that separate us from God's presence and peace. No wonder He fought them on the Israelite's behalf and gave them the conquered land.

Contrast the characteristics of evil represented by these spirit nations to the characteristics of God:

> *HASHEM passed before him and proclaimed: HASHEM, HASHEM, God, Compassionate and Gracious, Slow to Anger, and Abundant in Kindness and Truth; Preserver of Kindness for thousands of generations, Forgiver of Iniquity, Willful Sin, and Error, and Who Cleanses ...* Exodus 34:7a (SEAET)

When we look at it rationally, the contrast between evil and God is stunning. Who in their right mind would choose evil? The problem is that Satan is a wily adversary, never portraying his temptations in their true

---

24   Ezekiel 28:13-18
25   1 John 2:15-17
26   Luke 4:6,7

light but concealing them behind curtains painted with power, prestige, and pleasure. He uses the desires of our natural souls to deceive our hearts. The problem is our soulish nature. How does God respond when we fall to its enticements? He judges and punishes:

> ... *but does not cleanse completely, recalling the iniquity of parents upon children and grandchildren, to the third and fourth generations.* Exodus 34:7b (SEAET)

God is both merciful and righteous. He loves, forgives, and cleanses our sin when we turn to Him. If we do not, however, His judgment is sure. Mercy in one hand, consequence in the other. We choose moment by moment which side of God's nature will manifest in our lives. Too often I chose the world's temptations and reaped the judgment I deserved. Only my broken heart, confession, and repentance allowed God to end His separation from me. He loved me but hated what I had become and had no choice but to distance Himself from me. When I turned back to face Him, however, He was there waiting - just as He is now for you. How long have you been rationalizing your sin? How long have you been missing God? There may be a gulf between you, but it only takes one step to turn back into Him. Take the step that changes everything. Surrender to Him. Give Him everything and accept His peace in return.

God Turns from His Anger to Comfort Us

> *You will say in that day:* **"I will give thanks to you, O LORD, for though you were angry with me, your anger turned away, that you might comfort me.** *Behold, God is my salvation; I will trust, and will not be afraid; for the LORD GOD is my strength and my song, and he has become my salvation."*
> *With joy you will draw water from the wells of salvation.*
> Isaiah 12:1-3 (ESV, emphasis added in bold)

When I was in sin and unrepentant, God was angry. When I confessed and repented, God's anger abandoned its position, and He comforted me. I had to make the first move, however. Like a good parent, God loved me even when I did wrong and refused to admit it. Also like a good parent, He waited for me to come to Him. He let me deny, reject, excuse, rationalize, and deflect until all my defenses and subterfuges were exhausted. Then, when I surrendered, He turned back to me. My sin is mine and mine alone. No one else, not even God Himself, could take it from me. I owned it, and only I could surrender it. Once I did, God's anger abandoned its position in God. How is that possible? Simply because my surrender removed the cause of His anger. It no longer had reason to exist, and it no longer had standing in God's heart toward me.

When anger leaves, it creates a void that must be filled, and it is God's love for us that fills it. When a child confesses and repents, a loving parent turns to instruct, teach, love, support, and embrace. Our Father God is no different. This is the natural, deep, abiding love of a parent, and comfort is its expression as we are in the agony of our betrayal.

"Behold. God is my salvation: I will trust and will not be afraid; the LORD GOD is my strength and my song, and He has become my salvation." When I was living my double life of sin, I was constantly in fear. I feared discovery and the damnation of my soul, but most of all I feared the absence of God's love. Do you know what the absence of God's love is? It is the complete, total, absolute lack of hope. That is where I was, living day to day as an exercise in futility and knowing it well, knowing that the separation from God's love was complete and that only my surrender could change that. That sounds like an easy and obvious choice, doesn't it? Obvious, yes. Easy, no. The demons inside me were screaming, telling me all the lies that I was unworthy, I was the exception to the rule, and that for me God had a special place in Hell. This obvious decision was not easy, even as much as I desired it. It was, in fact, a battle for my life. Thank God that, deep inside, I knew they were lies. I knew the truth, and I believed the truth. I just had to act on it. I had promised God and myself that if He could see it in His heart to give me one more chance,

I would not let it pass. And then there it was, the question that changed everything.

When I confessed and repented, His song in my heart was instantaneous. The full revelation of my deceit took time to come out and I had to endure the Inquisition sessions, yet I had a new peace. Why? Because I knew where the pathway we were on would end. Do you know the feeling of hearing God's song in your heart as He sings over you? Have you experienced the sound and frequency of Joy, Happiness, Peace, Hope, and Assurance in your heart because of His heart's exhilaration at your return? It is a humbling and amazing thing. All those things that had been missing in my life were suddenly and gloriously present.

"With joy you will draw water from the wells of salvation." I love going to the well! God is always present, never absent tending some other matter; and the bucket is always full of fresh, invigorating water when I bring it up. But I must go, I must lower my emptiness into the well, and I must pull it up. It requires faith, to know that God is faithful. It requires desire, to want what God has for me. It requires willingness to do what is required. It requires strength to walk to the well when I do not feel like it, to pull up the bucket full of God's provision. It requires perseverance to keep on in the face of my sin and its devastation.

But oh, how sweet that water is! What a wonderful, glorious, delicious taste it brings! And what, you ask, is required to take the first step on this pathway from sin to God singing over you? Only one thing: Be willing to risk everything to gain everything.

God Intercedes

As I said earlier, I feel a certain kinship with David, redeemed sinner that he is. The "redeemed" part is what matters most, of course. David had the humility, heart, and strength to cry out for deliverance from his enemies, and God was faithful to deliver him.

But now, O Yahweh-God, make yourself real to me like you promised me you would. Because of your constant love and your heart-melting kindness, come be my hero and deliver me!

I'm so broken, needy and hurting. My heart is pierced through and I'm so wounded. I'm slipping down a dark slope, shaken to the core, and helpless.

All my fasting has left me so weak I can hardly stand. Now I'm shriveled up, nothing but skin and bones.

I'm the example of failure and shame to all who see me. They just walk by me, shaking their heads.

You have to help me, O Lord God! My true hero, come to my rescue and save me, for you are loving and kind.

Then everyone will know that you have won my victory, and they will all say to the Lord, "You have finished it!"

So let them curse me if they want, but I know you will bless me! All their efforts to destroy me will fail, but I will succeed and be glad.

So let my Satan-like accusers fail! Make them look ridiculous if they try to come against me. Clothe them with a robe of guilty shame from this day on!

But I will give my thanks to you over and over and everyone will hear my lavish praises.

For you stand right next to the broken ones as their saving hero to rescue them from all their accusers!

Psalm 109:21-31 (TPT)

These verses are poignant to me even today. There was a point where I wanted to pray this prayer—oh, how I wanted to—but felt it futile, given my abandonment. Like David, I was broken, needy, wounded, as if I was slipping down the last long, dark slope. I ached for God's touch, a word, a glimmer of hope, anything that I could grab on to, but it was not in me. If I had only known. In His mercy, Father God saw my despair and heart, and even though I had given up, He had not. God interceded for me. I was unaware of this until just recently. Sitting in my study one morning, I turned to this chapter quite unsuspectingly. I prayed as I always do, read God's Word, and meditated on these verses. My heart ached because this prayer had been in my own heart for so long, unspoken, but there nevertheless. I knew this prayer. I knew David's despair precisely because it had been my own. And as I sat there, wondering again about the connection between David and myself, thanking Father for saving one so undeserving as I, I heard His voice in my head:

"I knew you could not pray this prayer, so I had the Holy Spirit pray it for you. When you were too broken, He prayed for you. He was faithful, as I AM."

Now, these years past all the pain and despair, God is still revealing His mercy to me. It cannot be described, but I can tell you that it is real, tangible, and life-changing. God interceded for my life when I was too broken to do it myself. He commissioned the Holy Spirit to pray David's prayer over my life. That is the depth of God's love, that He loves us even when we have given up on ourselves or don't know how to find our way back to Him. God is not just waiting for you; He is rooting for you. You can know with certainty that He will be there when you turn into Him. So, why not turn? Why not lay it all down at His feet and let Him take your broken heart into His own? Read David's prayer as your own with a humble and transparent heart, and watch what God does.

How God Can Forgive Our Sins

One of the questions that I frequently asked myself and sometimes hear from others is: "How can a righteous God forgive us of our sins, especially our most horrible sins?" We find the answer to this age-old question in God's Word:

Make sure that your character is free from the love of money, being content with what you have; for He Himself has said, "I WILL NEVER DESERT YOU, NOR WILL I EVER FORSAKE YOU ..." Hebrews 13:5 (NASB)

Do you not know that you are a temple of God and that the Spirit of God dwells in you? 1 Corinthians 3:16 (NASB)

In him you also are being built together into a dwelling place for God by the Spirit. Ephesians 2:22 (ESV)

We are created beings. More than that, we are spirit beings first and physical beings second. He wrote a scroll for us, our earthly purpose, before sending us here to walk it out.[27] When we understand this, we see that God has a vested interest in our outcome. He is directly and intimately affected by our choices, decisions, and actions. If we believe that He dwells in us and we in Him, then we must recognize that He experiences everything we experience. He must. His Spirit dwells in us; He is in us. Think about that for a minute and ask yourself what you have caused God to experience in the last twenty-four hours. What about the last week, month, or year? He has experienced it all including what you've thought, looked at, listened to, felt, said, and done. If that realization doesn't sober you, then I am not sure what can.

So, we are in God, He is in us, and He experiences everything we experience. That doesn't answer the question—it makes it worse! How can God forgive us when our actions have so directly and profoundly affected Him?

The answer is in His heart. He loves us in ways we cannot begin to comprehend and at a depth that is unknown to the human condition. He loves us so much that He holds us in His heart even as we blaspheme Him with our words, thoughts, and deeds. He does have a personal stake in our lives, and because of that, His love motivates His mercy and grace to

---

27 Psalm 40:7-17. 139:16; Jeremiah 1:5; Hebrews 10:5-7

manifest in us and through us so that His creation may be healed. As we accept His judgment, forgiveness, and healing, we in turn express it into the world around us, His creation.

More than even that, however, is the most personal reason. He holds us in His heart. When we sin, His heart feels it, knows it, and is broken by it. His love motivates God to extend His mercy and grace to us. When we accept them through our confession and repentance, He floods us with His forgiveness. Because we are His creation, He can love us that much, and because we are in Him, His heart is healed, as well. We are not only His creation; we are part of Him just as He is part of us. Our healing results in His healing.

I am humbled by God's love for me. It is beyond every concept of love I have ever known. To have experienced His anger and separation only makes it that much more humbling. God turned away from His anger to save me despite my life. I praised Him with my lips while denying Him with my lusts and actions, yet He chose to offer me that last chance, and to judge and forgive me. He is an amazing God; His love is greater than we can understand. In many ways, this is only the beginning. There is another part of our walk back into our lives, and it begins with forgiveness. It is one thing to face God, whom we believe in but cannot see, and another to stand face to face with those we have hurt so deeply to ask their forgiveness. And it can be just as daunting and painful to extend forgiveness to ourselves. These moments of truth, however, are not an option for the one who desires complete freedom and healing.

CHAPTER TEN

THE MIRACLE OF FORGIVENESS

Six months after the revelation of my betrayal, Ruthie and I were in a tender yet difficult place. We had made progress, but there was still a long road ahead of us. Some days were good, some were bad, and a few were especially bad. One of those began with a call while I was in the office one morning. The call, what it did to me, and the evening discussions after I returned home were difficult, the most difficult since my initial confession and repentance. I would learn much about myself and forgiveness because of that call. It would not be easy, but it was essential.

The phone on my desk rang at ten o'clock in the morning. I knew instantly from the sound of Ruthie's voice that this would be a hard call and determined to see it through. Forty minutes later we hung up, and I was in crisis.

The call was completely one-sided. I cannot recall what I said, but I know it was very little. I listened to her pain as she poured out her heart, revealing previously unarticulated issues and feelings that laid bare the true depth of her wounds. At first, I was overwhelmed by the devastation my sin caused, and evil began to talk to me again. I started having thoughts of how her misery would end if I were just gone or if I asked God to abandon me to Hell and heal her. Satan was mocking and prodding me again as I listened to her anguish. It was everything I could do not to throw in the towel on the spot. The battle inside me, dormant for six months, suddenly raged again. I was on the verge of losing it completely. Then, in a last-gasp effort to stave off destruction, I started praying that God, who had brought us so far, would pour out new mercy on both of us, to heal us individually and as a couple. An excerpt from my journal notes that day:

> Lots of talk about the position we are in, what we must do, how narrow the path is, and that she can only trust God because she does not yet trust me. She told me how much she loves me, and it is only because of the depth of her love for me that she could stay and not leave. She did not stay because she had no choice, she stayed because she wanted to, because she loves me too much to walk away. She talked a lot about enduring the pain for both of us and for others who will be set free by our story, because no one else could.
>
> This one hurt. At the end I was devastated in spirit; crushed and full of remorse and sadness. Now, hours later in the afternoon I am barely able to function. I am still fighting the temptation to give up. I will not, but it is a fight of the spirit and heart. There is a part of me that is so ashamed, so guilty, that I feel absolutely unworthy and undeserving of her love and Christ's love. But their love is my only chance, our only chance. If I reject their love, even out of grief and self-persecution, then I reject life.
>
> I hate what I've done, but I cannot give up. I will not do that. I love her. I love God. I love Jesus. They love me, and I will not dishonor their love by hating to the death the one they sacrificed so much for. I have no idea how to go

> on from here other than to again submit to God in total brokenness and humility, and to ask that He pour out His mercy, love and healing on my wretched soul. He is my only hope. His salvation gives me strength, His love sustains me. He is my Savior.

That evening, we talked and prayed our way through the issues we dealt with earlier. I shared with her that I had been under attack but did not tell her how severe it had been. I humbled myself before her and God and begged for forgiveness and strength. I told her that Satan had mocked and ridiculed me as she spoke and throughout the rest of the day, and that he had tempted me to give up. I had not heard his voice since repentance and deliverance, but this was definitely him. I rebuked him in Jesus' name and declared victory.

Ruthie told me that she knew it would be tough for me and had prayed for me before she called. But she knew she had to do it. She had to get rid of the bitterness that was still inside her, and that this was God's way of cleansing her of the pain, hurt, and hatred. We prayed, opening our hearts to the Father, the Son, and the Holy Spirit, asking them to tabernacle in us. I thanked God for accepting my tabernacle as His dwelling place, making it holy, acceptable, and worthy of His presence in me. And then it was over. One of the hardest days had finally come to an end. God's peace began to settle in me, and I knew we had survived the test. It had begun with an assault against my very life and ended with new forgiveness.

Forgiveness. Just as our journey must begin with confession and repentance, it must come to forgiveness. Without it, there is no hope, no restoration, and no renewal.

Why Forgiveness Matters

Forgiveness is as important to the party who is wronged as it is to the offender. In their case, it allows them to release their anger, woundedness, hatred, and hopelessness. It sets them free to love again and be loved again. When we commit an offense of such magnitude against another as I did, we place their spiritual condition and future in jeopardy, just as we do our own. We imprison them in hatred, distrust, self-doubt, self-blame, lust for revenge, and many other evil domains. Of course we desire forgiveness, but we must understand that the offended needs to forgive us for their own benefit as much as ours. We should not, however, expect it to come easily or quickly. It may, and God can certainly do that if He desires, but it is not the norm.

Forgiveness is a process, and all processes have structure. The forgiveness process includes grieving what has been lost, blaming the other and potentially blaming oneself for triggering the offense in some fashion, or for not recognizing it sooner and facing it. There will be many what-ifs. The process must allow time for the back-and-forth which must occur as the offended and offender face every aspect and nuance of the betrayal head on. It's messy and it takes time. Both parties must be invested in the success of the process and committed to seeing it through. Without that, the road becomes much darker and uncertain. When the sacred oneness of the marriage relationship is broken, only its complete restoration can offer a path forward. Without real forgiveness, the restoration of oneness cannot be attained, cannot even be imagined. Two hearts were one. Now they are separate, and each is broken. A house divided will not stand. There is a lot of work to be done. In my case, I made a commitment to stay in the process no matter how difficult it became, because I knew Ruthie would need to work through things in her own way and time. I could not dictate how the process would evolve, its timing, or its outcome. All I could do was everything that was asked. God would have to do the rest.

Above all else, forgiveness is a matter of the heart. When trust is broken, it may not seem rational to forgive. Something stronger than rationale must be at work. Love matters, even when one cannot say with certainty that love still exists. The one who has been wronged will have a lot to work through and will need time to do that work, and it is most definitely work. Giving them the freedom to find their own way in their own time is a starting point. Being an active participant and contributing everything that is asked of you will help them. Expect hard questions, painful conversations, emotions, and anger. Expect it to take time. Understand also that time is one of God's great healers. Give them time to process and give God time to heal your broken hearts.

From the betrayer's perspective, there are multiple reasons why forgiveness is needed. None of them should include feeling blameless, vindicated, or anything less than fully transparent. Anyone with a truly contrite heart is going to be broken by their sin, and their brokenness will manifest in their feelings, words, actions, and even in their appearance. This brokenness is necessary but also dangerous if left to run unchecked. It is the seed of unworthiness, which leads to continuing self-hatred and all its associated evils. Paul instructs us on this point:

> *For the one who has caused me grief has not only grieved me but, to some extent, has caused you all grief as well. I believe that your united rebuke has been punishment enough for him. Instead of more punishment, what he needs most is your encouragement through your gracious display of forgiveness. I beg you to reaffirm your deep love for him. You see, I wrote previously in order to see if your hearts would pass the test and if you were willing to follow my counsel in everything. If you freely forgive anyone for anything, then I also forgive him. And if I have forgiven anything, I did so for you before the face of Christ, so that we would not be exploited by the adversary, Satan, for we know his clever schemes.* 2 Corinthians 2:5-11 (TPT)

There are two primary reasons forgiveness is so important: It frees both parties from the past, and it is the beginning of hope and trust for what must follow. It is the gateway to healing, restoration, and renewal.

GOD'S FORGIVENESS

Forgiving someone who has hurt you deeply can seem impossible to manage. When betrayal and pain batter us, forgiveness can be the furthest thing from our mind. Yet, it is the second step after confession and repentance in the healing and restoration process. How is it that God makes this most difficult thing so necessary, and why is it that it comes on the heels of confession and confrontation when we are so injured?

Perhaps it will help to look at why and how God forgives us our sins against Him. If anyone has a right to withhold forgiveness, one would think it would be the Creator who gives us everything and whose Son we crucified. Yet, He is a God of forgiveness when we turn back into Him. How does He do it?

He looks upon us through the eyes of Jesus, not His eyes as our judge.

> *When they came to the place that is known as The Skull, the guards crucified Jesus, nailing him on the center cross between the two criminals. While they were nailing Jesus to the cross, he prayed over and over, "Father, forgive them, for they don't know what they're doing." The soldiers, after they crucified him, gambled over his clothing.* Luke 23:33,34 (TPT)

On the cross, while nails were being driven through His body, Jesus forgave those who doomed Him to physical death and those who were carrying out the verdict. He knew their guilt but chose to forgive them anyway. He chose. That is the crux of the matter. He made a choice of the heart to forgive them. He chose love over hate. This powerful act demonstrates love's power. That same power is available to us when we choose to exercise it, but we must choose, and the choice must be from love, not a religious requirement or something that we do reluctantly or without honesty. Love is the most powerful force of nature, but only when it is real.

Later, after His resurrection, Jesus teaches His disciples about forgiveness. Pay attention to the power He placed in them:

> *Then, taking a deep breath, he blew on them and said, "Receive the Holy Spirit. I send you to preach the forgiveness of sins-- and people's sins will be forgiven. But if you don't proclaim the forgiveness of their sins, they will remain guilty."*
> John 20:22,23 (TPT)

The power He placed in the disciples is in us also. We each hold the power to forgive or condemn. You hold in your heart the ability to set your boss, your mate, your brother or sister, your neighbor, or anyone else free from their sin against you, or to condemn them with eternal guilt.

He forgives us in part for His own benefit, as well as ours[28]:

> *"I, only I, am He who wipes away your willful sins for My sake, and I shall not recall your sins."* Isaiah 43:25 (SEAET)

He forgives us for a purpose:

> *"... everyone who is called by My name and whom I have created for My glory, whom I have fashioned, even perfected;* **to liberate the people** *who are blind though they have eyes, and deaf though they have ears."* Isaiah 43:7,8 (SEAET, emphasis added in bold)

God's purpose is the redemption of His creation. In that, we are agents on assignment. When God forgives our sin, He forgives us completely, looking to Jesus on the cross and through His eyes to see us through love and not the condemnation we have earned. He chooses to remove our sin from His memory, remembering only the perfect sacrifice made for our sake. That is the choice we must make. Will we look at the one who wronged us through the eyes of Jesus on the cross, or through our own

---

28   See "How God Can Forgive Our Sins" in previous chapter.

hurting eyes? Will we choose to honor God's purpose, or choose our own? These queries raise another interesting question: Is it possible for us to forgive as completely as God does? If we are to forgive that completely, then we must know where to start.

Get Radical with Yourself First

Offense is seldom a one-sided equation. Before we can extend forgiveness to another, we need to deal with our part of the equation. This is important because our forgiveness of another must come from a clean heart to be complete. If not, there will remain in our heart the seed of discontent, offense, and blame. The fifth chapter of Acts offers important insight for us. Jealous of the apostle's popularity and fearing their effect on the populace, the high priest and his associates imprisoned Peter and other apostles. The angel of the Lord, however, freed them with a commission to stand and tell the whole truth of God's way to the people. Knowing that doing so could only escalate the conflict between them and the rulers, they chose to be obedient. As a result, the high priest had them recovered to face new charges. And then comes the reply of Peter and the apostles which must instruct us today:

> *If we have to choose between obedience to God and obedience to any human authority, then we must obey God. The God of our ancestors raised Jesus from death. You killed Jesus by hanging Him on a tree, but God has lifted Him high, to God's own right hand, as the Prince, as the Liberator. God intends to bring Israel to a **radical rethinking of our lives** and to a **complete forgiveness** of our sins. We are witnesses to these things. There is another witness, too - the Holy Spirit - whom God has given to all who choose to obey Him.* Acts 5:29-32 (TVB, emphasis added in bold)

Here, Peter nails our condition on the head, and his words convict us not only of our sins but also our unforgiveness. We are condemned before God by our thinking, our disobedience, and our hardened hearts. What are we to do? Peter and the apostles have an answer for us: a "radical rethinking of our lives" and "complete forgiveness."

A radical rethinking of something must begin and be motivated by an assumption that the thing is seriously out of alignment, else it would only need a small tweak or adjustment. "Radical" means that things are not right in a large way and the adjustment must be major in nature. One of our most common errors is to recognize a problem in our life and make only a minor or half-hearted adjustment when major overhaul is needed. We may feel good about ourselves for a while, but it is likely to be short-lived. We have not dealt with the problem; we've only obscured it. "Radical" means going deep, questioning our own beliefs, biases, and behaviors. It means getting serious and getting real. When something is seriously wrong in our life, it warrants a rigorous, transparent, and honest approach. We cannot question others until we have questioned ourselves.

Operating by our feelings alone is a dangerous game. It can lead us into deep, dark, and troubled waters, the currents of our feelings carrying us into unsafe harbors. We may enjoy a moment or season of pleasure, but the cost can be great. This truth even applies to our forgiveness life. When wronged, it is easy to strike back or even be purposeful in our unforgiveness. It is man's way. God, however, calls us to a more challenging response: forgiving despite the offense.

The key to this, in my experience, is submitting the issue, my feelings about it, my behavior, and my heart in the matter to unflinching analysis. When I hold my actions and attitudes up against the light of what I know to be God's way, then any part of the issue that I am responsible for becomes apparent. I call this process testing, and I find in invaluable. Testing myself, my beliefs, and my actions against God's way can be a humbling experience. It is also a critical one. Without it, I may not fully recognize what is really happening in a given issue or relationship and am thus likely to do more harm than good. I am not suggesting that thinking our way through a problem is the only way to arrive at truth, but I do believe it is an important part of the process. Our Creator gives us intelligence as well as the ability to experience through emotion. Too often, I fear, we are imbalanced in how we utilize these gifts to navigate the seas of life.

Radical rethinking requires us to lay down our assumptions, biases, and especially our emotions and to open ourselves to complete truth. It requires us to seek God's judgment of ourselves first with the same critical examination we apply to others, and to recognize and correct our own errors. Only then are we in a position to rightfully turn our attention upon others. Often, we will learn that they are not the only ones needing forgiveness.

COMPLETE FORGIVENESS

Now we can deal with the "complete forgiveness" part of Peter's guidance. We begin by not making our forgiveness contingent upon someone else's actions. As Jesus' forgiveness on the cross did not rely on the confession or repentance of those who wronged Him, neither should ours. I know, it is a hard thing. Our natural desire is for justice and vindication, yet God calls us to forgiveness—even when these are absent.

I know that I often thought of myself as willing and waiting to forgive if only it was asked of me. Even though I try not to qualify my forgiveness today, I probably still err in this at times. When we wait for someone to ask for forgiveness, we make ourselves dependent upon the request and disadvantage ourselves from multiple perspectives: We hold the offense in our heart longer than we should, the separation between us and the other person continues to work on both of us, and we miss opportunities that renewed fellowship and cooperation bring. The old saying "Pay me now or pay me later" applies here. Would I rather pay the price now and be done with it and enjoy renewed fellowship, or would I rather be right but separated from fellowship, paying the accrued interest of pain, frustration, and hurt? It seems an obvious choice, doesn't it? Maybe, while you are reading this, but I suspect that in the middle of the conflict your natural urge is to hold out. May I give you what I believe is good advice? Let it go. Just let it go. Forgive. Look through Jesus' eyes and forgive. Let go of the angst and sit in His peace. Isn't peace what we really want? It is only a forgiveness away. As God is healed when He forgives, we are healed when we forgive others. The seed of bitterness is killed by the fruit of love.

But how do we do this thing that we know is so good and yet so hard? All that is required is a simple prayer that emanates from a pure heart:

> "Father God, I ask You for a portion of Your forgiveness. Bestow on me, Lord, Your heart that allowed You to forgive those who crucified You. I know I have been wronged, but I do not want to hold on to this righteous pain and anger. Release me from it, Father, by filling me with Your forgiveness so that I can take it on as my own. Father, I forgive this person. I release them from the cell I've been holding them in in my heart and I set them free. Father, send a double portion of Your love and forgiveness to me and this person. Father, bless them with Your presence in their heart. Restore what has been lost between us so that it is even better than before. Father, I release them with no ill feeling, no lingering bitterness. I release them completely, Father, into Your care. I know they are wounded too, Father. Heal them for Your sake, their sake, and my sake. Thank You, Father. Amen."

This prayer must be a genuine appeal of your heart. When it is, when such a plea comes from the love of your heart for the Father and your fellow man and you desire to serve and please God first, then He can do amazing things, undreamed things, like setting you and your partner in separation free of animus and guilt, free to cooperate in God's plan for your lives and ventures.

Complete forgiveness means that once it is dealt with, it is done. Period. It is an unconditioned response to offense that leaves the offense defenseless because there is nothing left to be offended about. It has been removed by love and obedience to the Lord. Further, it creates new opportunities and pathways that could never exist without forgiveness. Forgiveness is a bridge to a changed future. That is the power we hold in our heart, and the power of our choice. We will see an example of it at work shortly.

FORGIVING OURSELVES

I spoke earlier of the struggle I had forgiving myself even after Ruthie and others forgave me and knowing that Jesus makes forgiveness possible through His obedience. That is all wonderful, but I believe there is another step in the process. It is one that can prevent us from completing our journey back into freedom, and it is this: True confession and repentance can only come from a broken and contrite heart. We must realize that our heart, the heart of the sinner, has been broken by the weight of our sin and its devastation. The work of forgiveness cannot be made complete until the heart of the sinner has been healed. Only then can full restoration and renewal occur. That is one reason why forgiving ourselves can seem harder than asking forgiveness, and certainly harder than forgiving others. When we come face to face with our sin and realize what it has wrought, it can be devastating. Those thoughts can be life-threatening as we struggle against unworthiness, the weight and guilt of our actions, and see in our loved ones the pain and rejection we heaped on them. Considering these, it is easy to hate ourselves. Forgiving anyone else for anything else makes perfect sense, but forgiving ourselves while knowing what we've done? That can be hard duty. How merciful, then, that God provides a way.

> So Jesus was saying to the Jews who had believed Him, "If you abide in My word [continually obeying My teachings and living in accordance with them, then] you are truly My disciples. And you will know the truth [regarding salvation], and the truth will set you free [from the penalty of sin]." John 8:31,32 (AMP)

As God looks through the eyes of Jesus to see us with love that enables Him to forgive us, so must we. Looking upon ourselves through the eyes of the One who gave His life for ours and knowing the love He holds for us in His heart, we can come to understand and believe that our broken lives are worth the sacrifice, not because they are broken but because they can be restored. Our acceptance of His love and sacrifice are in our surrender to His kingship and lordship over our lives. These acts of surrender to the only power capable of saving us are our entry into a new life. I accepted Christ as a young boy and yet I lived the life I lived. I was a citizen of two realms, but that is a fool's game. It is not possible to satisfy both masters. In trying, we simply conflict and condemn ourselves in both courts. We must choose. There is no other way. If you are like I was, a believer who has lost your way and are conflicted by who you know you should be and what you have become, your answer is only a breath away. Surrender to Him. Confess, repent, and give Him your heart anew. Let it all out and let His blood cleanse your heart. If you are one who has never faced this moment and known His love, then this is your chance, as well. He does love you, and He is waiting for you to speak from your heart to His. It is not hard, and there is no formula of correct words, indeed no requirement except one: surrender. Give Him all your pain and let Him embrace you. Lay down your sin and brokenness and step into Him. He is as close to you as the air that you breathe. Tell Him you love Him and desire Him in your life, and give everything to Him, your pride, your pain, your successes, and failures, and most importantly, your future. That is all that is required—the complete surrender of a broken and contrite heart.

Facing the cross of Jesus' obedience and accepting His sacrifice for our lives is the first step. Too often it is the only step, robbing us of complete victory that sustains us through future difficulties and temptations. It can help to envision the process our Lord went through after the cross. He surrendered His physical life, entered the tomb, and then rose back to life. That is His victory over death, and ours when we claim it fully. There is a dying to our sin life and a new, exhilarating freedom. Freedom to do what, exactly? Freedom to fall back into sin, to make small compromises that change our course, to look back and not forward? As Paul said, "No, I say no!" Christ has dealt with your sin once and for all. Leave it there on the cross. Die to it and walk out of the tomb as a new creation made whole and perfect by His love. Live a resurrected life! When we stop defining ourselves by our failures and see ourselves as one whom Jesus loves, then our hearts open to the breathtaking discovery of the wonder of Christ, our Lord and King.

RECEIVING FORGIVENESS

The notion of being on the receiving end of forgiveness can be disconcerting, even though it is what we desire. When the forgiveness is coming from the heart of God, the believer has a basis for its motivation. After all, it is in the character of God to forgive and restore His creation. However, when forgiveness is coming from a loved one, acquaintance, someone we know at work, or any other person, it can seem awkward. From personal experience I can tell you that there are a few guidelines which will be of great help. As described in earlier chapters, it was not long after the revelation of my sin that I had to ask forgiveness of several people outside of my family, for a variety of reasons. Facing the prospect of these conversations was another gut check. These were my closest friends, some I would even consider confidants, and others were important to my career. Yes, it was a gut check.

Before asking someone for forgiveness, I spent time before the Father in advance of the conversation to seek His guidance and blessing. When doing this, I placed my focus on the other individual: how I had wronged them (even if they did not know it yet), how I had broken trust between us, why I valued my relationship with them. I also asked God what He wanted the conversation to accomplish in their life and our shared healing. Seeking God's will and way through these prayers helped me understand each relationship through God's eyes and gave me a deeper appreciation and love for both the individual and the relationship.

When I was receiving forgiveness without having asked, I tried to follow the same process, even though it was compressed into real time. This, I learned, is an example of walking in two places at once, being in the Spirit before God at the same time I was standing face to face with my forgiver. Intimidating at first, I quickly found this to be an empowerment both for forgiveness and the relationship.

Here are the principles I used as I went through forgiveness, both when I initiated the conversation and when it was thrust upon me in the moment:

- Be open to forgiveness, regardless of how undeserving you may feel. This applies in any situation. If God has forgiven you, then there is no reason to feel unworthy of someone else's forgiveness.

- Remember that forgiveness is a gift from God and the heart of the one forgiving you. Coming from that place and with the significance that such carries is a sign of the strength of the relationship.

- Transparency trumps image and position. Don't soft sell your sin; tell it the way it is. Transparency, however, does not mean you need to share unnecessary details. Be transparent, but also be wise.

- This is not a time to justify or rationalize your actions. Own up to it without excuse. Accept that you sinned, ask Jesus to intercede for you with the Father, then be truthful without being hurtful or deceitful to others.

- Accept forgiveness with humility, graciousness, and gratitude. Use the experience and interaction to validate the best in the other person and the relationship. Be humble and thankful.

- If forgiveness should be denied, leave the door open. The person you've asked to forgive you may never do so, but without an open door, they are less likely to ever approach you on the subject again. Do not assume their "no" is a final answer. It probably took a long time for you to come to the place of repentance. Likewise, give them the time they need to come to forgiveness. Love them, uplift them, and encourage them in every possible way. You've made your choice and can live with its consequences. Give them space to do the same as you pray for their healing and restoration.

There is an instructive teaching about the power of forgiveness, which caused King David to turn aside from his assault on an offender in favor of exercising honor. It teaches us that the unexpected can change everything.

ABIGAIL BUILDS A BRIDGE

In 1 Samuel 25, we find an amazing example of the marriage between forgiveness and wisdom, and how they combine to change one's future. If you are not familiar with the story, this occurs shortly after Samuel's death. In the first scene (vv. 3-12), David sends emissaries to a rich man named Nabal seeking his blessing during the feast. Nabal, however, is a cruel-hearted man and rejects the request out of hand. This after David has treated his shepherds with honor and respect.

> *And Nabal answered David's servants, "Who is David? Who is the son of Jesse? There are many servants these days who are breaking away from their masters. Shall I take my bread and my water and my meat that I have killed for my shearers and give it to men who come from I do not know where?*
> 1 Samuel 25:11,12 (ESV)

David, of course, is not pleased. He orders 400 of his men to prepare for battle and begins riding toward Nabal. You might suspect that Nabal is not long for life, and you would be correct if not for his wife, Abigail. Learning of her husband's disregard for honor (vv. 14-17), she takes matters into her own hands. Sending messengers ahead to ward off what she knows must be coming, she loads provisions and follows behind them (vv. 18-20). Encountering David (vv. 23-31), she appeals to his better judgment, wisdom, and honor, the result of which is an amazing turn of fortune. Let's look at her action in more detail to see what it teaches us about forgiveness:

- v. 19: She is wise enough to recognize truth and strong enough to take responsibility.
- v. 23: She exhibited humility before the one wronged.
- v. 24: She takes full responsibility without offering an excuse or rationalization.
- v. 26: She reminds David of his relationship with God and how God has preserved him.
- v. 27: She honors David with the gifts she prepared.
- v. 28: She asks for forgiveness, as if it were she who wronged him.
- v. 28: She prophesies greatness, Honor, and Favor for David because of his submission and service to God.
- v. 31: She reminds David of the wisdom of restraint, to protect his own conscience and honor.

What is David's response to her intervention? We find it in the next verses:

And David said to Abigail, "Blessed be the LORD, the God of Israel, who sent you this day to meet me! Blessed be your discretion, and blessed be you, who have kept me this day from bloodguilt and from working salvation with my own hand! For as surely as the LORD, the God of Israel, lives, who has restrained me from hurting you, unless you had hurried and come to meet me, truly by morning there had not been left to Nabal so much as one male."

Then David received from her hand what she had brought him. And he said to her, "Go up in peace to your house. See, I have obeyed your voice, and I have granted your petition."
1 Samuel 25:32-35 (ESV)

Soon after, Abigail is further rewarded when God strikes Nabal dead, and David takes her as his wife. For our purposes here, that is the point of this story. Abigail acted to prevent great harm to her evil husband and family and in doing so secured a new future for herself and family, one that she could not have foreseen (vv. 36-42).

Forgiveness is a bridge to a new future. Abigail built one with her wisdom, courage, integrity, and humility. She did it, and you can do it, as well. Here is the thing, though: Building a bridge is hard work. It must be envisioned, believed in, and built through effort and sacrifice. That is how bridges are built, and it is how you must build your bridge to a better future.

I built many bridges as I dealt with the shame and guilt of my sin, some of them many times. Some event or word would trigger me, and I would be carrying the burden of my sin all over again. A critical point I came to understand was that incidents are not a sign of failure or weakness unless you allow them to be. Each time it happens is another opportunity to look at yourself through the eyes of Jesus as He paid the price for your freedom, and to honor His love for you. Stop in the moment, pray your confession and repentance, and thank Him for the covering of His blood over your life. Then begin again. The enemy only wins if you give in to him in hopelessness, and Jesus only wins when you surrender your burden of guilt to Him.

In the next chapter, we will look at the process Ruthie and I used in those early days when emotions were so raw. It wasn't easy, but it was necessary. We built our bridge one beam, one girder, one rivet, and one forgiveness at a time, and we know that with God's help, you can, as well.

CHAPTER ELEVEN

THE FORGIVENESS PROCESS

As Ruthie and I faced the realities of our situation, we knew that forgiveness was both desired by God and the only practical way out of the condition we found ourselves in. Both of us were in a vulnerable state. Recognizing that, our conversations were deliberate as we tread cautiously. We loved each other deeply even though trust between us was broken. Both of us desired healing and restoration, and both knew there was a long and dangerous road ahead. Committed to repentance and forgiveness, we struggled to find a way to address our injured hearts in ways that would not fracture our relationship completely.

One morning, I opened my Bible to read Paul's second letter to the Corinthians, and in it I found encouragement and wisdom.

> *For I made up my mind not to make another painful visit to you. For **if I cause you pain, who is there to make me glad but the one whom I have pained? And I wrote as I did, so that when I came I might not suffer pain from those who should have made me rejoice**, for I felt sure of all of you, that my joy would be the joy of you all. For I wrote to you **out of much***

affliction and anguish of heart and with many tears, not to
cause you pain but to let you know the abundant love that
I have for you.

Now if anyone has caused pain, he has caused it not to me, but
in some measure--not to put it too severely--to all of you. For
such a one, this punishment by the majority is enough, so **you**
should rather turn to forgive and comfort him, or he may
be overwhelmed by excessive sorrow. *So I beg you to* **reaffirm**
your love for him. *For this is why I wrote, that I might test*
you and know whether you are obedient in everything. Anyone
whom you forgive, I also forgive. Indeed, what I have forgiven, if
I have forgiven anything, has been for your sake in the presence
of Christ, **so that we would not be outwitted by Satan;** *for*
we are not ignorant of his designs. 2 Corinthians 2:1-11 (ESV,
emphasis added in bold)

What I was feeling in my heart was confirmed by the Word: Happiness
and joy could only come from Ruthie's heart. The one I betrayed was
the only one who could restore joy to my life. Ironically and somewhat
incongruously, I knew that the inverse was also true. The only one who
could restore her joy was the one who had so wronged her. Paul wrote to
the Corinthians, "out of much affliction and anguish of heart and with
many tears," and I can assure you that Ruthie and I experienced great
affliction and anguish. There were many tears from both of our hearts. We
spoke plainly without a hint of sugarcoating, yet we spoke with love and
transparency. We were honest and vulnerable, and we affirmed our love
for each other and God as we committed to finding a way.

The passage quoted above has much to capture our attention, but
I think two words in particular warrant deeper understanding: "... you
should rather turn to forgive and comfort him ..." Exactly what does that
mean? The Greek word for rather is mallon.[29] It conveys a meaning of
"going beyond what is required to include more, better, by far, and so

---

29   Strong's G3123

much the more." Forgive is the Greek charizomai,[30] whose definition includes "pardon, rescue, forgive freely, to grant." From the Greek, then, we can understand the instruction to mean "go far further than is required and rescue" the one who offends you (author's interpretation). Translating the Greek charizomai to Hebrew yields natan,[31] whose meanings include "to give with great latitude of application, to be healed, to deliver, and to restore." Perhaps "forgive" is best understood through its ancient Hebrew pictograph. It is a combination of two letters: Nun-Tav-Nun. Nun represents the seed of life. Tav represents the mark or the goal, which is the cross. When combined in the ancient Hebrew, נ-ת-נ, the expression of the letters can be understood as the "cross surrounded by life." There is God-given life before we encounter the cross of Jesus, and there is new life after our spiritual resurrection from sin by virtue of our obedience in going to the cross as Jesus did, dying to our sin, and being resurrected to new life. What we experience is nothing less than that—new, God-given life.

Such sacrificial love must indeed be love of the greatest kind. The very notion that Ruthie would forgive me was almost more than I could comprehend in the moment. Later, when I understood the full meaning behind the word and her obedience, I was humbled even more. Yes, her love rescued me, in so many ways that it is hard to fathom even now. As Christ sacrificed Himself for us, those who forgive us also humble themselves through obedience to pull our souls from the fire. It is that simple. Without such forgiveness, the sin will be forever on their heart and a barrier between sinner and aggrieved. But when it is given, it frees the aggrieved from a life of bitterness and loss, overwhelms the sinner, and defeats the evil one. There is no greater power than true love, especially not Satan's.

---

30 Strong's G5483
31 Strong's H5414

How the Process Came to Us

Two weeks after what is now known between Ruthie and me as "the big reveal," Will and Sylvia were back to support us as we broke the news of my betrayal to our sons. That visit is also when they shared the forgiveness process with us, which we adopted as our own and share with you here. This process is not the result, to my knowledge, of any professional counseling, book, or source other than by direct revelation by God to Sylvia. Will and Sylvia had been using this process to strengthen their own relationship and released it to us. This is not to say that seeking professional counseling is not desirable in situations like this. I do caution, however, that any counselor you might use should be chosen carefully. In today's world, even the word "Christian" appended to a counselor's title should not necessarily give confidence. At best, I would say it is nothing more than a place from which to start the vetting process to confirm their belief system is truly aligned with God's purposes and ways.

That said, there are many godly and committed counselors whose life work is helping grieving couples heal their relationships. They will naturally have their own preferred mechanisms and tools. Choosing your counselor is possibly the most important decision you will make after deciding to confess and repent. Make it prayerfully and carefully. It will in large measure determine the success or failure of your journey.

We were comfortable with Will and Sylvia because we knew them from the church we were a part of at the time. We respected their integrity, knew they were well-grounded, and trusted them to keep confidentialities and to support us spiritually. We honor them for their investment in our lives and thank them for being obedient to God's urging. Without them, we well may not have made it. With them, we had a chance.

Engaging the Process

A few pointers and cautions before getting to the meat of the process: Some of these will seem naturally apparent. All have been proved many times by our experience. We give them to you now in hopes they will ease your path. I am sure you will gain the wisdom of others as well as you walk your journey. It may at times be a hard thing, but it is also a good thing. Recognize these moments as such and count them as progress. There will likely be pain as you walk this path as it necessarily requires revisiting all that has gone before. It can be hard, and it can be emotional, yet it is a part of the cleansing and healing process. With that, let's look at our lessons learned.

It is a learning process: Expect to be in new territory in your relationship and communication. It will often be raw, especially in the early stages, but that is okay. Each of you should feel free to let it all out, and it is natural that the language will sometimes be harsh. Over time, as God works His healing, the language will change. Give each other permission to make mistakes as you learn how to communicate in a new way, and allow grace to rule when mistakes are made. It must be a part of the healing process.

Coaching: If one is struggling with the process or how to say something, then the other can be a coach. This requires stepping out of your participant role. In the coaching role, you must set aside your emotions to help the other focus on the correct process or language. Sometimes, this process can take time as the one being coached searches for and tests their thoughts and language. The one being coached should not take the coaching as an act of superiority but rather as coaching to lead to a better outcome for both of you. Once the immediate roadblock is resolved, the coach can step back into their participant role.

Extending grace: Both sides will need to extend grace to the other, allowing them to process, relate, and speak in their own way and time. Do not be concerned at the start if you need the principles or steps of the process to be repeated and reinforced. This is natural as the forces at work inside us contend for their position. Remember: grace and time. Grace and time. Grace and time.

Diligence: For this (or any other) healing process to work, it must be applied diligently and consistently. In doing this, do not let the process become routine. Each engagement is a new and different encounter, regardless of how many times you may have covered the same territory. Ruthie and I walked through the process thousands of times. Many of these were to forgive for the same offense, and that is okay. There are layers upon layers to be revealed and healed. Do whatever it takes with patience, love, and grace. That is your standard.

Nothing is too small: It can be tempting to let small things go without working them through the process, especially when emotions are on edge or you are walking lightly. Our advice is to face each issue as soon as it reveals itself. Small, even seemingly petty things are actually gateways to larger offenses. Dealing with them is part of the discovery process, both for the larger issue and to illuminate the power of forgiveness and healing. Small victories add up to large victories. Forgiving your spouse for not rinsing the dishes may seem ludicrous when viewed against the sin of adultery. Trust me, it is not. Every offense matters. Every forgiveness is a healing.

Avoid taking offense: It is natural that our defenses come up when facing a claim of offense against another, especially if it is something that has been dealt with previously or seems petty. That is a soulish reaction. The important thing to remember is that the offended is forgiving you because it is still an issue in their heart. You may have dealt with it previously, but deep hurts do not usually disappear in an instant. You might ask, if the prior forgiveness for this offense is real, then why are we facing it again? The answer is simple. There is a battle going on. Satan is fighting for his grip on each of you. He will contend for every ounce of your marriage and being, to destroy it and you. The prior forgiveness will face assault by old emotions. Just like a physical battle between two armies, assaults must be countered and victories re-won, sometimes multiple times. Understand that for what it is and engage with determination and grace to win the battle again. Forgive, receive, and watch evil die.

Avoid using the process as a weapon: This is the counterpoint to the above. When you have been deeply hurt and are feeling the pain of insult and injury, it is natural to want to strike out, to inflict like pain. Forgive when you need to, but test this need first. Are you really feeling an offense? Ask God to confirm it in your spirit or reveal it as a weapon of the enemy. Then, seek His peace in the matter and act accordingly. But what do you do when you feel or even know that the process is being used as a weapon against you? My advice is to walk the process with integrity from your perspective, regardless. Understand the pain and hurt that motivates it and kill it with love. Do not resist, and do not give the enemy an opponent to war with. Agree. Repent again. Ask forgiveness again. Humble yourself in love. Heal.

Encourage and affirm: Take every opportunity to encourage and affirm the other, both when engaged in the process and at other times. Do not hesitate to thank them for rinsing the dishes, for example. Every genuine kindness is a deposit in your love account. I do not suggest making light of encouragement. Honoring the efforts of others builds strength in the relationship, creates goodwill, and eases the path. Just like financial savings accounts, these deposits accrue interest. Over time, they will outweigh the offense accounts.

Be intentional about what replaces the negative emotions: In step three of both the offended and offender's verbalization, there is a list of positive attributes, including the Holy Spirit, Truth, Peace, Love, Joy, Grace, happiness, and bliss. These are foundational to healing and restoration. It is strongly advised that each of these be included every time you go through the process, with others added as desired by the offended party.

THE PROCESS

Here is a template of the process, followed by a scripted example.

The one who has been offended or feels the pain of a past offense starts by naming it and the emotions it causes, and asks to have these taken and replaced by God's presence:

> **Step One:** The person who feels wronged states the reason as a forgiveness. <u>name of the offender</u>, I forgive you for <u>name of the offense</u>.

Step Two: Father, thank You for taking the <u>name all the emotion(s) you are feeling</u>> from me.

Step Three: Father, fill me with the Holy Spirit, Truth, Love, Peace, Joy, Grace, happiness, bliss, <u>list all other attributes that are desired in place of the emotions</u>>.

Step Four: Jesus, I thank You for healing me.

Now, the one who is charged with the offense replies, backing up the one who was offended.

Step One: Yes, Lord. We forgive <u>offender's name</u>> for <u>offense</u>>, in Jesus' name.[32]

Step Two: Thank You for taking <u>name of the emotion(s)</u>> from <u>wronged person's name</u>>, in Jesus' name.

Step Three: Thank You for filling <u>wronged person's name</u>> with the Holy Spirit, Truth, Peace, Love, Joy, Grace, happiness, bliss, <u>and all other attributes that are desired</u>>, in Jesus' name.

Step Four: Jesus, thank You for healing <u>wronged person's name</u>>.

This simple process depends upon your transparency and integrity. When engaged with it is not the time to argue or even discuss the issue at hand. Name the offense and ask that it be taken away and replaced by God's presence through the Holy Spirit, Truth, and Peace. The one backing up the offended then comes into agreement. All of this without judgment, rebuttal, or contention. Remember, it is about what the offended is feeling, even if you do not necessarily understand it or agree

---

32 A comment here for clarification: Some may ask why the offender is speaking in third person here and not in first person. In this instance, the offender is backing up the offended, affirming their declaration. They are not making a statement of their own, they are supporting the one who has been wronged. In our experience, speaking in third person here helped build a bridge between Ruthie and me, as it emphasized that we were in agreement and acting as one.

with it. Allow them to shed the offense from their heart and have it replaced with healing.

There will, of course, be times when the one who committed the offense will begin the process. They may be feeling guilt, sadness, or some other emotion caused by their failure. When this happens, they can name the offense to the other person, who would then begin the process as outlined above. Alternatively, the offender can go first, stating the emotions and accusations being made against them in their spirit, and the offended can back them up.

The process may sound simplistic, but it is powerful when engaged with transparency and a desire for healing. It is best operated as a form of prayer. This is not just a conversation between the two of you; God is present with you. One way to experience the intimacy and power of these moments is to visualize yourself standing before God, as you did at the marriage altar, for example. With that in mind, here is an example from our history.

Ruth: Ken, I forgive you for adultery.
Father, thank You for taking the hurt, pain, anger, devastation, unworthiness, bitterness, hatred, and my broken heart from me.
Father, fill me with the Holy Spirit, Truth, Peace, Love, Joy, Grace, happiness, bliss, and knowing that I am worthy and desirable.
Jesus, thank You for healing me.

Ken: Yes Lord, we forgive Ken for his adultery, in Jesus' name.
Thank You for taking the hurt, pain, anger, devastation, unworthiness, bitterness, hatred, and broken heart from Ruthie.
Father, thank You for filling her with the Holy Spirit, Truth, Peace, Love, Joy, Grace, happiness, bliss, and knowing that she is worthy and desirable.
Thank You, Father, for healing Ruthie.

Expect emotions to be raw when dealing with such a devastating experience. Put your heart on full display in response. Take responsibility. Let your love be apparent and your faith real. Understand also that you will walk through these many, many times. There will be large issues like the original sin, and seemingly small ones like not rinsing the dishes. How can something that small and insignificant warrant engaging this process, you ask? Because that which is insignificant to you has significance to the other, such as being interpreted as, "He doesn't care about anything I do or the time it takes me to do it." You will come to this point time after time and the correct answer will always be the same; act from love with a desire to honor, love, uplift, and encourage. Let these be your genuine response.

In Part One, I described my life and the depth of my desperation and sin so that you would know just how dark it was and understand that if God did this for me, He will do it for all sinners who confess and repent. In Part Two, I described how He redeemed me, and we dealt with the big issues: confession, repentance, deliverance, love, and forgiveness. Now, we will turn our attention to the final part of this book: the overcomer's walk of faith and perseverance, and living out our freedom in Christ.

PART THREE

A NEW LIFE

The one who conquers, I will grant him to sit with me on my throne, as I also conquered and sat down with my Father on his throne. Revelation 3:21 (ESV)

CHAPTER TWELVE

WHAT IT TAKES TO BECOME AN OVERCOMER

Most of us will, at one point or another, wish our lives were different, that we could abandon what is wrong and begin anew. Many will wish; too many do not believe it possible. Whatever it is in life that constrains us seems to have a hold that cannot be broken. When we get to this point it is because we have lost hope and fail even to try, giving up on ourselves and our future. Others will try but fail, eventually giving up on the quest. What makes those who give in to hopelessness different from those who persevere to win the victory of freedom and peace? I believe it is this: a desire in the heart that refuses to accept that there can be no hope. As a wise person once told me, "There are times when the facts just don't matter." Overcoming is born of a desire that will not relent no matter the hardships and trials one endures. That desire is the heartbeat of Hope, and it can be nourished and encouraged even during our trials.

It Takes a Broken Heart

For years I had been crying out to God seeking deliverance, but especially so in the last two years of my captivity. When it happened, it was sudden. I had promised myself that if the chance ever came, I would not let it pass, no matter the consequence. When the question was asked, my decision had already been made. I simply followed through on what I had promised God, myself, and indirectly, my wife and family. Knowing that the consequences would be severe, I took this monumental step with complete peace because I knew it to be right. My desire for freedom was so deep that I had already decided to endure the aftermath of confession, no matter how God chose to respond. For decades I had been trapped between the person I had become and the person I desired to be. I could not continue and did not want to, even though I knew the ramifications would ripple through the rest of my life. I was done with it, come what may.

The path to this tipping point was long and difficult, and made possible only by two facts I knew to be true: God loves me, and Ruthie loves me. Certain of their love, I could not be certain of the future, but Love gave Hope a chance. I decided to bet on those two, Love and Hope, and I went all in. I had come to the point where nothing else mattered.

It was the desperation of a broken heart that brought me to this point. It would not be the last time I would feel its pain. The Inquisition sessions with Ruthie were heart-wrenching. The betrayal and pain in her face and voice pierced my heart like a fire-sheathed lance. Every remembrance of my deceit or sorrow at where my life had brought us was cause for my heart to break again. Even as we began to rebuild our relationship, there were times it was tough. Each question meant having to relive my sin, and each forgiveness was a fresh start. There were many fresh starts.

The truth is this: Our sins do have consequences. When the consequences manifest and how we must pay our debt are matters of divine providence. Surrendering to that fact and submitting to what is required of us is the only way out of bondage and into freedom. Trying to control, manage, or manipulate the process is the sign of two things: a heart that has not yet surrendered completely and sure failure.

Love is a matter of the heart above all else, and it is there that one must break before healing can begin. Surrendering one's heart is no easy thing, in life or spiritually, but it is the starting point for all that follows.

True love must come from a pure heart, one that is unencumbered by deceit, one that has surrendered itself to the One who loves more than we can deserve and despite what we have become. He is willing to restore and renew us, but His pure heart can only work with one that is broken and empty of its desire for the world.

It Takes Humility

As I began my walk back into a good relationship with Ruthie and God, I determined to do whatever was required of me. In the moment, I did not necessarily agree with each mandate, but that did not stop me from honoring my commitment. I had promised my wife and my God that I would do anything, and that is exactly what I would do. It wasn't always easy. In fact, it was never easy. If it had not been for my commitments to them, I would have rationalized my way around some of what was required, but those commitments were sacrosanct. I could not lie or otherwise deceive, and I would not refuse. My commitment would stand, even at the expense of my pride. Especially at the expense of my pride. I had come to understand that it had become my enemy. Pride is not always a bad thing. It can motivate us to accomplish important things, to take care of ourselves and our families, and honor our commitments to others. However, it can also lead to destruction. Unrighteous pride becomes a gateway into one's temptations, lust, and greed. I learned I had to rule my pride, I could not allow it to force me into deceiving those I hurt so deeply. If I was to be successful at this new start, I had to be successful from the start.

My first opportunity came two weeks after my confession to Ruthie and our friends. I called our two sons and told them we needed to have a family council with just us, no wives or children present. When they arrived, they were confused and put off by the fact that our two friends, the couple mentoring us, were there. Then I told them why we were gathered, that I had been addicted to pornography and in affairs with other women for years. I asked their forgiveness for abandoning them and their mother emotionally, for not being a good father, and for the lies and deceit that supported my lifestyle. It was an emotional time to say the least, and I was uncertain how they would react. I was shaken on the inside, then relieved when they forgave me and offered their love and support. Our elder son and I had planned time away together in the mountains the following week and I was not certain, statements of love aside, that he would still want to go. He did, and it turned into an important experience for both of us as we shared our hearts along with enjoying nature and being together for the week. We cried, we laughed, we prayed, and we started to heal.

At the time of my confession, I was sitting on the board of directors of a professional association. It was the honor of my life to that point. It was hard to step away, yet I recognized that the position had become an idol to me. At that realization, I knew leaving was the only right thing to do. I also apologized to those closest to me, friends, and co-workers, whom I had deceived when arranging and carrying out my many sins. These were humbling experiences. Yet, what I experienced in each case was forgiveness, which humbled me even more.

As humbling as these experiences were, they do not compare to humbling myself before my Creator. To know and understand the scale of my sin and its destruction, to know in my heart how truly unworthy I was, and to yet experience the joy and bliss of redemption, restoration, and renewal is beyond description. There are no words, only an eternally grateful heart.

Humility is required to come before the throne of God. There is no place for pride there, and it is there one seeks to live life in its highest form. From the ashes of what we have wrought for ourselves we bow before the throne of the Almighty. From ashes to the glory of His presence, that is the magnitude of change that God works in our life when we surrender all to His mercy. As the twenty-four elders cast their crowns before the throne,[33] we cast the charred works of our lives. We surrender our pride and offer it to Him as a sacrifice. In return, God grants us undeserved mercy, grace, and favor.

---

33 Revelation 4:10

While the humbling of a broken and contrite heart is a necessary process, it is important to understand the true power behind humility. The Bible is full of references, but my favorite is the Twenty-Third Psalm. In the fifth verse we find these words:

> *You prepare a table before me in the presence of my enemies; you anoint my head with oil; my cup overflows.* Psalm 23:5 (ESV)

As David prays to God he says, "You prepare a table before me..." Imagine that, Yahweh, the God of Creation, the Eternal One, sets the table and prepares a feast of Rest and Peace that He serves to David. David the sinner is served by God in an act that boggles our earthly minds. Here, Father God is not only honoring one who loves Him but is also teaching us what humility really is. It is not a false thing meant to elevate one in the eyes of others or to feed our pride; it is a bowing of the heart to honor, love, and serve. David wasn't perfect. I am not perfect. You are not perfect. Yet, God waits for us to enter the Rest and Peace of His feast table where He can love on us with Love that is perfect. God loves you so much that He is inviting you to sit at His table and experience His love.

From a personal journal entry at the time:

> *Jesus looked straight at the people and said, "What do you think this verse means: 'The worthless, rejected stone has become the cornerstone, the most important stone of all?' Everyone who falls in humility upon that stone will be broken. But if that stone falls on you, it will grind you to pieces!"*
> Luke 20:17,18 (TPT)

> "Falls in humility on that stone" speaks of abandonment and surrender to Christ. If we do not do this, then our sin and pride crush us. It is our glory to be broken over Jesus, the cornerstone of our salvation. Better His glory than ours, better His salvation than our sin. Better to be broken upon the stone that is Christ.

It Takes Faith

Behold, his soul is defiant; it is unsettled in him. But the righteous person shall live through his faith. Habakkuk 2:4 (SEAET)

For I am not ashamed of the gospel, for it is the power of God for salvation to everyone who believes, to the Jew first and also to the Greek. For in it the righteousness of God is revealed from faith for faith, as it is written, "The righteous shall live by faith."
Romans 1:16,17 (ESV)

Our lives prove that we are not capable of living righteously on our own. If one has sinned, and we all have, then we are convicted by our own actions. Refusing to admit that truth further convicts us through our arrogance. Even those among us with the strongest of wills are not able to overcome their sins on their own. We must repent, and our faith must be based in the power of the One we repent to in the belief He has the authority to free us, or it is itself baseless. We must have faith and live by our faith. Faith in what or whom, you ask?

Faith in ourselves, in our own constitution, is not enough. Likewise, faith in others cannot be the answer, unless the other we choose to have faith in is perfect, and none are. Faith in inanimate objects and symbols is also a fool's errand. If they are created by man and his self-generated beliefs, then they are false, because no man among us is perfect and thus no one among us can create perfection. If one chooses to believe in creation as a natural occurrence, then they choose to worship and have faith in something they believe occurred randomly, which makes no sense. If creation is so perfect, then why are we so imperfect, and why would creation tie its wellbeing to man's coattails? The question stands: Why would one choose to believe in any of these inferior gods? I believe the primary reason behind all rationalizations and false constructs is that choosing one of these alternatives allows us to decide what is right and what is wrong, and thus allows us to define our personal brand of righteousness. The result is a universal belief that what is right for me and what is right for you are matters of individual discretion if we do not harm one another. That, obviously, is something mankind has not been able to accomplish in all its eons of trying, as our history, world, and lives of chaos prove.

What then, whom then, are we to have faith in? There is only one plausible and true answer. It is not open to rationalization simply because it is Truth. All that we see and know is created, and it is the Creator in whom we are to believe. If not the Creator, then there is only one other choice, the deceiver, the great counterfeiter, whom we choose when we do not choose the Creator.

Christians know this, of course, yet many fail to live in righteousness, choosing instead to go their own way while telling themselves that everything will be okay in the end. Why is that? In part, a large part I believe, it is because of the doctrine of Grace. Many of us have been taught to believe that because we are Christians we are covered by grace, so our sins are forgiven. I believe that is an incorrect understanding of the principle of Grace. We will discuss this in greater detail later, but for now, accept that point as a hypothesis. If it is correct, then the question of whom or what we should believe in must still be answered. The answer is simple: We are called to believe in, have faith in, and trust the One who created us. The Eternal One who is the heart behind all that is, and who is also our "what," the Perfect One whose creation is perfection, or at least was, until man got in the way. He has been saving and restoring us ever since that first sin. We still sin, but He still loves us as a good father, providing for us despite our failures.

One of the struggles I faced after deliverance was a crisis of faith, not in God but in myself. I questioned my ability to have the kind of faith that God desires of His believers. The kind of faith that moves mountains, heals, and restores—absolute faith in His ability to do absolutely anything. My sin had been so evil that I questioned how the God of Mercy could allow Himself to trust me to have faith of any meaningful sort. I had it backwards. I wasn't struggling to trust God; I was struggling to trust myself. This was a massive issue for me, and it took some time before

I came to realize that God will always honor our faith in Him. Over time, just like going to the gym, exercising one's faith builds up our faith. God never drops the bar when spotting us. We may not always understand His response, and it certainly may not always be as we desire, but it is always in God's nature of righteousness and caring. So it was that over time I began to see changes in my faith life. An answer here or a changed circumstance there, that is all it took. I paid attention as I went to God in faith on matters large and small. I knew He was capable but questioned if my faith was strong enough that God would honor it.

I suppose to clarify it, one can say it as simply as having faith in faith. And that is what I decided to do. When one looks at the life of Jesus, we do not ask where the faith came from that make His miracles possible. He is God, after all! Of course what He desires or decrees will happen. He is God! Jesus has the confidence and faith He has precisely because He is God. He knows the end from the beginning and the beginning from the end of everything. His confidence comes from knowing, and ours comes from knowing that He knows. We may not always understand but can be certain that He does, and that is where our faith hits bedrock, in knowing that the Eternal One knows all and has all power.

Great is our Lord and abundant in strength; His understanding is infinite. Psalm 147:5 (NASB)

It Takes Work

It is not enough to know; one must act. To become an overcomer, we must accept that obedience, perseverance, and endurance are intrinsically linked. The only path to success honors these as we walk out our salvation and righteousness. Overcoming is not easy. Facing the trials and temptations that will challenge us is hard work. Take heart in knowing we have a secret weapon! The Word is not given to us for the sake of knowledge alone. Knowledge and understanding left alone at the altar without action are incomplete.

*Don't just listen to the Word of Truth and not respond to it, for that is the essence of self-deception. So always let his Word become like poetry written and **fulfilled by your life!** James 1:22 (TPT, emphasis added in bold)*

*Not only that, but we rejoice in our sufferings, knowing that **suffering produces endurance**, and **endurance produces character**, and **character produces hope**, and **hope does not put us to shame**, because God's love has been poured into our hearts through the Holy Spirit who has been given to us.*
Romans 5:3-5 (ESV, emphasis added in bold)

By "action," I mean doing, obeying so that our life testifies for righteousness, persevering through trials and struggles so that our witness is magnified, and enduring through time to signal the reality, depth, and truth of Christ's victory in our life. In doing these, we allow our lives to glorify God. It is a turning away from ourselves and into the person of Christ, letting Him face the world in our place, secure in the certainty that His strength is greater, His will purer, and His endurance eternal. We do not need to do it ourselves, and we do not need to do it alone. Faithfulness to live our lives in Christ and through Christ enables us to persevere and endure. In these, we establish the truth of our new way, The Way fulfilled.

We must tear down the altars we've built in our lives. All sin, but more so repetitive sin, creates altars in our lives. Whether it is sexual immorality, gossiping, or any other sin, it becomes our idol when we worship it by dwelling on it, desiring it, lusting for it, and acting on it. We may not think of it that way, but that is exactly what we do with each choice to commit sin; we worship at the altar of our sin. Overcomers are given explicit directions on what to do with these altars:

You shall utterly destroy all the places where the nations that you are driving away worshiped their gods: on the high mountains and on the hills, and under every leafy tree. You shall break apart

their altars; you shall smash their pillars; and the sacred trees shall you burn in the fire; their carved images shall you cut down; and you shall obliterate their names from that place.
Deuteronomy 12:2,3 (SEAET)

"Utterly destroy," "break apart," "smash," "burn," "cut down," and "obliterate." This is serious language. There is no room for compromise, allowance, accommodation, or options. As the Israelites were commanded to eliminate false idols and altars in their worship, we are commanded to eliminate them in our hearts. It might be greed or a lust for power that causes us to scheme and deceive, or it could be overblown pride. Whatever it is in your life, these false gods and their altars are to be destroyed. They exist because sinners give themselves to them, thus creating legal right for them to tempt and torment us, and to accuse us in God's court. The overcomer cannot coexist with them; they must be overcome by the blood of Jesus and the overcomer's righteous walk.

It is possible to be delivered by God but not occupied by Him, leaving our house open to intruders. Jesus tells us exactly that in the teaching about the return of an unclean spirit:

Let me tell you what will happen to this wicked generation: When an evil spirit comes out of a man, it rattles around through deserts and other dry places looking for a place to rest - but it does not find anywhere to rest. So the spirit says, "I will return to the house I left." And it returns to find that house unoccupied, tidy, swept, and sparkling clean. Well, then not only does one spirit set up shop in that sparkling house, but it brings seven even more wicked spirits along. And the poor man - the house - is worse off than he was before. This evil generation will suffer a similar fate.
Matthew 12:43-45 (TVB)

The picture Jesus paints for us here is that of a house which has been cleaned until it is sparkling. It is in immaculate condition, but to no purpose. It is unoccupied with no one living there to protect it, so it sits ready and waiting for someone or something to claim it. Habitation speaks of permanent residence, including the legal rights associated with residence. When we accept God's deliverance but fail to allow His continuing habitation because of our pride or lack of attention, we dishonor His mercy and endanger ourselves. Someone or something will fill our heart. If not God, who, what? For our house to be kept clean, God must be in residence, fully and completely. He does not rent out extra rooms; He claims all of our house. He desires to live in us, to inhabit our entire being. The overcomer is called to be His dwelling place, His mansion, His tabernacle.

As the priest of our own life, we must care for the tabernacle. The believer, one who has accepted Christ as Savior and Lord, is the tabernacle of the presence of God. Building and caring for the tabernacle of His presence is our calling and responsibility. As God commanded Moses, so He commands us. We are to anoint our lives with holiness, righteousness, and sanctity.

> *You shall take the anointment oil and anoint the Tabernacle and everything that is in it, sanctify it and all its utensils, and it shall become holy. You shall anoint the Burnt-offering Altar and its utensils; you shall sanctify the Altar, and the Altar shall become holy of holies. You shall anoint the Laver and its stand, and sanctify it.* Exodus 40:9-11 (SEAET)

Only when we have anointed ourselves through surrender does His presence come to rest in us. He will not bless chaos, arrogance, or disobedience. The task given Moses to erect the temple was hard labor, as is our task of erecting our new lives.

From the rabbinical notes on Exodus 40:17-38[34]:

> Now, they would see *their* Tabernacle enveloped in holiness, the Tabernacle that was built with *their* gifts, made by *their* hands, erected by *their* prophet, made possible by *their* repentance, assuring them that God's Presence would forever remain in *their* midst—if they would but continue to make it welcome.

Anointing ourselves with obedience and holiness creates the overcomer's life. Our hard labor builds a landing place for His glory, where it can live and breathe every moment of every day. The God of all creation dwells in the believer, making them the habitation place of His presence.

A broken and contrite heart, humility before God and man, faith, and faith put into action—these are the requirements of one who desires to overcome brokenness. It does not matter what form brokenness may take in your life. The way out is the same for all: surrender, desire, intent, faith, and action. When you have come to this point and settled your heart on its quest for freedom, then you are ready to begin. Next, we will examine five protocols that will put feet to your commitment.

---

34 *The Stone Edition of the Artscroll English Tanach: The Jewish Bible* (Brooklyn, Mesorah Publications, Ltd., 2011), 157

CHAPTER THIRTEEN

FIVE PROTOCOLS OF THE OVERCOMER

These five protocols are spiritual engagements which activate the power of the Word of God in our lives. They include cleaning up the rubble of our life, putting on the white robe of righteousness, taking our sins to the altar as a sacrifice to God, becoming a living sacrifice, and cleaning up the generational sin pattern of our lives. Each is taken directly from Scripture, which is a living being. When we approach God's Word with this understanding and attitude, we enable it to come to life in us. We understand this as it relates to Christ's sacrifice for the redemption of our sins, but it is just as true for the appropriation of the power of these ancient truths. Too often we look at God's Word, especially the Old Testament, as a history text. That is only its surface, its shallowest part. When we pray and meditate on Scripture, asking God to reveal the hidden secrets He has placed in it for our benefit, we step through the gateway of revelation. Here we discover Scripture in its living form, and it is this that draws us into the truths and power hidden in its depths.

These protocols are not rituals. They become real in our life when we engage them with our heart in pursuit of relationship with them. We activate them through our prayerful desire and intent to experience each as we journey back through our life and forward into our destiny. They are not one-time things, rather a new lifestyle as we continuously capture and deploy their truth and power in our lives. These five, done with purpose, sincerity, and surrender, help unlock our future in Christ.

Emptying Out Egypt

The third chapter of Exodus ends with these words: *"... and you shall empty out Egypt."* In Ezekiel 39:10 (SEAET), we find this instruction expanded with explanation: *"They will plunder those who had plundered them and despoil those who had despoiled them—the word of the Lord HASHEM/ELOHIM."*

We know that this instruction was given to the Israelites just before their exodus from Egypt, and we know that the Israelites were faithful in following the instruction as their Egyptian captors rushed to give them the riches of their personal possessions as they departed. From this, Israel was established as a nation of wealth from its very beginning, a blessing of God drawn from the spoils of those who had enslaved them.

We understand the history of this word, but what does this instruction mean to us today? How is this ancient scripture alive today, and what are we to do with it?

My spirit jumped one morning as I read this passage. "You shall empty out Egypt." Each time I re-read the phrase, my spirit jumped again. What was God telling me, and why is this word important to me and so many others today? As I meditated on this passage over the next few days, God revealed its truth for modern man.

We have all been enslaved by various things. For some of us, the experience has been mild. We have suffered no addictions, our families are whole and loving, our place in life seems secure and safe. Sure, we occasionally do something we know we shouldn't, but they tend to be small things or personality characteristics. We think of these as just being "the way we are." Others, however, suffer deeper and darker realities. Addictions to drugs and alcohol, eating disorders, pornography, adultery, abandonment, lives of crime and hatred—these are tough circumstances. God's Word has the same answer for all: "Empty out Egypt." His love redeems us, but we have work to do. It is the work of emptying ourselves of the sin, unforgiveness, doubt, and unworthiness of our lives. These are the things that capture our souls and rob us of the fullness of life God intends for each of us.

When we read the Exodus story, we see three main components: the exodus itself, the wilderness experience, and entering the Promised Land. The Israelites were in Egypt for 430 years,[35] the latter portion of which they were in bondage as slaves. One would think that leaving such persecution would be unanimously held as a good thing, but not all Israelites agreed. Some were comfortable with their state even though their lives were defined by bondage. One could say that they were comfortable with their familiar spirits, just as we are often comfortable with ours today. Many people, including many believers, lack the courage required to escape the bondage of their sin. They lack courage because they lack faith or are too caught up in the pleasures of sin to desire freedom. When one steps into their faith, however, they step into their own exodus and redemption. My own testimony shows that faith is the critical element, even when it must be exercised in the aftermath of failure. I tried many times to leave my sins behind, and I failed many times. I could have let those failures define me. Instead, I chose to believe God is bigger than my sin and put my trust in my faith in Him to try again. The exodus experience is one of redemption, and it is an exhilarating experience when one is in the midst of its victory. The wilderness, however, awaits.

It is too easy to step back into our soulish nature, which remembers and desires the unrighteous pleasures of our past. Living by the desires of our soul is what gets us into trouble in the first place, and we are often tempted to revisit them, especially in today's society where social norms seem to change by the hour and nothing is considered taboo, and where temptations are everywhere we turn our eyes. Television, movies,

---

35   For a good explanation how long Israel was in Egypt, see https://www.answeringenesis. org/bible-questions/how-long-were-the-israelites-in-egypt/.

advertisements, music, and pop culture all present an image of the beautiful life in which there is no sin, only pleasure. Even billboards, bus stops, and ads for the mundane sell the false notion that life is defined by wealth, sexual pleasure, and an unlimited array of possibilities wherein anything goes all the time. Be careful. As my father used to tell me, "To tolerate everything is to value nothing." To guard our newfound freedom, we must first guard what it will tolerate, because what we choose to tolerate will become our new normal. That is the lesson of the wilderness. Do not surrender your freedom to what used to enslave you.

After forty years of wandering, the Israelites finally entered the Promised Land. What did it take for them to leave the wilderness and enter into God's promise? They had to exercise their belief that what He promised was true. They had to exercise faith, that He would deliver their enemies into their hand. And, they had to live righteous lives that honored God. When they surrendered themselves completely to His love and provision, they lacked nothing. They lived prosperously and peacefully in times of obedience. But when they turned to their souls for guidance and justification, they fell into idolatry and great sin, and God responded with judgment. The Israelite story is one of repeated cycles of obedience, sin, repentance, forgiveness, and favor. In that, it is like our own lives. Our promised land of freedom and God's favor is dependent upon our complete surrender to His love and provision.

The work of emptying out our personal Egypt's is the work of cleaning out the rubble of our lives. Our hearts must be changed, our desires cleansed, and our walk straightened. There can be no compromise, no "That doesn't really matter," or "God doesn't care about that." It all matters, and He cares. So where do we begin? There is only one starting point: our relationship with Father God. Developing intimacy there leads to intimacy in all other righteous relationships, and the desire to please Him above all else leads us to want to rid ourselves of all unrighteousness. We must purge our heart of sin. How do we do that? Only by immersing ourselves in the righteousness of Father God. In Him, no unrighteousness can exist. Live in Him, breathe His breath, and allow Him to show you the way. Empty out your Egypt and live a life full of blessing and love. Make holy choices and enter your very own Promised Land.

BEING CLOTHED IN WHITE GARMENTS

In the third chapter of Zechariah, we find Joshua the high priest standing before God:

> *Then he showed me Joshua the high priest standing before the angel of the LORD, and Satan standing at his right hand to accuse him. And the LORD said to Satan, "The LORD rebuke you, O Satan! The LORD who has chosen Jerusalem rebuke you! Is not this a brand plucked from the fire?"*
>
> *Now Joshua was standing before the angel, clothed with filthy garments. And the angel said to those who were standing before him, "Remove the filthy garments from him." And to him he said, "Behold, I have taken your iniquity away from you, and I will clothe you with pure vestments."*
>
> *And I said, "Let them put a clean turban on his head." So they put a clean turban on his head and clothed him with garments. And the angel of the LORD was standing by.*
>
> *And the angel of the LORD solemnly assured Joshua, "Thus says the LORD of hosts: **If you will walk in my ways and keep my charge**, then you shall rule my house and have charge of my courts, and I will give you the right of access among those who are standing here. Hear now, O Joshua the high priest, you and your friends who sit before you, for they are men who are a sign: behold, I will bring my servant the Branch. For behold, on the stone that I have set before Joshua, on a single stone with seven eyes, I will engrave its inscription, declares the LORD of hosts, and I will remove the iniquity of this land in a single day. In that day, declares the LORD of hosts, every one of you will invite his neighbor to come under his vine and under his fig tree."*
>
> Zechariah 3 (ESV, emphasis added in bold)

We think of God's prophets and the high priests as being holy, but they are not perfect, neither then nor now. Joshua, a high priest worthy of God's calling and blessing, was clothed in filthy garments before grace was shown to him. We are no less unrighteous today. We each carry the burden of our sins; high priests carry the sins of a nation. Standing before the throne of God in such manner is humbling to say the least. In this passage, we see a model for the experience:

> v. 1: Joshua stands before God as Satan accuses him.
>
> v. 2: God rebukes Satan, for Joshua is a chosen one.
>
> vv. 3-5: God removes Joshua's iniquity and clothes him in righteousness.
>
> vv. 6-10: God issues His promises of redemption, restoration, and rulership.

Any sinner who has been delivered and changed by the mercy of God's love will attest to the validity of this process. I know that my own experience is a mirror reflection of Joshua's. As high priest, he carried national accountability, whereas I stood for my own sins and, later, for those of my bloodline. The power of God's mercy is not conditioned by our position, however. It is the same for all: complete and victorious no matter our position in life, no matter the gravity or depravity of our sin. God does not deal in half-truth or half-forgiveness. He is an all-or-nothing God. Only when we abandon our sin can God reverse the laws of earth so that we fall upward into His mercy. The phrase "pure vestments" refers to righteousness. It is a gift from God. Our responsibility is to walk it out in our lives by making holy choices. Righteousness is a gift, but holiness is our responsibility. It is the fruit of right hearts and right actions. It is the overcomer's way.

> *He who overcomes will thus be clothed in white garments; and I will not erase his name from the book of life, and I will confess his name before My Father and before His angels.*
> Revelation 3:5 (NASB)

Taking Our Sin Up the Altar

Early one morning, I was reading about Ezekiel's vision of the Third Temple.[36] I happened to be reading from the Tanach and turned to the reference section where I found a diagram of the plan view of the temple as interpreted by Rabbi Rashi. I was stunned when I recognized its similarity to the Hebrew letter Hey. The more I looked at it, the stronger the sense of revelation became.

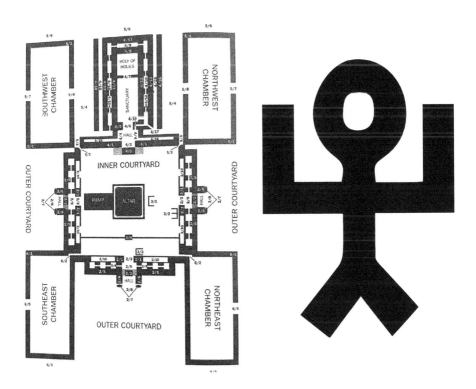

The letter Hey means Ruach (divine breath), Revelation (mysteries revealed), and Seed (creative power), and is used as a statement of exclamation: "Behold!" It is God's language exclaiming, "Behold, here I AM!" The temple plan view has the same outline shape as the letter Hey. In other words, God declared His glory, "Behold! Here I AM," even in the

36 *Stone Edition, The Artscroll English Tanach: The Jewish Bible* (Brooklyn, Mesorah Publications, Ltd., 2011), 1336

shape of His temple! In this, He declares himself to be the source of divine breath that brings life, of revelation of the fullness of His kingdom, and the creative power of His Spirit.

Note that the altar is positioned in the center of the inner courtyard, a place of great prominence and importance. The altar is where the sacrifice takes place. It is here that we, each the priest of our own life, must deposit our will, desires, life, agendas, beliefs, and sin as sacrifices to God. It is here that all that separates us from our Father is consumed by His holy fire, becoming sweet incense before Him.

We cannot simply walk up to the altar and deposit the hubris of our life. We must first climb the ramp that elevates one from ground level (our earthly experience) to the elevated level of the altar (Heavenly realm). Walking up that ramp can be one of life's great efforts. I know that I started this climb many times before finally getting there, and I am still making that walk. It is not a one-time thing; it is an every-time-I-sin thing. It is easy to have the thought of doing something hard, but each sacrifice must be carried up the ramp before it can be burned as a sacrifice. The load must be borne on our own shoulders, as no one else can take it up for us. This bearing is a matter of desire, will, faith, strength, and endurance, each a gift of God's grace. The act of following through faithfully in this work is, in fact, a pre-sacrifice as we commit ourselves to experiencing God's forgiveness and healing. Before forgiveness, however, comes obedience to the act that places our burdens before Father God. If one does not make that climb, if one fails to try or gives up on the way, then there can be no sacrifice. Without a sacrifice, there is nothing for God to destroy with His fire, and if God does not consume the sacrifice, then there has been no sacrifice, and we can have no peace. The greater the sin, the harder the climb, but it is worth it untold times over. This is the surrendering of all that separates us from God. Christ died to set us free, but only we can surrender to Him.

Becoming a Living Sacrifice

Jesus is our high priest, and it is to Him we submit ourselves to be cleaned and made pure for the sacrifice. If you have studied how the priests cleaned the sacrificial animals, you know it was not a pleasant thing. But there is a reason and purpose for each step in the process, and we can adapt these to our own surrender.

We begin by acknowledging Jesus as our high priest and submitting ourselves to Him as a sacrifice, abandoning our own will to place ourselves in His hands. Dying to ourselves is a necessary step of course, but it is only the first. What follows is a natural act as man sees it but a miracle of cleansing in the spiritual sense and realm. Like everything else the overcomer does, one does this through faith with the intent of a heart that desires to know, please, and honor God.

I begin my prayer by accessing the spiritual realm of God's presence, and then repeating the act one more time to enter His presence. Once there, I recognize Jesus as my high priest and submit to His authority, asking Him to cleanse me. Then, I pray my way through the cleansing process. I ask Him to divide me down the middle and open me up as a way of exposing everything that is in me. I surrender my legs to Him as a way of surrendering my walk with the world; when I surrender my head to Him, it is symbolic of surrendering my thoughts, beliefs, and will. Then, I imagine Him cleaning me with His perfect blood, His hands washing each organ and eventually putting me back together. I pray through each organ, asking Him to cleanse and purify it as I describe its relevance to my life with Him, e.g., how my heart is full of love for Him, but I desire more love, greater love, and to know His heart's desire for me. When I am finished, I imagine Him putting me back together. My legs now represent a renewed strength and purity of walk in His way. As He puts my head back on my shoulders, I imagine putting on the mind of Christ, and as He closes me, I see myself as restored in purity and purpose.

While the imagery may be gruesome to some, it reflects the sacrifices of old and how they were conducted. I think of it as a type that I can leverage for my own experience and benefit. It is not something to be repulsed by, not if one desires to be cleansed and set free. It is not a substitute for Jesus' sacrifice but an acknowledgment of its power and purpose, and it is not a physical act but a spiritual one. As such, it is infinitely more powerful and real, manifesting itself in our spirit, thought, desires, and walk. It is something to run toward, giving the Savior an opportunity to administer the full power of His own sacrifice into our lives.

Resolving Our Sinful Past

Any personal sin, generational sin, or unrighteous spirit such as unworthiness, self-hatred, greed, gossiping, coveted-ness, jealousy and others of their ilk that separate us from righteousness must be dealt with.[37] We must take responsibility for our past because no one else can.

To put it simply, if something in your life is not righteous, then it is yours and only yours to deal with. Our challenge is to exercise dominion over the spirits that seek to tarnish our life, and we can only do so through God's mercy and grace. Our battle is in not allowing sin to control our attitudes, beliefs, or actions. We may know this intellectually, but the proof is in our walk. One thing I've learned people are very good at, Christians included, is fooling themselves. As you think about what spirits are or may be operating in your life, take a hard and objective look. Do not assume that issues or spirits you've dealt with in the past have not returned. Test yourself, your thought process, and what your soul is telling you, and ask the Holy Spirit to reveal truth to you. Do not be surprised or discouraged to learn that old spirits and demons have returned, or if you discover some you were not previously aware of. That is okay. It is a good thing because now you know they are there, and you can go after them. One last word of caution before getting into practical steps: If you have a sin issue or know there is an unrighteous spirit in you, do not ever disregard it because you think it is under control. "Under control" is a lie from the soul, a temptation and rationalization to let it

---

37   Grant and Samantha Mahoney have a very good teaching on this subject, available at https://www.moed-ministries.com/shop/Deal-with-your-junk-p127634428

slide. Control is never the issue. You either have an issue that needs to be dealt with, or you don't. If you don't, then no control is needed. If you do have one, however, then the illusion of control is double jeopardy. Trying to control something implies that doing so is in your power (it isn't), and it is an admission that you are choosing to allow it to remain present.

Okay, let's move on to a couple of practical steps we can apply to deal with our sinful past.

Tracing generational sin: We each carry our own sin, but we may not realize that some of our sin comes from our forefathers and that our sin will likewise be passed on to our future generations. Whether we realize it or not, this truth has been in operation since the very beginning. The sin of our ancestors creates a legal right for the sin's spirit to operate in future generations until it is dealt with. Each succeeding generation experiences the sin in their own life, perpetuating its hold on the bloodline's future. An alcoholic or abusive father spawns the same traits in a son; abandonment results in a broken love line and children who do not know what it is to be loved or how to love ... and the beat goes on. The legal right the original sin creates must be dealt with by confession, repentance, and forgiveness. Until it is, it has a right to operate. This is not a new concept. It is, in fact, God's way.

> *The Lord is slow to anger and abounding in steadfast love, forgiving iniquity and transgression, but he will by no means clear the guilty, visiting the iniquity of the fathers on the children, to the third and the fourth generation.* Numbers 14:18 (ESV)

After my deliverance, I began to understand the implications of generational sin. As I learned more, I began to question how generational sin affected my own life and to fear for my sons and their families. One of the things I learned is that generational or hereditary disease can be an indication of sin patterns that flow from generation to generation. That prompted me to think about what I could recall of my family's health history. Although I regrettably do not know a lot about my family's history,

I do know a little. One evening, I sat at my desk and thought through what I knew about our generational health. At the end of the evening, I had a pretty good road map sitting before me.[38] Later, I mapped what I had developed of our family health history against known spiritual causes of disease.[39]

	Spiritual Cause	Scripture	Paternal				Maternal		
			Self	Father	Aunts Uncles	Grand Parents	Mother	Aunts Uncles	Grand Parents
Anger	Rejection, Lost Hope, False Accusations, Pride, Envy	Eph 4:26,27	✓	✓					
Alcoholism	Need to be loved	Isa 41:13 Isa 53:5 Psa 107:19,20			✓				
Cancer	Bitterness, Self-Loathing, Need to be Loved, Abandonment	Prov 18:21 Matt 6:9-15; 7:1,2; 12:36 Jhn 20:23 Rom 2:1 Psa 26:2 Heb 11:1,6		✓	✓	✓		✓	
Type 2 Diabetes	Fear of failing others, Fear of failure, Fear of man, Performance and drivenness, Inability to receive love, Unloving spirit, Spirit of death	Prov 15:13; 17:22 Matt 22:37,39 2 Tim 1:7 1 Jhn 4:11,18	✓	✓		✓			
Depression	Self-accusation, Self-centeredness, Self-introspection, Self-pity, Guilt, Shame, Fear, Anxiety, Stress	1 Jhn 4:18; 2 Tim 1:7 Matt 22:37 Prov 15:13; 17:22 Jhn 14:27 Jer 16:14	✓	✓	✓				
Cardiovascular System (Angina, Hypertension, Heart Arrhythmias, Mitral Valve Prolapse, Coronary artery disease, Strokes)	Fear, Anxiety, Stress	Job 3:25 Luk 21:26 Eph 4:26,27 2 Tim 1:7	✓	✓	✓	✓	✓	✓	✓
Psoriasis	Self-hatred, Lack of self-esteem, Conflict with identity, Shame, Sexual immorality	1 Thes 5:23 Rom 8:15 Lev 12, 13	✓	✓		✓			
Negative thoughts	Dependence on self, Unforgiveness, Fear, Guilt, Shame	Phi 4:8,9 Psa 94:19 Heb 4:12 Isa 26:3	✓	✓	✓				
OCD	Guilt, Self-hatred, Fear	2 Tim 1:7 1 Pet 5:7 Rom 12:2 Phi 4:8 Isa 41:10	✓	✓	✓	✓			
Dissociative Identity Disorder	Fear	Mar 5:9 Jam 1:8 Eph 1:4 Luk 8:2 Jhn 14:12-14 1 Jhn 4:18	✓						
Suicide	Self-Hatred, Hopelessness, Shame, Guilt	Jam 4:2 Matt 5:21 2 Cor 5:17-19 Eph 4:21-24	✓		✓				

38   Wright, Henry, *Exposing the Spiritual Roots of Disease* (New Kinsington, PA, Whitaker House, 2019)
39   Wright, Henry, *A More Excellent Way to Be in Health* (New Kensington, PA, Whitaker House, 2009)

When I looked at what the evidence told me about my family, I knew experientially that it was true. The evidence did not lie. When I considered it against what I knew of my family's history, the verdict was stunning. Since my confession and deliverance, I have been working my way through spiritual healing, and continue to do so. Can I say that I am completely healed? Not yet. Can I say that I am in a much healthier place than before? Without question. Can I say that my relationships with God and family are stronger? Absolutely yes! It is a process of desire, intent, and faith. I desire to be clean and whole; my heart's intent is to see it through to completeness with integrity to honor God, and I have faith that my Father is capable, willing, and on the job.

Praying through generational sin: One evening in 2016, Ruthie and I were in our living room praying together. I was asking Father God to reveal to me the sin patterns of my own life when the Holy Spirit directed me to expand my prayer to include generational sin. I understood that I was to take these sins on as if they were my own and confess and repent for each sin. I knew that I was to stand for my family line; in fact, I was the only one who could. I did not know where to start, seriously. Most of my family were solid Christians. They had flaws, of course, but serious sin? I did not know of any. But the Spirit prompted me, and I began to earnestly seek God's revelation. Two hours later, I was exhausted and completely wrung out emotionally and physically. I had traveled in the Spirit and witnessed first-hand many of the sins of my family, including robbery, murder, adultery, and hideous immoral perversions from decades and centuries past. Not only were these sins revealed to me, but also the lasting impacts that followed them. I now understood why there was a spirit of poverty in the family, for example, and where the roots of unworthiness and negative thought patterns grew from.

Overcoming is hard work. It is the journey to a new life on a pathway formed through faith, humility, effort, and perseverance. When you begin, surrounded by the dense jungle of your dark sin, you must take up the task of creating and walking this new path. God is waiting for your confession, repentance, and that first step of obedience. He will provide everything you need, but only you can do the work. As you do, your faith will increase, and you will become witness to the life-changing love of God. He, after all, is the One who protected Cain after he murdered Abel.[40] Why did He protect the first murderer? I believe the answer is this: Because He knew what was yet to come. He knew the future. That is one reason why the God of Glory whose heart is full of compassion for His creation can forgive and restore us despite our sin, because He knows what we do not. He knows our future, that which He destined for us. The overcomer's task is to discover and walk out their new future, their new life.

To discover our future and walk it out sounds like a tall order. How can we do that? In the closing chapters we will learn about additional tools and wisdom from God's Word that will help us build new patterns in our thinking, behavior, and relationships. First, however, we will look at the importance of what we believe and how critical that is to our future.

---

40 Genesis 4:13-15

CHAPTER FOURTEEN

WHY DOCTRINE MATTERS

I may not be the only person to experience horrific life failure, but I am the only one for whom I know the whole story, including the effects of failed doctrine. I grew up in a mainline protestant denomination from literally the day I was born and accepted everything I was taught as truth. But it wasn't all correct. This chapter looks at two specific doctrines that bore bitter fruit in my life, Grace and Cessation, and one that rescued me, Mercy. I am no theologian and I've never been to seminary, but I know what I was taught by good people who were sincere in their beliefs, who loved me, and who wanted only the best for me. I also know the truth of what I have experienced and the marvelous power of Mercy.

Before going further, I should state clearly that my decisions, the life they led me into, and their consequences are no one else's responsibility other than my own. These were my choices and my sins. I knew better. I did the things I did knowing they were wrong. If ever a person deserved what such a life would naturally lead to, it was I. Only God's Mercy could save me from myself and what I wrought. That said, the theology I grew up under had flaws in it that I would not recognize for decades. When I did, it set in motion a series of events that would eventually result in my quietly-stated confession. Before we look at specific doctrines, let me explain why I think this is so important and how I've come to evaluate teaching, doctrine, and prophecy.

We Are Responsible for What We Believe

Too many believers accept anything they hear from the pulpit, see on YouTube, or read in the latest popular book. Abandoning our responsibility to test and prove what we are taught is risky business, leaving us open to being influenced incorrectly or adopting false teaching and doctrine. Just because someone has a position, a big ministry, or other platform does not mean they necessarily have it all right. The Word tells us we are responsible for what we choose to believe:

> *As I urged you when I left for Macedonia, I'm asking that you remain in Ephesus to instruct them not to teach or follow the error of deceptive doctrines, nor pay any attention to cultural myths, traditions, or the endless study of genealogies. Those digressions only breed controversies and debates. They are devoid of power that builds up and strengthens the church in the faith of God. For we reach the goal of fulfilling all the commandments when we love others deeply with a pure heart, a clean conscience, and sincere faith. Some believers have been led astray by teachings and speculations that emphasize nothing more than the empty words of men. They presume to be expert teachers of the law, but they don't have the slightest idea of what they're talking about and they simply love to argue!* 1 Timothy 1:3-7 (TPT)

I know this truth from personal experience, having been influenced by false doctrine even though active in church for virtually my entire life. How are we to keep from falling into this trap? A few years ago, I adopted two strategies: First, instead of listening to a wide number of folks, I looked for a small circle of teachers who are well-grounded, seeking deeper truth through the Spirit, and in relationship with each other. They may not agree on every detail, but their teachings are consistent, and they edify each other. My second strategy was to develop a method of testing what I take into my own belief system. Here are the four questions I use.

Does the teaching contradict or support what is written in the Word? This is a litmus test for me. The Bible is a small book and only a portion of what God intends for us, but it is a plumb line for everything else. There cannot be any disagreement between a word that is given, a revelation, or a doctrinal teaching and the Word of God. The Almighty speaks to us in many ways, but none of them should contradict His inspired Truth.

What does the Spirit tell me regarding the virtue of a teaching? For much of my life, I listened to and accepted as gospel what church leaders taught. Pastors are called to the ministry, so it is easy to assume everything they say is from God, but pastors are human and have their own biases. I have learned to turn to the Holy Spirit for confirmation, to test what I am being taught.

Do I discern any sort of agenda in a teaching or its motivation? Unfortunately, not all teaching is purely motivated. I am not a fan of "health and wealth" or "hyper grace" theology that promises all our needs will be met because God's love is so big He won't hold us accountable or bear to see us in need or want of anything. Even worse are those who promise spiritual covering in exchange for financial support, as I believe no man can provide spiritual covering for another, not even a pastor, prophet, or apostle. Only God can be our covering. On the same plane in my view are those who seek to change beliefs as a social engineering mechanism. Motivations and agendas that seek to elevate a person, organization, or cause over God the Father and His Word are sure signs.

What happens when I put the teaching into practice in my own walk? No matter how strongly we believe and how diligently we apply incorrect teaching, it cannot bear good fruit because the seed itself is spoiled. In contrast, all good teaching should bear good fruit in our lives. If the teaching is correct but does not bear fruit, then it is a matter of faith and/or application. Good fruit proves that good seed has been nourished and applied correctly in our daily walk.

It is too easy to fall into the trap of believing what we want to hear. The Word of God is not intended to justify our actions or make us comfortable; it is meant to challenge our beliefs, what we say, and what we do, all to conform us to God's truth. We are accountable for what we believe and how we act. The best way to meet God's standard is to follow His Word and make holy choices, trust what the Holy Spirit tells us is correct, and act accordingly. Abdicating responsibility for our beliefs and actions is not possible. We may follow incorrect values, teachings, or beliefs, but the buck stops with each one of us. We cannot point the finger elsewhere. Take responsibility for what you believe and do, letting God be your judge, not man.

With this in mind, let's now look at three specific areas of teaching. Two of these, Grace and Cessation, planted incorrect beliefs in my life, which I allowed to take root to my detriment. The third, Mercy, saved me from complete ruin.

GRACE

Pulling out of my driveway during the early pre-dawn hours one morning, I thought about the hour-long drive to the office that lay ahead and hit the audio system "play" button. In many ways, I count this moment as the beginning of my journey back into truth and a new life. I had selected Eric Metaxas's biography of Dietrich Bonhoeffer[41] as my new listen. With my daily commute, I had plenty of opportunity to listen to recorded books. Choosing this book was not by accident. I was curious about the man and his times and hoped that in it I would find clues to my own time and the answer to a question that both nagged at me and scared me. Over the next several days, it seemed as if I stepped back in time to relive history and experience the life of this giant of the faith. What I learned through his arguments to his own contemporaries confirmed my fears and suspicions about the doctrine of Grace I knew in our time. This

---

41 Metaxas, Eric, *Bonhoeffer: Pastor, Martyr, Prophet, Spy* (Nashville, Nelson Books, 2010)

excerpt from the review I wrote on Goodreads.com only suggests the scale of impact the book had on me:

> *All of that is interesting from a historical perspective, but this volume's most memorable impact is much deeper in my own experience. Of late I have been challenged by the common Christian definition of Grace, causing me to question my own security. In the end I cannot deny the pure simple logic and wisdom of Bonhoeffer's philosophy of Costly Grace. In it I find challenge, truth, inspiration, and confidence. In it I find a purity of thought that resonates with the Word.*[42]

What is not in my review is what was going on in my life at the time. I knew that I was a sinner, that the truth of my life made my public face and persona a lie, and I was desperately afraid that there was no pathway to redemption and freedom. At the same time, I had not yet come to the point of surrender, still desiring and living a life that caused me to despise myself because I was unable to stop what I was doing. Could Bonhoeffer possibly illuminate my dilemma in the light of God's grace? That was what I was really interested in finding out.

To summarize what I had been taught and believed to this point, it was that grace is a gift from God's heart to the believer, which ensures the believer's eternal salvation from the moment of accepting Christ. While God desires us to live a sinless life, His grace covers us in the event we fail. Everyone fails, of course, but no matter—grace has it covered. The expectation was that we will give perfection our best shot but not worry too much when we fail. We are, after all, only human. God knows this, and that is why He releases grace when we need it. I was taught that we are saved by faith through grace. This statement is correct, but the interpretation I was living under was not. One day, a pastor asked if I believed that once we are saved we are always saved. I recall my answer clearly: "If we are saved through grace, then it must be through grace alone and

---

42   https://www.goodreads.com/review/show/267604346

not by our behavior. Once it becomes a matter of behavior, then it is by definition through our works and grace is made null and void. Grace is superior as we are too weak to earn salvation by our works, so it must be grace alone, and grace has no time limit."

Boiled down to the basics, I believed that there could be no eternal consequence of sin for one who has accepted Christ as their Savior. Even murderers, rapists, and the vilest offenders were assured of an eternal life in Heaven if they had accepted Christ either before or after their sin. For our purposes, let's focus on the one who is a believer and then sins, even knowingly and egregiously as I did. We even have a name for such a person; we call them a "Carnal Christian." Of course, no one intends to be such, until they are.

If correct, this doctrine would amount to a "get out of jail free" card for any believer, for any sin, at any time. But it is not correct, and I believe it is one of the most significant errors and misrepresentations of doctrine that exists. It is responsible for a false belief system that traps untold millions of people in a false security. The notion that we are not accountable for our beliefs, decisions, and behavior and are thus free to live as we choose without consequence contradicts God's Word on every count. If such were the case, then sin would cease to exist in all practical manner as there would be no penalty. If there is no penalty then there cannot be a reason not to do whatever the soul desires, beyond natural preference for another action, because there could be no consequence. Carried to its logical extension, such a system would negate the very concept of sin. The more I considered this the less sense it made. How could a righteous God allow such a huge loophole in His doctrine? He didn't. Man has twisted truth to his own purposes and sold the bill of goods. Bonhoeffer states it well when he compares what he refers to as "cheap grace" and "costly grace."[43]

> The essence of grace, we suppose, is that the account has been
> paid in advance; and, because it has been paid, everything can

---

43   Bonhoeffer, Dietrich, *The Cost of Discipleship* (New York, Touchstone, 1995), 43-45

be had for nothing. Since the cost was infinite, the possibilities of using and spending it are infinite. What would grace be if it were not cheap?

Cheap grace therefore amounts to a denial of the living Word of God, in fact, a denial of the Incarnation of the Word of God.

Cheap grace means the justification of sin without the justification of the sinner. Grace alone does everything, they say, and so everything can remain as it was before.

Cheap grace is the preaching of forgiveness without requiring repentance, baptism without church discipline, Communion without confession, absolution without personal confession. Cheap grace is grace without discipleship, grace without the cross, grace without Jesus Christ, living and incarnate.

Listen now as he describes true grace, costly grace:

Costly grace is the treasure hidden in the field; for the sake of it a man will gladly go and sell all that he has. It is the pearl of great price to buy which the merchant will sell all his goods. It is the kingly rule of Christ, for whose sake a man will pluck out the eye which causes him to stumble; it is the call of Jesus Christ at which the disciple leaves his nets and follows him.

Costly grace is the gospel which must be sought again and again, the gift which must be asked for, the door at which a man must knock.

Such grace is costly because it calls us to follow, and it is grace because it calls us to follow Jesus Christ. It is costly because it costs a man his life, and it is grace because it gives a man the only true life. It is costly because it condemns sin, and grace because it justifies the sinner. Above all, it is costly because it cost God the life of his Son: "ye were bought at a price," and what has cost God much cannot be cheap for us.

Grace is costly because it compels a man to submit to the yoke of Christ and follow him; it is grace because Jesus says: "My yoke is easy and my burden is light."

Finally, I had found a description of grace that I could believe in, and it convicted me to the core of my being. I had known that I was a sinner, and now I knew the depth of my betrayal of Christ. I had been living a life of cheap grace. My heart ached then for myself as it aches now for the multitudes still believing in and trapped by the lies of cheap grace. I wonder, are you one of those, one like I was? If you cannot answer that question with an immediate and resounding negative, then you should take a hard, deep look inside. Are you living a life of one filled by the Incarnate Word of God, one in which even your most secret moments and desires edify and proclaim Him? Lay down your burdens, your sins, your hidden, soul-fed desires, and take up His cross, take up His life, take up His walk. That is Christ's call to the unbeliever and the sinning believer alike. The peace that surrender brings into our lives the moment we accept His call is beyond description. Ask me how I know.

Now that we know what grace isn't, let's talk about what it actually is, beginning with the Merriam-Webster Dictionary definition[44]:

grace (noun)
   a: unmerited divine assistance given to humans for their regeneration or sanctification
   b: a virtue coming from God
   c: a state of sanctification enjoyed through divine assistance

The definition identifies the source of grace ("divine"), its purpose ("regeneration or sanctification"), and its type ("virtue"). To put the dictionary definition into usage, we would say that God gives grace to us

---

44 https://www.merriam-webster.com/dictionary/grace

when needed so that we can be sanctified. To be explicit about sanctification, we can add that the purpose of grace is to maintain our sanctification so that our relationship with God can be maintained in a state of union. The point here is that grace is not a "get out of jail free" card we can play whenever we choose to sin, and we certainly should not believe that God is playing it on our behalf. It is His assistance, given to us freely, for the express purpose of maintaining our sanctification, as clearly articulated in Scripture.

> *What shall we say then? Are we to continue in sin so that grace may increase? May it never be! How shall we who died to sin still live in it? Or do you not know that all of us who have been baptized into Christ Jesus have been baptized into His death? Therefore we have been buried with Him through baptism into death, so that as Christ was raised from the dead through the glory of the Father, so we too might walk in newness of life. For if we have become united with Him in the likeness of His death, certainly we shall also be in the likeness of His resurrection, knowing this, that our old self was crucified with Him, in order that our body of sin might be done away with, so that we would no longer be slaves to sin; for he who has died is freed from sin.*
> Romans 6:1-7 (NASB)[45]

Reading the scriptural definition and explanation of grace makes its purpose clear: It is God's provision of everything we need in all circumstances to enable us to be dead to sin. Our goal is the sinless life of Christ. When we fail in that, our response is confession and repentance to restore our relationship, and a bearing of any consequence we have created for ourselves with humility and a contrite heart. Grace is our bulwark against committing sin, not a promise of no consequence when we do sin.

---

45   See also Acts 20:32; Romans 6:14,15; 2 Corinthians 9:8

Cessation

Cessation doctrine denies the working of the Holy Spirit through man to manifest what we commonly refer to as gifts of the Spirit. Under Cessation, all such gifts ended with the death of the last Apostle. Before we go further, let me object to this disqualifier. If it were true, it would mean that God, our Creator, in all His majestic power, is powerless to manifest His will in our lives through the Holy Spirit. It would mean that God has limits, and if this one, then what other limits has He placed on Himself? I know of only one in total, and that is that God respects our exercise of our own will, even when it contradicts His. I do not believe He limits Himself in any other way. We could get into a long discussion of why or why not it is correct,[46] but let me summarize for the sake of brevity. The doctrine of Cessation was developed by John Calvin in response to the Roman Catholic Church program recognizing and codifying miracles. In other words, it was a man's response to another man's doctrine or program. In this, it was strategic in nature, meant to deny a competing doctrine, and a product of man's intellect, reasoning, and belief.

I can hear you asking, "Why is this important? Why should I care about a theoretical difference of opinion about doctrine?" Belief in this doctrine denies God's ability to manifest Himself in our lives through the Holy Spirit. This would mean, for example, that God could not speak through man to prophesy, that the Holy Spirit in us could not communicate with God through a spiritual language, and that God could not use man as a divine healing instrument. To use a sports analogy, it would mean that God sent the Holy Spirit to the bench, telling Him he was out of the game ... for the rest of time. It would mean that God voluntarily made Himself less omnipotent, and it would mean He loves us less than the ancients. Neither is true.

As Ruthie and I were nearing marriage, my father counseled me that wherever we would attend church, it should be a New-Testament-believing

---

46   For an in-depth review of Cessation and Continuance (Cessation's opposite), see John Noe's excellent paper at http://www.prophecyrefi.org/wp-content/uploads/Cessation-Theology.pdf

body. By this, he meant it should be one that believed salvation comes by faith through grace, and not be one that believed in or exercised the gifts of the Spirit. I also recall the sensitivities of the time. A local sister church split when some members began to speak in tongues, and another over miraculous healing. It caused division in the Body of Christ, separated friendships, and even divided families. For a long time, I assumed and believed that the teaching I was raised under was correct, that these "gifts of the Spirit" were really tools of the Devil to divide and conquer the church. When I say "a long time," I mean the first sixty-two years of my life. Many tried and failed to convince me otherwise, including Ruthie. How, then, did I realize and accept the truth?

In the period leading up to my confession, we began attending a prophetic church. It was out of my comfort zone, but I realized that I saw nothing which contradicted the Word. The gifts were acknowledged and would occasionally manifest, but they were never the focal point or at odds with what I believed and understood. On rare occasions, I witnessed healings, and that was definitely out of my comfort zone. But I knew the people and their conditions. I knew their pain, and I knew their faith. When the healings lasted and I saw the changes in their lives, I had to acknowledge that they were real. Then I began to recall incidents from my own life, times when I knew God had spoken to me directly and through others. I began to process what I was learning and experiencing, and my belief system opened the door to, "It could be real." Shortly after and without a quest on my part, I received the gift of tongues. Now I was really in unchartered territory. I had to decide. Was what I was experiencing real and true, or was what I was raised to believe correct? I turned to the Word of God for evidence.

Now there are varieties of gifts, but the same Spirit; and there are varieties of service, but the same Lord; and there are varieties of activities, but it is the same God who empowers them all in everyone. To each is given the manifestation of the Spirit for the common good. For to one is given through the Spirit the utterance of wisdom, and to another the utterance of knowledge according to the same Spirit, to another faith by the same Spirit, to another gifts of healing by the one Spirit, to another the working of miracles, to another prophecy, to another the ability to distinguish between spirits, to another various kinds of tongues, to another the interpretation of tongues. All these are empowered by one and the same Spirit, who apportions to each one individually as he wills. 1 Corinthians 12:1-4 (ESV)[47]

I was convinced. Scripture clearly instructs us that the Spiritual gifts are for believers, all believers, to be manifested in service of God's cause and for His purposes. For Cessation doctrine to be correct, God would have to be different today than He was then, less powerful, and Jesus' exhortations would have to be for believers of a specific time and not for all believers for all time, none of which is supported by the Word of God.

With this new understanding came the realization that the Holy Spirit now had access to my heart, access that was previously denied by the lack of truth, understanding, and belief in my life. I realized that as the Spirit now had access to me, I also had access to Him. It is a two-way pathway, and I determined to travel it. My approach to understanding the Holy changed. I no longer simply wanted to know about God, but now wanted to know Him in a much more personal way. I shifted from being a casual observer of the doctrine I had been fed all my life, to pursuing God's heart with all my heart. I no longer desired knowledge for knowledge's sake; rather, I desired intimacy between my heart and God's heart. That was my new first order of business, but I also knew that new knowledge, revelation, and experiences would result as the fruit of an intimate relationship with the very being of God. Soon enough God would act, letting me know that the change in my heart was resonating in Heaven.

---

47   See also 1 Corinthians 12:27-31, 14:1; Ephesians 4:11-14; John 14:12; Hebrews 13:8

MERCY

I was reading and understanding the Word differently these days, and one evening I was reading in Proverbs when a verse I am sure I had read hundreds of times without understanding began to draw me in. As I meditated over it, I asked the Spirit to reveal what was hidden for me in this moment, searching for its truth, praying that God would speak to me in some way.

> *It is the glory of God to conceal things, but the glory of kings is to search things out.* Proverbs 25:2 (ESV)

As I continued meditating, I felt myself enter into the word "search." I was amazed at the experience. Nothing like this had ever happened to me. "Search for it. Search for it. Search for it" repeated over and over in my mind in a voice not my own. Search for it, yes, but for what? I was looking in the Spirit, straining to see without knowing what it was I was trying to see.

Suddenly, the darkness became darker, the mood quieter, and a reverence and stillness filled me. I stopped everything, just hovering there in the moment, now wanting simply to capture the experience, to make every instant of it mine. In the middle of the darkness, a dim light began to glow. Just a small, dim, yellowish light. Then I saw something else. It looked like an ancient scroll. Old parchment, aged and wrinkled in places. I had seen images of scrolls, of course, but never one like this. It had ancient writing on it in dark gray ink and in a language I could not read. As I looked at it, the image became clearer. I waited, hovering beside the scroll, searching for what God was trying to show me. Abruptly, the scroll was torn in half, and the right side of the scroll disappeared. Just as suddenly, a fresh half-scroll took the place of the missing half, and I watched as a line of stitching with blood-red thread appeared, sewing the two halves of the scroll together, one old, one new. A monogram symbol formed in bold type and appeared adjacent the red stitching, and this I did understand. It was an Old English style lowercase initial for my first name, with a cross bar added to the vertical staff of the K. As it appeared, a voice inside my head said, "A king's glory is to search out the meaning and more. Simply knowing and understanding are meaningless if not walked to maturity." I understood this, also. My life had been a shambles but God, in His mercy, was giving me a second chance. The monogram represents my kingly position in Christ, the line of stitching represents the divide between my old life and my future. The stitching is God's mercy purchased at the price of Jesus' red blood. I knew what this image was depicting—my old past joined with my new future, and I knew what I must do: search to discover my new destiny and walk it out. God's mercy was in action in my life, represented by a line of blood red stitching on ancient parchment. God's mercy was giving me a second opportunity, a new journey, and a new future.

The good news for me, and for you, is that I am not the first to be saved by God's mercy, and I am certainly not the last. His love for us is the motivation behind His compassion for our lost lives, His mercy the instrument of His heart which acts on our behalf. It is not that He does not see and know our sin; it is that He loves us despite it—so much so that He promises restoration when we turn back into Him.

The ancient prophet Hosea gives us a powerful picture of God's mercy in action. Israel has once again abandoned God, and He is angry, so angry that He gives Hosea the unusual command to marry Gomer, a prostitute, even though both God and Hosea know she will continue to be unfaithful. Hosea obeys, and the expected happens. God establishes the name of each child to show Israel how they have treated Him:

*Eternal One: I want you to name this boy **Jezreel** because I'm just about to punish Jehu's dynasty for all the blood Jehu shed at the city of Jezreel. I will bring an end to the monarchy in Israel. Here's how I'm going to do it: I'll destroy their army and break their bow when they fight the Assyrians in the valley of Jezreel.*

Gomer became pregnant again, and this time she had a girl.

*I want you to name her **Shown No Mercy**, because I'm not going to show any more mercy to the people of Israel. I won't forgive them anymore.*

After Gomer finished nursing Shown No Mercy, she became pregnant again and had another boy.

*Eternal One: I want you to name him **Not My People**, because these people aren't Mine anymore, and I am not their God.*
Hosea 1:4-6,8,9 (TVB, emphasis added in bold)

God named Hosea's children Jezreel, No Mercy, and Not My People. Yes, God was so angry that He renounced Israel as His children. Even so, He promised a new future.

But things won't always be this way. Someday there'll be so many people in Israel that they'll be like the grains of sand at the seashore - too many to count! It shall turn out that in the very place where it was said to them, "You are not My people," they will be called "Children of the living God." Hosea 1:10 (TVB)

Sometimes, as in my wilderness experience when I was seeking God and not finding Him, we can understand His anger, disappointment, and rejection. We have, after all, sinned and blasphemed Him. And yet, His promise is still there, waiting for us to respond as He courts us in the midst of our broken helplessness.

*But once she has nothing, I'll be able to get through to her. I'll
entice her and lead her out into the wilderness where we can be
alone, and I'll speak right to her heart and try to win her back.
And then I'll give her back her vineyards; I'll turn the valley of
Achor, that "Valley of Trouble," into a gateway of hope.
In the wilderness she'll learn to respond to Me the way she did
when she was young, when I brought her out of Egypt.*
Hosea 2:14,15 (TVB)

We believe the wilderness we find ourselves in is a place of hopelessness. God, however, uses it as a place to meet us, entice us back into His
arms, and re-establish His hope in our lives. There is good news in this!
If you are walking in the wilderness now as I did for so many years, take
cheer, for God is courting you. You may not recognize His presence in
this trial because you are focused on your sin, your pain, and your loss of
hope, but He is most assuredly there with you, waiting for you to turn
into His heart.

The rest of Hosea is filled with the story of Israel's journey through
the wasteland of their own wisdom, strategies, and actions. But when they
finally turn, listen to God's response.

Hosea's appeal to the people:

*Return, Israel, to the Eternal, your True God. You've stumbled
because of your wickedness. Think about what to say, and come
back to the Eternal One. Say to Him, "Forgive all our sins, and
take us back again. Bring us into Your good grace so we can offer
you praise and sacrifice, the fruit of our lips. ..."*
Hosea 14:1,2 (TVB)

And God's promise:

*I'll heal their apostate hearts so they won't turn away from Me
again; I'll love them freely because I won't be angry with them
anymore.* Hosea 14:4 (TVB)

The people will return from exile and sit in My shade once again; they'll flourish like grain; they'll send out shoots like the vine. And their fame will be like the wine of Lebanon. Hosea 14:7 (TVB)

The story of this book is real. It is a story of a life of promise that went far astray, resulting in great sin, guilt, shame, and loss. But it is also a story of great love, forgiveness, redemption, restoration, and renewal. I am fortunate to have found my way out of the darkness and that Ruthie elected to stay by my side. I know that, and it humbles my heart every day. I also know this: Our God is bigger than we imagine, His love deeper than we can know, and the freedom of His forgiveness life-changing in ways we can only dream about. He is real. His love is real. It is the most powerful force in creation, and He is waiting to bestow it upon you.

His mercy saved me; let it save you. It does not matter what you have done or where you are coming from. Come home. Lay down your fears and come home. Take the step that changes everything. Whatever it is, confess it and repent. Present your broken and contrite heart to God and watch what He does. His strength is greater than your weakness, His mercy bigger than your sin. He loves you. He believes in you. He's rooting for you. And He's waiting for you.

It's time to come home.

CHAPTER FIFTEEN

COMING HOME

Coming home. That has a nice ring to it, doesn't it? It does indeed, and it is a sweet experience for those who make it. There will be bittersweet moments as we make the journey, moments we would rather not encounter, such as the first time we face a friend or family member and tell them our truth. The overcomer must, at times, be in the role of the prodigal son. Not everyone will be accepted back with such love and generosity of heart as the original, but that will be the choice of others. The overcomer's choice is to humble himself or herself and make the walk back in humility.

These moments are necessary. Each is a waypoint as we navigate our way back into relationships and a new life. Along the way, we will learn more about ourselves and the God of mercy who rescues us, discover hidden depth in others, and overcome obstacles that seek to deter us.

LEARNING ABOUT MY FATHERS

Like you, I have two fathers: my Heavenly Father and my earthly father. One was real to me. I saw him every day, talked with him, played pool with him, looked up to him, and obeyed him. He was a good father. He worked hard to provide for our family. He was a deacon and teacher in the church, a loyal and generous friend to many in need. He was dependable and had a good heart. He was a child of the Great Depression, and it left an indelible mark on him, one I could see in his actions and read on his face virtually every day. There was a negative mindset; assumptions always ran toward negative options. Yet, he had a deep humility and great faith. Honesty and integrity were hallmarks of his life and what he expected of everyone around him. He did not know how to express love. I know he loved me, but there were few tender moments in our relationship. He would say that if he didn't love us, he wouldn't work so hard to provide for us. He grew up working hard as a child, fought in WWII, and had worked hard ever since. You could say that all he knew was work, family, and church life. For him, life was about effort, doing the right thing, and never crossing the line. He had a strong will and fought with determination for what he believed to be right, even when it set him against friends.

My Heavenly Father was also real to me, but in an abstract way. I know that sounds like a contradiction, but it is the best I can do to describe it. I believed He was real but had never seen Him or knew anyone who had. Then, one day, I heard Him speak to me. I knew it was Jesus speaking and I responded. I accepted Christ as my Savior that afternoon when I was six years old. I know that may sound too young to some, but I remember that afternoon as clearly as this morning. It was real. I heard His voice and answered His call. I knew exactly what I was doing and why. Over time, however, the intimacy of that moment faded. Church became routine. I checked all the boxes and did all the right things. I participated in all the programs and believed that I was a solid Christian. But the realness of that moment lost its hold on my heart. As it faded, the world with all its attractions and expectations took preeminence,[48] I went to church to learn about God, not to know Him, and I did not expect to encounter Him during my day-to-day life.

---

48   Isaiah 64:6

My two fathers are the same in some ways and yet are drastically different. One day a couple of years ago, with the benefit of hindsight, I began to ponder my relationships with them. When I compared them (How unfair was that to my earthly father?), I could see clear similarities and differences in their persons and my relationship with them. It looked like this:

Earthly Father	Heavenly Father
Honest and forthright	Honest and forthright
A man of integrity	A God of integrity
Compassionate and giving	Compassionate and giving
Quick to take and hold offenses	Quick to forgive and forget
A closed heart once offended	Always willing to open His heart
Stern	Fair
Unapproachable	Inviting
A distant relationship	Desires intimacy
Striving, hard work and effort	Does everything from a position of rest and peace
Judgmental	Just
Quick to temper	Long-suffering
Disappointed in me	Loved me despite who I became

If my father had known of my sin, I am sure he would have eventually called me his son again, but it would have been tough, and there certainly would have been no fatted calf and feast. That response could only come from a father who finds pride and joy not in a perfectly-lived life, but in the son who has failed but is now overcoming, returning home in humility, searching for forgiveness and love. What a joy, then, that we have such a Heavenly Father.

JUBILEE AND THE PRODIGAL SON

In Leviticus 25, God instructs Moses on the form and purpose of Jubilee. This is the initiation of God's law of forgiveness and rest in all areas of man's life.

"You shall count seven weeks of years, seven times seven years, so that the time of the seven weeks of years shall give you forty-nine years. Then you shall sound the loud trumpet on the tenth day of the seventh month. On the Day of Atonement you shall sound the trumpet throughout all your land. And you shall consecrate the fiftieth year, and proclaim liberty throughout the land to all its inhabitants. It shall be a jubilee for you, when each of you shall return to his property and each of you shall return to his clan. ..."
Leviticus 25:8-10 (ESV)

As you read the rest of the chapter, you will understand the full breadth and depth of Jubilee. It touches every important part of life, including how the land is to be given rest, debts are to be structured, slaves are to be treated, and how forgiveness is to be a central theme of life to sustain families and society. It is a system that emphasizes humility, integrity, fairness, and compassion. It is a system that emphasizes the value of each person regardless their state in life, and one that seeks always to restore freedom. No story illustrates the fulfillment and perfection of this better than the parable of the prodigal son, found in Luke fifteen.

You probably know the parable well. Even some non-believers have likely heard it so often they can teach it at some level. This parable, however, is about living it, not simply knowing it. The overcomer must walk the parable out in their life, turning it from a concept taught in ancient Scripture into the reality of their life today. While there is much to this process of walking it out every day, there are a few key things to keep in mind.

The younger of two sons in the parable is a rebellious lad and asks his father for his portion of the inheritance so that he can go and do as he pleases with life. I am sure he had grand plans. I recall that in my youth my best friend and I had visions of re-creating the Route 66 television series, in our own way, of course. Two young guys on the road, a classic car, and no real responsibility except to have fun and enjoy the trip. I imagine the young man of Jesus' parable had a similar mindset. Life, however, had different plans. Let's pick it up at verse seventeen of Luke fifteen.

We Must Come to Ourselves

*"But when **he came to himself**, he said, 'How many of my father's hired servants have more than enough bread, but I perish here with hunger! ...'"* Luke 15:17 (ESV, emphasis added in bold)

Yes, life has a way. We must all come to ourselves, meaning that we must awaken to the reality of our life. A few like me will have a lot of waking up to do. In one sense, that makes it easier. For us, it is easier to realize that something is amiss precisely because it is so amiss. Obviously, that is good and bad. We come to the realization but have a long way to go. The road will be longer and rougher. Knowing that may make it hard to start the journey because of guilt, shame, fear, or a depth of hopelessness. Others may have a more difficult time realizing their state simply because it doesn't seem to be that bad. It is easy to look around and tell ourselves that our sins do not seem so bad in comparison. Life looks good and feels good. Maybe it isn't, and maybe it is. It is all a matter of perspective, and your position changes the view. We all have sin in our life. We are called to "come to ourselves" in a manner that breaks our heart when we realize what we sacrifice to attain the counterfeit pleasure of a sinful existence. Coming to ourselves is that moment of encounter with the truth of our life, and our broken heart is the sweet fruit of the encounter. You might ask how a broken heart can be sweet fruit. Good question. Here's the answer: when it causes us to face the reality of our life and surrender it with a contrite heart before God.

If you are struggling with questions about this in your life, I ask you to do one thing: Think about where you are positioned. Your position changes the way you see yourself and the life you are living. Are you positioned in the world and looking through the eyes of the world? Try moving. Position yourself in Christ, hanging on the cross and being crucified in Him, and look at yourself and your life through His eyes as He hangs there, paying the price for your freedom. The price has already been paid, but you must collect on it. He loved you enough to lay down His life for you. Do you love Him enough to honor His sacrifice with your acceptance? Let your heart become broken. Surrender to His love, and begin the journey home.

WE MUST ACT

> *I will arise and go* to my father, and I will say to him, "Father, I have sinned against heaven and before you. I am no longer worthy to be called your son. Treat me as one of your hired servants. And he arose and came to his father." Luke 15:18-20a (ESV, emphasis added in bold)

We must act despite our fear, shame, and guilt. Nothing can happen until we overcome inertia and take the first steps. The Parable of the Prodigal Son lays out a pathway that we can follow in our own circumstance. First, he got up, meaning that his first action was to recognize his condition and decide to do something about it that only he could do. He stood up. That alone is a significant thing. It is a signal and encouragement to yourself that you have sunk as low as you are going to sink. When you stand you engage action with emotion and as simple as it may sound, it is powerful. Stand with determination and conviction and take the first step forward. Notice the prodigal son's humility as he returns to his father. He does not ask to be returned to his old station in the family line. No. Instead, he asks to be treated as one of the servants, without qualification of what he is willing or unwilling to do. In doing this, he signals to others that he realizes he was wrong and is taking responsibility for his actions, asking for acceptance not as who he used to be but as he is now.

We Must Give Others the Freedom to Make Their Choice in Response

"But while he was still a long way off, his father saw him and felt compassion, and ran and embraced him and kissed him. And the son said to him, 'Father, I have sinned against heaven and before you. I am no longer worthy to be called your son.' But the father said to his servants, 'Bring quickly the best robe, and put it on him, and put a ring on his hand, and shoes on his feet. And bring the fattened calf and kill it, and let us eat and celebrate. For this my son was dead, and is alive again; he was lost, and is found.' And they began to celebrate. ..." Luke 15:20b-24 (ESV)

There is much to encourage us in this parable that Jesus teaches. We can understand that the wayward son's father was looking forward to his return even though he had abandoned the family. Despite the pain he caused, his father was still searching and hoping for his return. His welcome was not at all what he was expecting. The father's reaction was not based in the depth of his son's sin; rather, it was a measure of the father's love and compassion. The father's joy at his lost son's return came from his heart, overpowering all the other feelings and emotions that would surely be present in such a situation and relationship. Not only does he accept him back as a son, but he is not subtle about it, either. There is a celebration to be had here, despite the pain of what had gone before.

And then there is the older brother. His reaction is not so accepting. Instead, he reacts in anger and rejects his returning brother (vv. 25-30). We may judge him harshly for his reaction, but I dare say it would be the reaction of most people in such a situation. And that is an important part for the overcomer to think about as they journey back.

We cannot control how others will react, and we are not responsible for the choices they make. Each person must make their own decisions and take their own actions. It is unrealistic to expect everyone to react as the father in the parable did. There will be "older brothers" who harbor disappointment, hurt, abandonment, and anger over our sin. As God's grace allows us to overcome, we must allow His grace working through us to give others time, space, and reasons to lay aside their bitterness.

I am incredibly fortunate that Ruthie loved God so much that she could listen to Him and not the world. She was not just hurt by my betrayal; she was shattered to the core. Yet, she forgave me and committed herself to walking at my side as we started the healing process. It wasn't easy and, truthfully, sometimes it still isn't easy. It isn't as if there was a turning point where the past dropped out of memory. There are consequences to our sin even when we are forgiven. Walking out those consequences is part of the journey home. Not everyone will be willing to walk the road with you, but the fact is that their decision is theirs alone, and the accountability for it rests in them. The overcomer can only do what is their responsibility. Our choices must be based in what God our Father is asking of us. Only our obedience to this call can redeem us and set in motion the opportunity for others to make their decisions. Without our obedience, we rob them of their own opportunity to honor God's heart. There are no guarantees when one walks this path, but there is always Hope. Our faith must be in the Hope of Christ and His mercy towards us and those around us.

A Kiss, A Robe, A Ring, Shoes, and a Fatted Calf

It is too easy to read Bible stories and parables as nothing more than anecdotes or analogies and miss the deeper meanings. The Parable of the Prodigal Son is a perfect example of what is hidden in front of our eyes, which we should be alert to and recognize when it presents itself. As we read, we should always be asking: What is that about? Why is that there? What is hidden in this that makes it important? What is God really saying? For the overcomer, understanding the symbolic meaning of this story not only adds richness to the story but hope and faith to our own future.

Let's start with the father in the parable running toward the returning son, embracing and kissing[49] him. He didn't wait for him to arrive and grovel, he ran to meet him, cutting the distance and time between them. That can only be love, compassion, and rejoicing in action. His joy at his son's return is so great that the pain of his leaving is set aside, and he demonstrates this by kissing him. In Hebrew, the word used here for kiss means to attach oneself and arm the recipient with weapons. In other words, the father is signaling to everyone that the son is returned to his full stature and place and is under the father's protection. We can put ourselves in the returning son's place. We may not be certain how those around us will react, but we can be fully confident that our Father in Heaven will drop all and run towards us when He sees us returning. We can anticipate His embrace and kiss as His sign of redemption and restoration, not just to us but also to all who witness His effect on us.

He put the best[50] robe on him. The son was returning as a complete mess. Everything he had taken was lost, and he had nothing to offer his father as a gesture of love and respect. His father, however, offered gifts to him! The robe was a symbol of position. This was not just anyone—this was the father's son! And it wasn't just any robe. It was the best robe, richly made, finely detailed, colorful—the kind of robe not a commoner but a person of position wore. It said to everyone within eyesight that he was first in succession, rank, influence, and honor. Why did the father give him the best robe? To restore him to his former position, to change the way others saw him and responded to him, and to change the way he saw and thought of himself. To tell him, "You think of yourself as worthless and useless; I see you as you were meant to be."

He put a ring[51] on his finger. A ring is a symbol of authority. It carries honor, purpose, and power, signifying the authority of the wearer to act on behalf of and in the name of the one who issued the ring. The ring was used to seal legal documents and treaties. It gave instant credibility to the

---

49   Strong's G2705: To kiss earnestly.
AHBL H5401: A mode of attachment, to arm with weapons.
50   Strong's G4413: Foremost in time, place, order, or importance.
51   Strong's G1146: Finger ring.
AHLB H2885: A seal, signet ring.

wearer as an ambassador of higher authority. Your Heavenly Father has rings waiting to fit your fingers.

He put shoes[52] on his feet. One of the father's first actions is to put new shoes on his son's shoeless feet. Shoes and feet represent our walk, our future, our destiny. We see the failures of our past and the troubles of our present. Our Father sees our future and begins to prepare us for our new destiny.

He killed[53] the fatted calf. Remember, the sacrificial animal of old—be it lamb, calf, or bull—had to be perfect and without blemish. The sacrifice was a trade of perfection for imperfection. Jesus Christ offered Himself as that sacrifice for you and I, the Perfect One taking our place on the cross, offering Himself in trade as atonement for our sin.

Here we have a beautiful image of the forgiven son with his full inheritance restored. A new robe (position), a new ring (authority), new shoes (destiny), and the sacrifice of another (freedom). The overcomer in Christ knows this joy, to be redeemed, restored with a new inheritance and destiny. Yes, that is what your Creator is offering you. Turn and you will see Him facing you, waiting. Face Him, step into Him, and become lost in His embrace.

MATURING OUR DELIVERANCE

I recall well the afternoon of my deliverance session with Pastor Mike a few weeks after my confession. Ruthie and I had been working through things. We were near the end of The Inquisitions, and our friends Will, Syl, Toni, and Georgia were counseling and supporting us. The time had come to meet with our pastor and ask him to intervene with God on behalf of my freedom, our freedom. I did not know what to expect, but it was not the dramatic experience I thought it might be. I remember what was said, but mostly I remember the freedom I felt. I left that session

---

52 Strong's G5266: Slippers.
AHLB H5274: To fasten up, secure.
53 Strong's G2380: To sacrifice by fire.
AHLB H6999: Turn into fragrance by fire as an act of worship and sacrifice.

knowing something had changed and wondering what would come next. I did not feel exhilaration, but a sense of calm confidence. Most importantly, however, I knew that it was just a beginning.

Deliverance is great. For some it can be euphoric, even. When the initial experience drifts away, however, the overcomer will be left to realize there is work to be done. A lot of work. We've been given a gift, a new life, but we must give ourselves over to it completely and take up the task of making it real every day. The gifts God gives to us require work to sustain and mature them. It is our responsibility to take an active role in the maturing of our faith, character, spirit, and gifts. How do we do that? Thankfully, God has already thought of it and, through Paul, offers us a guide:

> I'm writing to encourage you to **fan into a flame** and rekindle the fire of the spiritual gift God imparted to you when I laid my hands upon you. For God will never give you the spirit of fear, but the Holy Spirit who gives you **mighty power, love, and self-control.** 2 Timothy 1:6,7 (TPT, emphasis added in bold)

We are encouraged to "fan into a flame" the fire that has been placed in us. The Greek word used here is anazopureo,[54] which renders three main components: It refers to a living thing, fire, and repetition. Left alone, the fire of our deliverance will die out. By blowing on its hot coals with our desire, intent, devotion, and effort, we exercise faithfulness to God's intention for our life. Desire is the key. When we desire something enough, we pursue it relentlessly. Pursue the full measure of your deliverance by fanning its flames with your breath. Breathe new life into your life through your desires, intents, thoughts, words, and actions. Feed it with your heart, with your words, with your faith, and with your actions. Let the breath of God that lives in you speak into your circumstances and heart. Listen to what He says and believe Him, not the deceiver.

---

54 Strong's G329

Keep the standard of sound words you have heard from me, in the faithfulness and love that are in Messiah Yeshua. **Guard the good that has been entrusted to you,** *through the Ruach ha-Kodesh who dwells in us.* 2 Timothy 1:13,14 (TLV, emphasis added in bold)

In these two verses, Paul challenges us to take responsibility for what God has freely given us. We are to "keep the standard of sound words" as a way of keeping them alive in us, nourishing and preserving them in our hearts and spirits to quicken them. Part of that includes guarding the gift. Anyone who has ever pulled guard duty will tell you it is not a passive activity. To guard properly, you must be constantly searching for the enemy and be alert to his plans and desires, and you must be armed with the knowledge of God's desires and the power of His Word, ready to engage at the first sign, trusting the very breath of God that is in us to empower us in His service.

When Is a Hard-Fought Victory a Loss?

One night I had a dream, something I never used to have, really. This dream was long and intricate, too long to recount here except in summary. In this dream, Ruthie and I were living in an East Coast city, possibly Philadelphia. We encountered a group of people who were excited about a new line of products and urging us to become part of their group. When we examined what they were selling closely, however, we recognized that it was not at all as they said. They claimed it was made of pure marble and alabaster, but we saw that it was made of a cheap grade of fiberglass. It was a complete fake. Later, we were walking down a city street when we came upon a group of people gathered by the roadside. It was the same group, except the leaders were missing. Everyone was sad. Then, a train moved slowly down the middle of the street. It had open cages with bars and trolled slowly past the crowd. Inside the cages were the leaders of the group who deceived people. They were imprisoned and being put on display. They were beaten, broken, weak, and defeated. Their friends and family still loved them and were there to see them, but the prisoners were completely beaten and lost. In their midst was an innocent man who was taken in by their lies. He was innocent but had been judged guilty by association and was imprisoned with them. His heart was breaking in despair. Then these words came to me in a booming voice:

When is a hard-fought victory a loss?

When is a hard-fought loss a victory?

At first, I thought this dream was about my life. I could see myself in this scenario. But the Spirit corrected me, and I came to understand that it was about those who have been deceived, who have fallen for the false goods and those who sell them. As I continued to process the dream, I realized it was about Truth compared to its counterfeit. Truth is exactly as it says it is: strong and enduring. Counterfeit truth is weak and eventually ineffective. It has no staying power. One is light, the other darkness. One is full of power, the other weak. The lie of the counterfeit will be revealed for all to see, and those who perpetrate it on humanity will be dealt with harshly and eternally. I understood this was not just about mankind in general but about the church, as well. Truth is real and it matters. I believe the biggest issue we face today is Truth Decay,[55] in the world and in the church.

When I set out to resolve the riddle, I came to the following:

When is a hard-fought victory a loss?

- When it passes. It is exhilarating but fleeting. There is always another battle to be fought.
- When your energy is spent, robbing you of what it takes to win the next battle.
- When it comes at too high a cost—a Pyrrhic victory.

---

55   The term was coined by Michael Rich, CEO of The RAND Corporation, headquartered in Santa Monica, CA, as a way of discussing the erosion of truth in society in general and politics in particular.

- When its spoils divert you from continuing the fight and its greater rewards.
- **When you've fought for the wrong thing.**

When is a hard-fought loss a victory?

- When you remain true to the cause despite losing. (Integrity)
- When you continue to fight hard in the face of defeat. (Fortitude)
- When you learn about yourself and what you are capable of. (Confidence)
- When you learn about the enemy and their vulnerabilities. (Intelligence)
- When you are sure of the cause and proud of the effort. (Passion)
- When your courage surprises you. (Discovery)
- When you give all you have to give. (Sacrifice)
- When you care more for Truth or principle than you do for safety, victory, or gain. (Commitment)
- **When you've fought for the right thing.**

What have you been fighting for? Why are you in the fight? I will tell you that my life exemplified the false victory that was really a loss, until I surrendered. Then I stepped into a new arena, a new fight—the fight for my life. I began to fight for the right thing. It's not easy, but it is virtuous and sweet! I do not know who you are or what you are facing, but I tell you this truth without qualification: God is bigger than the trial you face, and His mercy stronger than your enemy. Surrender to Him and begin to fight for the right thing.

THE OVERCOMER'S WAY HOME

> *"But if they **own up to their sins** and **acknowledge the sins of their ancestors**, if they **admit that they have been unfaithful to Me**, defied Me, and rebelled against Me - which*

*prompted Me to turn against them and scatter them among their enemies - if they **humble their uncircumcised hearts** and **offer reparations for their sins**, then I will remember My covenant with Jacob, Isaac, and Abraham, and I will also remember the land."* Leviticus 26:40-43 (TVB, emphasis added in bold)

In this short passage, the overcomer finds a checklist for returning home. Coming to grips with the truth of their sin, recognizing generational patterns and responsibilities, confessing with humility, and working to restore trust are the big boxes that each of us must check off. There are no shortcuts. The second hardest part of this journey is facing those we must face. The hardest part will be seeing some of them reject us. Again, that is their choice, not ours. We will still love them and desire them in our lives. More importantly, however, we must honor their position in our life and their right to make their own decision, asking God to restore the relationship when they turn away. With prayer, love, transparency, and a righteous life, we give them every reason to return. It all comes down to our confession, repentance, humility, righteousness, and forgiveness. That is the path we must walk.

Revelation - Our Roadmap to the Future

Our walk also requires faith. As I have mentioned before, my upbringing in the church did not emphasize or even teach the prophetic, and it largely denied the power of the Holy Spirit to act in our day-to-day lives. It should come as no surprise, then, that these were notions that I had to grow into, and that growth took time. Attending prophetic churches was a stretch for me in the beginning, but what I saw and experienced there made growing and trusting first possible and then rational. My experiences and observations proved the truth of what I was witnessing. This in turn made listening to and accepting revelation and words from others easier to accept. The more I accepted them, the more they proved true. The more they proved true, the more I began to trust them. This may seem natural to most, but to me it was a big change. To my surprise, I received several prophetic words about my healing, our marriage, and what the future would bring. I did not get these all at once; they came in small bites over time. As I listened and believed, God was faithful. Each was a confirmation of what had gone before, and I could see just a little bit further, the next step. Each next step was a test of faith. Would I believe? Would I honor the word with obedience? Would I agree to be vulnerable, to put myself and my life out there?

These are questions every overcomer must wrestle with. The answer may be obvious reading them on this page, but when it is your turn to step out in obedient faith, it may be another matter. My counsel is this: Trust God. Believe God. Follow God. If you receive a revelation from Him, believe it. If you receive a word from a trusted source whom you know is connected to God, test it to prove it. Then, live according to it. Take it into your heart and adopt it as truth, as a foreknown fact. When the facts don't add up, trust God. Always trust God. It is not a passive trust He is looking for but an active one. Simply waiting for Him to do something is no trust at all. It is a loyalty test of God. Active trust believes and acts, even when it does not seem rational in man's knowledge and wisdom. This may sound crazy to you, but I testify that there are times when the facts just don't count. God counts.

These revelations, words, and prophesies present themselves to us in their own proper place and time. They may not seem to be connected or relevant to each other, yet each points to our next waypoint on the journey. Sometimes, we will look back from a far distance down the path and recognize how God guided each step of our walk. It is better, however, to be alert for and cognizant of how each of these moments fits into an evolving pattern as we experience the journey. This is not to try to predict what is in God's heart for us, but rather for the purpose of being careful to maximize each experience, to get the full measure of God's intent without unknowingly letting it slip by. The key to this process for me has been learning to trust and engage the Holy Spirit, who is our counselor and confidant. I have unlimited confidence in the Holy Spirit's ability to discern truth and His capacity to engage with me in this manner. It is a relatively new thing to me, and it is wonderful.

Our future lies before us, waiting to be reclaimed. That is the work of the overcomer, reclaiming what was supposed to be and what was once lost but is now so close. It requires desire, intent, purpose, commitment, and dedication. It doesn't happen in the blink of an eye, and I have yet to see a flash of lightning followed by instant perfection. What I do see, however, is the path forward into a future I could not have imagined. So great is God's grace, even for me, even for you. But we have work to do, the day-to-day, I'm-going-to-change-the-world kind of work, beginning with you and me.

CHAPTER SIXTEEN

REBUILDING OUR CITY

The last few years have been quite a journey, and I know that it has only just begun. Along the way, there has been an almost never-ending string of changes, both external and internal. Life is much different now. I am at peace with who I am and where I am. Our marriage, always a work in progress, is healthy, loving, and still growing. If I were asked whom I most admire, love, and desire to please, there would be two persons: Jesus my Lord, and Ruthie my wife. I am not sure it is possible to explain how different a place this is opposed to where I was. I will simply say it is beautiful and wondrous.

There is still work to do, of course. There will always be work to do. Life is not a static thing. It evolves with literally every breath and thought, and we must be constantly aware of its course. More specifically, we must be constantly aware of the source and motivation of our desires and the purposes of our decisions. These are the things that chart our journey through life. Being intentional about them matters. That is what this chapter is about, partnering with God in our restoration.

Filling the Void

As Ruthie and I continue to grow into each other, we are learning to replace old habits that were destructive with new ones. Given where I've come from, this is especially true in my case. There is a potential dark side to deliverance. It creates a void which in turn presents opportunity to evil. Something will fill the void, and if we aren't careful and diligent, that something will be our old demons made big, new enticements, or a combination of both.

> *"When the unclean spirit has gone out of a person, it passes through waterless places seeking rest, but finds none. Then it says, 'I will return to my house from which I came.' And when it comes, it finds the house empty, swept, and put in order. Then it goes and brings with it seven other spirits more evil than itself, and they enter and dwell there, and the last state of that person is worse than the first. So also will it be with this evil generation."*
> Matthew 12:43-45 (ESV)

Obviously, we prefer to fill the void with healthy, life-producing things. In my case, I made seeking greater intimacy with Father God and Ruthie my mission in life, so to speak. By that, I mean that I made these a life priority. I began to focus on my spiritual connections with God, Jesus, and the Holy Spirit, and I began to do small things that deepened my heart connection with Ruthie.

Why did I do these things? The obvious answer is that they are good things to do. Also, I knew and understood the truth of what Jesus said on the issue. Further, I understood that whatever I chose to fill the void the absence of the demons created in me, it had to be a positive thing, not just a busy thing. I wanted to do things that would change my life as well as fill it.

So, I determined to pursue God, not just because it was a good thing to do but because my heart ached for Him. I didn't want to just know about Him. I wanted to know Him as a Father, as a friend. I didn't want to just pray my desires and needs to Him as if working my way through a checklist; I wanted to have personal conversations with Him as I would my best friend, to know His desires, to hear His joy and pain, and to learn how I can bless Him with what I do. This pursuit has and is taking my spiritual life in new directions, some of which I have already discussed. I am learning to see and hear in the Spirit, which is something I never would have imagined possible. Along with that, I am learning to trust what I see and hear, to plumb the depths of what God presents to me to gain deeper understanding of what He desires of me. And, strange to say it still seems, I am beginning to understand that there is a prophetic side to me that I never realized existed.

When we turn into God, He will surprise us in ways we do not expect. He will challenge us to become more than we thought possible. Confession? Repentance? Deliverance? Forgiveness? Yes, they are all awesome, but they are only the beginning. When you seek God's heart you will find it, and it will take your breath away.

And then there is my relationship with Ruthie. Oh, how I love her. Sometimes I remember her as she was when we were dating, and I recall how captivating and beautiful she was. Then I look at her today and fall in love with who she has become, more beautiful than ever, strong in her faith and will, and wise beyond understanding.

I've learned that the occasional small thing goes a long way, something that hasn't always been obvious to my self-centered self. A couple of examples:

Ruthie is famous in our family for her month-long birthdays. She just declared it one day decades ago and it has been so since. Her birthday is on the third of the month. We start celebrating on the first and it lasts all month. We are not in the habit of giving lavish birthday gifts, but small things work just as well. Taking this one step further, I decided a few years ago that we could celebrate her birthday on the third of every month. Again, nothing big, just small things that say, "I love you." It might be pink roses, a movie she likes, or a spontaneous drive, and sometimes we have fun with it. I once hid three Hershey Kiss candies in several places throughout the house without telling her. She discovered them as she went about her day, and she loved it. She opened a cupboard and there were three Kisses waiting for her, then she found three Kisses in a drawer of her desk, and later three Kisses waiting for her in the shower. This isn't an every-month thing, but it is a way to let her know how I feel about her. And to be honest, the joy it brings to my own heart is part of the deal. I love pleasing her.

Another change I've made is to engage with healthy activities to fill the few empty hours I have. I make a point of getting out to walk and hike local trails. I love getting out in the country for landscape photography, and I've started taking on tasks that I used to pay someone else to do, like clearing our property of brush. You get the point. Idle time is dangerous time. Make sure you fill it with things that encourage, uplift, and develop you, not things that enslave you.

All of these are important. Focusing on our relationship with God, the ones we love, and the things that keep us spiritually, physically, mentally, and emotionally healthy—these are ways that we put off our old habits and life and put on the new us.

> ... to put off your old self, which belongs to your former manner of life and is corrupt through deceitful desires, and to be renewed in the spirit of your minds, and to put on the new self, created after the likeness of God in true righteousness and holiness.
> Ephesians 4:22-24 (ESV)

This is not to say that we have arrived. Life is a journey that never ends, ever. We can feel good about our progress in working alongside God to change who we are but can never forget that we have further to go. This, I believe, is one of the greatest gifts God gives us. No matter who we are or where we've come from, no matter how humbling our failures or great our successes, God always has more for us. He has in His heart a plan for you and me that even the highest of us cannot fathom, and that is the great joy of life in His embrace. It just keeps getting better.

> *Not that I have already obtained this or am already perfect, but I press on to make it my own, because Christ Jesus has made me his own. Brothers, I do not consider that I have made it my own. But one thing I do: forgetting what lies behind and straining forward to what lies ahead, I press on toward the goal for the prize of the upward call of God in Christ Jesus.* Philippians 3:7-14 (ESV)

FELLOWSHIP WITH BELIEVERS

Part of filling the void in your life is being in relationship with believers of like mind. It is an important part of the Christian life and your future. I have been in church most of my life, including my sin life, and I was a part of many groups and even led some. However, the men's groups I was in rarely got to the meat of the matter. Mostly, they were social groups where men were afraid to get real. We would drink coffee, have breakfast, talk the good talk, and do everything we could to get out without being transparent, vulnerable, and honest. Yes, I had a lot of friendly sessions of this sort—men talking without saying anything. Going to church or a group meeting is not the definition of fellowship. It's not the where that matters, it's the what. Fellowship is about relationship.

The Word tells us fellowship among believers is important not for its social component alone, but because we share a responsibility for and to each other:

> *And let us consider how to **stir up one another to love and good works**, not neglecting to meet together, as is the habit of some, but **encouraging one another**, and all the more as you see the Day drawing near.* Hebrews 10:24,25 (ESV, emphasis added in bold)

After deliverance, I wanted to be in relationship with other men as part of my walk into maturity. I realized, however, that groups like those I had been a part of in the past would not meet the test. They were places to hide in plain sight. I had done that, and I didn't want to do it again. I wanted reality, genuineness, and the pursuit of God's heart. I knew I had to find a different kind of group. It did not happen quickly, but eventually I joined a group of men who soon became like brothers. After two years, I was asked to co-lead a new group. That took some prayer! Me? Lead a group of mature believers? Really? Yes, really. I am amazed at the depth of God's love among these men. Each group (I am still in the first) meets twice a month using video-conferencing technology. I've only met three of the men in person yet love all of them like brothers. These are not your typical men's groups. These guys are real, bold, and completely transparent. These groups do not sit around and try to impress or fool each other. We engage with the Spirit of God, seek Him, and boldly go where He leads. The agenda is His, never ours, and it is thrilling. Recently, I was corresponding with one of the men following a session. Here is what I wrote to him:

> I am sure that every man carries the burdens of life's troubles and mistakes, some more than others. Sometimes, these can become part of our personal identity, the way we see ourselves. But it is not the way God sees us. He sees us standing righteous and true before Him, not because of how we live our lives or our experiences but because we are in His presence (Isaiah 6). That is what I am most thankful for, His presence.

> I loved last night; it is still resonating in me. The fellowship was awesome. Really enjoyed hearing from some of the quieter ones and humbled by the whole notion of what God has called us to. That is an intimidating thought, yet it is our purpose as believers whose calling is to not just believe

but be active agents. 'Who, me?' 'Yes, you' He says. Imagine that. So here I sit, a retired career guy who failed God and my family so often and so profoundly throughout most of my life, getting used to the notion of what God has called us to, me included. It is not an honorific or prestige thing. It is a calling, a responsibility, and an accountability ... and a humbling one at that. I am so happy ... joyous ... at being in this company of men who love YHVH so. In the breakout session during the last facilitator forum, I said that I am in awe of the men in the two groups and consider each more mature than myself. Dale chuckled when I said it, but I was serious. Each one seems a giant of faith and wisdom to me. I see in them the fruit of much of what I missed. They inspire me and I am better for their friendship. Yes, I am thankful for a merciful God who would connect me to men such as these, and thankful for the opportunity to travel with them in His company. Our God is an awesome God.

Someday you will read about my journey and be amazed that one like me can be allowed in the room (or Zoom as it happens) with the rest of you. I've got stuff in my life. It took me a long time after deliverance, which wasn't that long ago, to let go of it. I felt unworthy, guilty, and ashamed. If I stop to reflect on the past I can easily fall back into that darkness. I choose instead to rest in His presence and trust Him, to believe in what He says about me and not what the enemy says. I choose to see myself as a son of the Almighty God who rules supreme, a beneficiary and carrier of the inheritance of the King of Kings, as a forgiven and beloved son.

I am also a member of a study group that meets weekly and have two longtime friends with whom I meet on a regular schedule. Each of these groups and relationships is important to me. God uses them to nurture my life. Fellowship is important for believers, yet too often we trivialize it through routine.

Get serious and get real about relationship and fellowship with other believers, intentionally seeking them and asking the Holy Spirit to guide your search and make the right connections. Remember, you are not looking for a social group. You are looking for the connections that God Himself has chosen for you to guide you, mature you, and nourish you.

Rebuilding Trust

One thing the overcomer must understand is that forgiveness, as good and important as it is, is not trust. The two are distinctly different. Just because someone forgives you for what you've done doesn't mean that they trust you not to do it again. The overcomer needs to understand not only that this is true but also why it is true and have a plan for rebuilding trust. This is true whether the violation has been on a deep personal level, a business level, or in any sort of situation where you've failed to honor a relationship.

By having a plan, I do not mean a checklist or empty promises. I mean a commitment to the one offended, yourself, and most importantly to God to do whatever it takes.

As I sat in our den that morning, I was wondering if I would escape unscathed. Our friends would soon be departing, and time was running out. If I was going to be unmasked, it would have to happen soon. Almost before the thought finished in my head, the question was asked. I wasn't running toward the moment, but I wasn't running away from it, either. Part of that moment was an instant commitment inside my spirit. I thought, "This is it. I will be honest and truthful, and there is nothing I will not do to save our marriage. Nothing."

To turn the phrase around, what I was really saying to myself and later to Ruthie was, "I will do whatever you ask of me. It doesn't matter what it is or if I agree or not. If it's important to you and our healing, then it is done."

That is where I began, with that commitment. I knew it would be hard and that I would not always agree, but it was a small price to pay for our freedom.

Forgiveness is given. Trust is earned. It doesn't happen instantly. Trust is built over time through transparency, genuineness, and consistency of action. All relationships require being vulnerable, and this is never truer than when a relationship has been broken and is being healed. The forgiveness offered by the offended is a down payment on the future of the relationship. The experience after forgiveness will determine your future and possibly the future of the relationship. Break your commitments and it won't go well.

The way I came to view it is like this: The forgiveness that Ruthie extended to me was the seed, while her trust would be the fruit of that seed and changes in my life and character. There would be no fruit if any of the components were missing. Everything rode on each one of them.

So, I did what I was asked to do. Almost all of it I agreed with, but not everything. It didn't matter. I walked away from an important professional position because Ruthie thought I had made an idol of it. I asked forgiveness of friends who had no idea what had been going on, revealing the sordid past to some I worked with, admired, and respected the most. Many of them asked why I was revealing my sin and apologizing to them. I did not tell them it was because I was told I had to. I told them it was because it was the right thing to do, and it was. I promised that nothing would come between us and our future, and I meant it.

Rebuilding Our City

In many ways, we can compare our lives to that of ancient Jerusalem. It was the shining example of God's provision and peace, a thriving city full of hustle and bustle, full of life. Then something happened. The people became tired of God, bored by His standards for life. They became disenchanted and sought other pleasures, denying in their hearts that God was real and true. They began to worship other gods, to enjoy forbidden fruit, and soon enough their beautiful city was in ruins, and they were captives under oppression in a foreign land. I don't know about you, but that is certainly an apt description of my own experience. Did I know it and understand it at the time? No, and I suspect the Israelites of old did not, either. Then I was in captivity, desperate for a return to God and His love, and powerless against the enemies that surrounded and subjugated me.

I needed a Nehemiah, someone who would take up the cause of my freedom. When Ruthie forgave me, we both knew that our work had just begun and that we had to start somewhere. Sometimes, the best place to start something new is from the rubble of the old. It sounds counterintuitive, but there is good, solid, re-usable material even amid the rubble. If the offended has forgiven you and given you another chance, it says two things: They believe you are capable of changing, and they believe there is enough good in the circumstance to make it worth the effort. I was forgiven, but our lives and marriage lay in ruins everywhere we looked. As each of us looked into ourselves independently and at our marriage as a couple, we had to survey the wreckage and determine what could stay and what had to go. We had to clear away the rubble and begin to build with the good pieces that were left in the wake of the damage. It took determination, willingness, commitment, effort, and most of all, grace.

The first four chapters of Nehemiah tell the story of the rebuilding of Jerusalem. The nation of Israel was enslaved in Babylon, but God puts it in Nehemiah's heart to ask for favor from the king, not just for permission to rebuild Jerusalem, but for protection and resources, as well. Nehemiah, who was the king's wine steward at the time, turned out to be a pretty good leader and builder. We can learn a lot from him.

The walls of Jerusalem were in shambles. The city and the few poor souls who lived there were vanquished by the oppressors that surrounded them. They were unprotected, defenseless, and vulnerable. Sound familiar? Does this sound like your life and situation? I know it did mine.

And what does Nehemiah do, whom does he appeal to? Before he appeals to King Artaxerxes, he appeals to God the King. He reminds God of His love for Israel, he prays confession and repentance, he reminds God of His promise to restore the people when they turned back to Him, and he gains God's favor. As a result, King Artaxerxes, now unwittingly acting as God's agent, agrees with Nehemiah's requests, and sends him to investigate the conditions of Jerusalem.

After arriving, Nehemiah conducts an inspection in secret, traveling around and through the city at night when no one was aware, when no one could hinder his investigation. What he learns is not encouraging— it is even worse than he expects. Not only is the city broken, but its inhabitants are demoralized and weak.

I know how I felt in the early days after my confession. I was most definitely demoralized, weak, and wondering what would become of my life and my family. I've never known another time like that, and I imagine it was not much different from how the occupants of Jerusalem felt. Yet, Nehemiah tells them that God sent him to them, and it is time to rise up and rebuild. Naturally, the enemies that surrounded them are not ambivalent. They accuse Nehemiah of rebelling against the king. His reply?

"The God of heaven will make us prosper, and we his servants will arise and build, but you have no portion or right or claim in Jerusalem." Nehemiah 2:20 (ESV)

What Nehemiah told the enemies of Israel is that a higher power was sponsoring his mission and assuring its success, and that Israel's enemies had no place in it and no right to it. This is exactly what we say to the demons who have occupied our lives when we begin the rebuilding process. There may be a lot of rubble lying around, but there is good material there, material to build with. Your job, then, is to sort out what is good and can be used for the rebuilding effort and get to it with commitment and faithfulness.

As you read the rest of the story, you will discover the secrets of Nehemiah's leadership and the Israelites success. Nehemiah understood the power of his positioning and was not shy about exercising it. He and the people were impassioned in their desire and effort. They prepared, persevered against difficulties and long odds, and their resolve and commitment did not waver. When their enemies came against them, they invoked God's wrath, calling on Him to turn their curses and plans back upon their own heads. They set guards and deployed forces, and the leaders stood behind the laborers in unity and support. Half of the people worked to rebuild while the other half stood ready to fight.

This story will sound very familiar to overcomers who have been there themselves. To those of you who have not yet experienced this part of the journey, I say you should be looking forward to it. Yes, it is hard and sometimes exhausting work. Yes, your demons and enemies will attack you. But I tell you this also: No matter how broken your city is, no matter how burned and devastated, no matter how demoralized you may be, our God is bigger, mightier, everlasting, and powerful, and He is on your side. Trust in Him, believe in Him, and get ready to do the hard work of rebuilding your relationship and your life. Build a beautiful new city and live in peace.

We Are Still a Work in Progress

Ruthie and I love each other dearly. When we tell people that we've been married for over fifty years we routinely hear amazement, how unusual it is in this day, and compliments. Oh, if they only knew. But the truth is that love is what sustained us through the decades of hard times. And now we are in a much different place. God is faithful, and yet we are still growing, still overcoming. This is not to say that we are in a bad place; it is just that, like all couples, we are different people. In our case, the differences can be stark and thus require continual attention. I suspect that will always be the case for us, as it is for many.

For starters, our personalities, our "wiring diagrams," are direct opposites. Ruthie is open and gregarious; her heart is available to almost everyone. God gave her a big love and she exercises it daily. Every morning, she asks God to give her divine appointments so she can minister to people. He rarely disappoints. She is warm and compassionate, and her emotions are never far from the surface. I used to joke that she would cry at Smurf cartoons, because she did. I didn't understand, and now I do. She is an emotional creature; it is one of the gifts God put into her to enable her to touch people's lives. And she does, often. There are times when she gets her heart broken by those she opens herself to. I see the depth of her pain and it hurts, but it never stops her. Her life is completely organic and freeform, for one never knows where the next moment will take her or those around her. Me, on the other hand ... not so much. I am quiet, reserved, and analytical. I appreciate the value of routines that help me stay focused and productive. When I meet someone new, it takes a while for the relationship to develop. My friendships are relatively few but run deep, and my loyalty to them is important to me. But people do not typically bring their personal problems to me or tell me their entire life history within five minutes of meeting me as they do with Ruthie. She is a walking example of God's heart. I am practical and pragmatic, a strategic thinker, and completely comfortable inside my own head. God has a lot of work to do with me still, but I am learning and changing.

One of the areas we still struggle with is communication. You would think that after five decades we would have figured it out. We're still working on it. Again, we are wired differently, so we think and speak differently. Ruthie speaks in a stream-of-consciousness manner while I am more structured and succinct. Sometimes, she doesn't connect the dots when I speak in my abbreviated style, and sometimes I get lost listening to her. Naturally, it can be frustrating for both of us. We have learned to remember that these occasional frustrations do not mean that we don't love each other. It simply means that God gave us different personalities. In His wisdom He put us together, so we know He has a plan for us beyond her love being central to my deliverance. There is no doubt in my mind that that was the biggest reason He put us together. She is my Nehemiah. But He also had another reason: to mold these two completely different people into one to form a complete person so we can fulfill His plan for our lives.

There is another, more recent issue we deal with on occasion. I am recently retired and now we are in the same house 24/7, nearly 365 days a year. We are seldom more than a few feet from each other, especially in this time of the COVID-19 pandemic. We are learning to give each other space when needed, and God is faithful in this, as well. It may seem like a small thing, but it is a big adjustment.

So yes, we are in a different place in our relationship with each other and our relationship with the Lord. It is awesome ... and there is still work to do. All that really means is that we are still overcoming, still learning, still trusting, still believing, and still becoming. And we love what we are becoming.

Two of the most important changes for the overcomer are how they see themselves and where they live, not in the physical realm but the spiritual. Our identity and where we choose to live spiritually are everything to our future, and these are where we turn our attention next.

CHAPTER SEVENTEEN

OUR IDENTITY AND HOME IN CHRIST

I began this book with a description of my early life and journey into the depths of sin even while presenting the image of a normal life to the world. Recall that I said I spent my life "hiding in plain sight." What a joy it is, then, to share that I am now hiding in a different place, inside the person and position of my Lord. This does not mean that I am perfect or that life is perfect, but it does mean that I have a different perspective. I see my God and the world in a different light. My relationships with each are different, and my identity is different. While not perfect, I am changed. This is what it is to live in Christ: a new identity, a new purpose, and a new security. As I close this book, these will be my last encouragements. My life is changed, and I am a different person because of God's mercy and grace. I pray, trust, and believe you will be, as well. However, before we look at this miracle of miracles, living in Christ, let's take a moment to remember where we've come from.

HOW WE GOT HERE

Our miracle began in the darkness of our desperation. I do not know your story, but I know my own all too well. It is not dissimilar from that of the ancient Israelites as told in Second Chronicles, chapter thirty-three. I encourage you to open your Bible now and read along as I relate my own journey through their experience (the scriptures below are taken from The Voice translation). Use this reading as a guide to walk your own journey through sin and into forgiveness and redemption. I will caution you now that some of the language you are about to read is blunt and unvarnished. Sometimes it is best that way, to portray the stark truth of our life in ways we can grasp and use as a lever to change our course. It may be helpful for you to do the same. Do not sugarcoat your story. Be honest, blunt, and transparent with yourself. It will help you see where you've really come from. Here is my journal entry one morning six years after my deliverance:

> I am especially struck by the resemblance of my own story to Manasseh's.
>
> Manasseh corrupted Judah and the people of Jerusalem until they were more evil than the nations whom the Eternal had destroyed before the Israelites. Their minds were so full of sin that they didn't hear the Eternal asking them to return to His ways.
> (vv. 9,10)
>
> I too was addicted to my sin, desiring, and lusting after it literally 24/7 for years. When I was asleep, I was dreaming it. When I was awake, I was daydreaming or planning it. I was driven by the lusts and even their depravity. And this is exactly what this is: Addiction. Like the Israelites, I had lost control and lost touch. Nothing else mattered, I had to have the next fix. Knowing this and knowing how ungodly I had become, I surrendered to it. It wasn't hard, because I believed God must have given up on me. How could He possibly redeem one such as I? Not believing that His love

could be more powerful than my sin, I surrendered to what got me there.

To get Manasseh's attention, the Eternal used the Assyrian army to express His anger. The commanders captured Manasseh, forced a ring through his nose, bound his limbs with bronze chains, and carried him to Babylon as if he were an animal. (v. 11)

Like Manasseh, my sin led me into bondage with a ring through my nose, bound in chains, the spirits of my oppressors gloating over my misery. I served their every desire, each time sacrificing at their altar, each time reinforcing their hold, each time denying that God could reclaim me or even want to.

From this position of complete powerlessness, Manasseh finally humbled himself and begged the forgiveness of the Eternal God of his fathers. He heard Manasseh's prayer and found it sincere; He returned Manasseh to the throne in Jerusalem. From that day forward, Manasseh never doubted that the Eternal God was the True God. (vv. 12,13)

This is the power of a broken and contrite heart: To change God's heart, motivating Him to intervene and rescue one such as Manasseh and myself. The condition of our heart is everything to Him and by extension to us. When He moves we are made breathless by His mercy. Save me? Maybe. Restore me to my throne? How is that possible? Only by the Eternal's love and compassion. I know this firsthand. I am learning about my throne, small as it may be today. There is more to come, and I depend upon His glory magnified in that day.

Having returned to his father's work... (v. 14)

The description of Manasseh's post-redemption work is breathtaking. Following his father Hezekiah's model, he built the city walls, stationed commanders at each city to protect them, started purging the nation of sin, removed false idols from the temple, restored the Eternal's altar and made sacrifices of praise and peace. There is a lesson here for us. When God restores us, it is for a purpose - to magnify His glory with honor.

His prayer, the True God's compassion, and a record of his sins, unfaithfulness, and the locations of the high places and cultic statues, before he humbled himself, are written in the chronicles of Hozai. (v. 20)

We are redeemed, rescued, restored, and even re-purposed ... but ... the record of our sins is recorded for all time. God may choose not to remember, but the record is written in Heaven. How necessary then that we devote our lives to overwhelming the evidence of our darkness with new evidence of the Light, not out of fear or striving, but from a heart of abandonment to God's cause and His glory. In doing this we must be who God intends us to be, not some super-saved sinner. Be who God has created and called you to be. Live within His desire for you. Let it be your new natural without being driven or striving in your own power. God operates from His seat of rest. Sit there with Him, commune with Him, and do day by day what He calls you to. Day by day, in rest, in Him.

As you can tell, even six years after deliverance, my emotions and remembrance of my past were intense. I pray they will always remain that way. I trust these words as signposts marking where I used to be, and I never want to forget them. I do not ever want to return, but I want to remember the signposts as God's warning signs of danger and of His redirecting my path. I pray He will do the same for you. Re-purpose us He has, and it is time to turn our attention to our future.

A NEW PURPOSE AND PURSUIT

If you are then raised up with Christ, reach out for the highest gifts of Heaven, where Christ reigns in power. Be concerned with the heavenly things, not with the passing things of earth. For, as far as this world is concerned, you are already dead, and your true life is a hidden one in God, through Christ.
Colossians 3:1-3 (JBP)

We've all seen movies and heard stories of people who, for whatever reason, are put into witness protection. It may be a criminal who testifies against others, a witness, or a victim. Regardless of their position, they are given new lives in safe environments in exchange for their testimony. As overcomers, we experience a spiritual version of this which will have practical application and effect in our daily life. Our circumstance is changed. Where we once lived disobediently, we now seek to know God's will and way, and to be faithful in practicing them. We are no longer enemies of Christ but are now His agents. We have a new purpose, to live lives that magnify His name and glory, and a new pursuit, intimacy with the One who created us, loves us, and redeems us. In doing this, we "reach out for the highest gifts of Heaven."

Some who go into witness protection programs decide giving up their old identity is not acceptable in the long run. They surrender their security to return to their old location or lifestyle. They return to old habits, old relationships, and old vulnerabilities. Often, the result is predictable and sad. How does the overcomer avoid old temptations when they come calling? We maintain our standing through faith in His power to overcome our temptations and through obedience. Notice our faith is in His power, not our own. We've already proven where our power and strength will lead us, and we do not want to return. By believing in His power, however, we overcome our temptations through faith, trusting God to face them in our place. I find that one of the benefits of this approach is that the responsibility is on His shoulders, not mine. I do not have to fight those battles and neither do you. By allowing God to face them, we need only face God and do as He desires. Our focus is on knowing His desires of us and obeying them, not because we are running from something, but because we are running into Him. That is our new purpose and pursuit, to live lives that honor Him by living in and through Him, being hidden in Christ who is hidden in God. It is like having a multi-layered protection system surrounding us. Who doesn't want that?

A New Identity

For some overcomers, like myself, letting go of the past can be hard. We not only accuse ourselves by our guilt and shame, but there is another voice accusing us, as well:

> *TRANSGRESSION [like an oracle] speaks to the wicked deep in his heart. There is no fear or dread of God before his eyes.*
> Psalm 36:1 (AMP)

Yes, the unholy spirit of Transgression has a voice, and it speaks to us. It will accuse us, tempt us, taunt us, and ridicule us. Sometimes, we remember what we used to be and take our sin nature on as part of our identity, even when we know we have been cleansed and forgiven. It can be tempting. Being familiar with our past and old identity it can seem comfortable, especially in stressful times. It can even seem honest; after all, we are calling it like it is, right? Wrong!

How does the overcomer overcome this assault? By remembering what we used to be, what life under the rule of evil was like, how God in His mercy redeemed us, and whom He has called the new us to be. We may remember what we were, but we dream and live for who we are now.

We remember and put our faith in God's promise, that with our new life comes a new identity. We are sons of the Most High God.

> *Celebrate with praises the God and Father of our Lord Jesus Christ, who has shown us his extravagant mercy. For his fountain of mercy has given us a new life--we are reborn to experience a living, energetic hope through the resurrection of Jesus Christ from the dead. We are reborn into a perfect inheritance that can never perish, never be defiled, and never diminish. It is promised and preserved forever in the heavenly realm for you!*
> 1 Peter 1:3,4 (TPT)

The inheritance that is promised to the believer is perfect and cannot perish, be defiled, or diminish. It is "promised and preserved forever" for the overcomer who believes in the risen Christ as his or her Savior. It is not the inheritance of a king's son, rather, of the King's sons. If you have Christ in your heart as your Savior, then this passage is speaking about you—not someone who is perfect in every way, but you!

If all of Heaven sees you as a son of God who is assured the King's inheritance, why don't you see yourself that way? Yes, it can be hard to let go of our past, but we must know that holding on to it disrupts God's plan for our future. He rescued us for a purpose, and we must let go of the old and adopt the new as our identity. We are called to a godly life and given everything we need to live it, and that is our new identity. We are favored sons who have returned and been showered with precious gifts.

> *How precious is Your steadfast love, O God! The children of men take refuge and put their trust under the shadow of Your wings. They relish and feast on the abundance of Your house; and You cause them to drink of the stream of Your pleasures. For with You is the fountain of life; in Your light do we see light.*
> Psalm 36:7-9 (AMP)

It is time to realize who we are, and to live the new life we are called to. It is time to rejoice!

Building Our New Life

We read earlier how Manasseh followed Hezekiah's example in restoring Israel after it had fallen away from God. Now, let us turn to 2 Chronicles 29 for the story of Hezekiah's reign, which was Manasseh's pattern. It offers the overcomer a model for the rebuilding and restoration of our lives.

> *he opened the doors of the house of the LORD and repaired them.* (v. 3, emphasis added in bold)

For many of us, the first act will be re-opening the doors between us and our Lord. They were closed because of our sin, standing as symbols of our broken relationship with God and our Savior. Relationships require communication, something that is hard to maintain when the doors are closed. The doorway of our relationship with God must be re-opened and repaired; it must be made useful again. What this will require will be unique to each of us, but I suspect each will know what it means for them. I know I did. I had been looking at that closed door for years, and I knew who closed it: I did. My sin separated me from my God. When it came time to open the door and re-establish communication, it had to be opened from my side. How did I do that? I began calling out to Him, appealing for a hearing before His throne. Granted the hearing, I surrendered. You have already heard that part of the story, but I remind you that my surrender was total and complete. I held nothing back, from Ruthie or from God. My broken heart spilled its contents, and the sincerity of my heart won His mercy. That is where it all started. That is where it must start, with a broken and contrite heart that surrenders, holding nothing back. A word of advice here to those who are skeptical at this point: You may as well surrender it all because God already knows. You will not be telling Him anything new, but you must tell Him.

*Now **it is in my heart to make a covenant with the LORD**,
the God of Israel, in order that his fierce anger may turn away
from us.* (v. 10, emphasis added in bold)

What is the first order of business after the connection between the overcomer and God is put in order? It is to make a commitment, a covenant with Him that we will be obedient to His will and follow His Word. We often think of a commitment as a promise. A promise, however, can too easily be ignored or rationalized away. The word covenant[56] carries a different weight. It speaks to a "compact" that is made by passing between pieces of flesh or being in league with someone else. In other words, a covenant is not a one-sided thing. You are in it together with the one you covenant with, intricately interwoven with them, and they have a voice in how the relationship is honored. In Hezekiah's case, his covenant was with the Lord, and it was motivated by the desire in his heart for the relationship between the Israelites and the Lord to be restored. The doors to the relationship had been opened and repaired, now he was pledging that his participation in the relationship would be honest, righteous, and enduring. The notion that we can make a half-hearted covenant with the Lord is a false notion. The covenant must be real, and it can only be real if it is a true desire of your heart. This is the bedrock that your new relationship with God rests upon.

*"All the utensils that King Ahaz discarded in his reign when
he was faithless, we have made ready and consecrated, and
behold, they are before the altar of the LORD."* (v. 19, emphasis
added in bold)

At Hezekiah's command, the priests restored service utensils in the Lord's house to their former beauty and function. What did that mean in their experience? It meant that they had to first find what had been

---

56 Strong's H1285, from H1262 (in the sense of cutting (like H1254)); a compact (because made by passing between pieces of flesh): - confederacy, [con-]feder[-ate], covenant, league.

hidden, then work to polish away the layers of filth and grime. Finally, they had to consecrate them to the Lord, making them acceptable to Him. If you know anything of Jewish temple protocol, you know that this was not simply an act of cleaning. It was also symbolic and real in the spiritual realm. These simple physical acts had spiritual meaning and weight.

Who is the priest of your life? Who will do the work of uncovering, cleaning, burnishing, and restoring your life? That, I believe, will be a partnership between you and God. As you face the true condition of your life and begin to restore it through your commitments, decisions, faith, and obedience, God will partner with you. He will be as faithful to provide everything you need in this work as you are in doing it.

> *Then Hezekiah the king rose early and gathered the officials of the city and went up to the house of the LORD. And they brought seven bulls, seven rams, seven lambs, and seven male goats for a* **sin offering for the kingdom** *and* **for the sanctuary** *and for* **Judah**. *And he commanded the priests, the sons of Aaron, to offer them on the altar of the LORD.* (vv. 20,21, emphasis added in bold)

We know Hezekiah completed the process by ordering the preparation and presentation of the sin offering. The commandment[57] for this was well established; it was not something they made up. Every step in the process had a purpose: to symbolize the acts of confession and repentance, and to engage their participation in the process. It was not a mere formality or ceremony. It had meaning because their humbled hearts surrendered to God. In their case, they brought the specified animals to the priests as atonement. What do we bring to God today in our time, and how does a sin offering make a difference? Why is it necessary?

---

57 Leviticus 4 and other passages speak to unintentional sins. The following references, however, command sin offerings for specific sins. See Leviticus 5:1; 6:1-7; 19:20; Ezra 10:18,19; Numbers 5:5-31.

Part of the answer to these questions is in defining who our offerings are for. We know Scripture says they are for the kingdom, the sanctuary, and for Judah. I suggest they are as important for us today as they were for the Israelites, but what and who are these to us? The kingdom is the kingdom for us as it was for them. In this sense, our offering is part of restoring our relationship with God and signifies our new life covenant with Him. The sanctuary represents us. Our offering not only signifies restoration of our relationship with the holy, but also a new relationship with ourselves. We have a new identity, a new future, and no longer define ourselves by what we used to be. Finally, we make the offering for the full restoration of our tribe, our family. They have been wounded by our sin, and our relationships with them have been damaged, if not lost. We may never see restoration in some of them, but our offering opens the door. They will decide if they choose to walk thought it or not, but they only have that option if we do our part first. Christ is the offering to God for our sin. We are free because He was that perfect sacrifice. Our offering, then, is to the One who set us free. What can we possibly offer in exchange for such mercy? I think you know the answer by now: our heart, broken, contrite, humbled, transparent, and sincere. This is our offering. Despite our sin, what God really cares about is the condition of our heart. He can work with a heart that has laid itself down before Him, and so can those closest to us. It is the offering of our heart that matters.

Putting On Our New Life

> ... to put off your old self, which belongs to your former manner of
> life and is corrupt through deceitful desires, and to be renewed in
> the spirit of your minds, and to put on the new self, created after
> the likeness of God in true righteousness and holiness.
> Ephesians 4:22 24 (ESV)

It is time to put on our new self, our new identity, and new life. It is time to be renewed in the likeness of God. Some may question what that means; others may question how it is possible. The answers are relatively simple in nature but require strength and commitment to achieve. Being renewed in the likeness of God means that we take on His nature by living the life He desires for us. That means believing His will for us is better and His provision for our life greater than what the world promises, and that He loves us so much He is willing to do all this for us. In response, we live our life in His love and provision. It means laying the burdens of life before Him to walk in peace, trusting Him to meet every need. It means taking His Word into our heart as the foundation and guiding light of our life, judging every feeling, thought, word, and action against it, using God's truth and Word as our measuring rod for everything in life. It means rejoicing in His love and mercy, and it means taking practical steps to cement our new life into place.

An example of practical steps from my own life: After my confession and repentance, I had to face my old self and examine it closely. I did not like a lot of what I saw. I knew that my sexual addiction was not my only addiction, and I knew that each of these was influenced in some measure by my compulsive personality. I examined my life and the things in it and saw potential gateways back into darkness. They didn't look that way on the surface, but I knew where a simple game playing addiction led me, one slippery step at a time. So I looked, judged, and closed the gateways. I abandoned social media, except for one outlet which had no connection to my addictions. I stopped blogging because I had become trapped by how many views it got each week, the pressure to produce content, and the blog's importance to my identity. Even years later, I realized another gate was still open. A lifelong fan of music in general and jazz in particular, I one day realized that music and its frequencies were impacting me. I would hear a favorite song and remember a time and place and then have to deal with that moment. I made another decision, this time deleting everything but Christian and classical music from my collection, which was substantial. I do not know what your addictions are, but I do know this: Part of putting on your new life is putting down the things in your old life that are unworthy of or dangerous to the new you. It is time to "put on the new self, created after the likeness of God in true righteousness and holiness." Part of that is separating ourselves from the things that entice us back into old thought patterns, habits, and desires. Holiness is in making right decisions and taking right actions, and righteousness is the life that results. God empowers the first and rewards us with the latter as we honor Him. This is the new life, one that honors God's heart and Word, rejoices in His love, mercy, and peace, and lives to serve and glorify Him. This is where our joy comes from, the bliss of a life lived within God's heart, allowing His joy to flood over us.

Our New Life - Oneness IN Christ

When we put off our old self, we must put on something new. After a lifetime of living the life of a carnal Christian, I came face to face with the prospect of putting on my new life. It is both a conscious thing and a life-style thing. I say a "conscious thing" because, especially at the beginning of my new walk, I was innately conscious of everything around me, each choice that faced me, each decision and action. Over time, it becomes a lifestyle without becoming routine or mundane. Do I make mistakes? Of course I do, but I am ever more conscious of them and quick to deal with them. The overcomer will choose to walk this path with desire, intent, and commitment. It is part of becoming one with the One who redeems us.

I think of John 17 as the "Oneness Chapter."[58] If you have not read this recently, or ever, then I ask you to do so now. In it, you will find Jesus' heart and provision for your new relationship with Him, which is the same as His with His Father. Think about that for a moment! Not only does He desire that relationship with you, but He also prayed to His Father and specifically asked that God honor His request for our oneness with the two of them. As you read this passage, read it as if Jesus is praying specifically for you, because He is. Read this aloud, listening to your voice and the love Jesus is expressing for your life, and respond to Him with your own heart.

---

58   See also John 14:10, 20

*"And I ask not only for these disciples, but also for **all those who will one day believe in me** through their message. I pray for them all to be **joined together as one even as you and I, Father, are joined together as one**. I pray for them **to become one with us** so that the world will recognize that you sent me. For the very glory you have given to me I have given them so that they will be **joined together as one** and experience the same unity that we enjoy. **You live fully in me and now I live fully in them so that they will experience perfect unity**, and the world will be convinced that you have sent me, for they will see that **you love each one of them with the same passionate love that you have for me**. ... "* John 17:20-23 (ESV, emphasis added in bold)

In the moments before He was betrayed, Jesus prayed this prayer for you. With Judas and the high priest's guards en route to take Him, He made this remarkable appeal to God, opening the doorway to your oneness with them. When I read this prayer with that thought in my heart, I was humbled to my very core. Jesus knew what I was, yet He prayed for my restoration and completeness in Him, just as He is doing now for you.

God and Jesus exist in oneness because it is an intrinsic part of their nature. They cannot help but be one because of their unique relationship. With His prayer, Jesus invites us into that relationship, to live our lives in complete harmony with them. It is not something we do; it is who we become. As we turn our life over to the One who paid the price for our sin, He opens His arms to take us in. He lives in the Father, and through our faith He lives in us. As He lives in us, we live in Him. As He lives in the Father, we live in the Father through Him. Oneness.

This is our destination as overcomers. We step out of the world and into Christ, and through Him into God. We are surrounded by, one with, the Holy.

What an amazing place to be. What an amazing freedom. What an amazing victory over everything in your life. What does it take to enjoy this peace? Only one thing: faith in Jesus Christ, who was obedient to the cross for your sake. If you are a believer who has wandered away from God, if you have denied Him out of anger, fear, or unbelief, or if you are encountering Him for the first time, now is the moment. Join me in this prayer and make it your own.

Prayer

> Father God, thank You for loving me so much that You made a way for me, even me, to come to You. Jesus, thank you for Your obedience, Your heart for me, and Your desire to set me free. I surrender to You. I lay everything down at your feet. Everything. My sins, my pains, my fears, my guilt, my shame, and my unworthiness. I give it all to You, Lord. I surrender. Fill me with Your presence. Fill me with Your love. Fill me with Your peace, Lord. Show me the way into Your heart. Amen.

My prayer for you is that no matter what it is that separates you from God, your family, and your future, you will find the desire and courage to take the step that changes everything. Put your life in the hands of the One who gave Himself for you and let Him work His miracle of healing and restoration. Find His peace in your heart, become one with Him, and let Christ live His life through yours.[59]

---

59   2 Peter 1:3-11

Mercy's Kiss

Mercy kissed me, even though I used to be a blasphemer, a persecutor of believers, and a scorner of what turned out to be true. I was ignorant and didn't know what I was doing. I was flooded with such incredible grace, like a river overflowing its banks, until I was full of faith and love for Jesus, the Anointed One! I can testify that the Word is true and deserves to be received by all, for Jesus Christ came into the world to bring sinners back to life--even me, the worst sinner of all! Yet I was captured by grace, so that Jesus Christ could display through me the outpouring of his Spirit as a pattern to be seen for all those who would believe in him for eternal life. 1 Timothy 1:13-16 (TPT)

How great is God's mercy, you ask?

Even me, even you!

POEMS

In the period closely following my deliverance, I wrote several poems. This was unusual, as I've never been that interested in poetry and had never tried to write poetry. Yet these came to me, typically during moments of introspection and communion with God as I considered what God was doing in my life, how great His mercy is, its effects upon my life, and how Ruthie's love and strength held the gateway open for me. I am forever grateful to God and Ruthie, the two forces in my life.

I cannot claim that what follows is good poetry. I am one who can truthfully say that I wouldn't know good poetry if it walked up to me and said hello. I can claim that these come from the heart. They still have the power to move me to tears and to great joy. They are borne out of my pain, sorrow, and great bliss, and I hope they honor the One who has done so much for my life. I love Him now in ways I've never known.

Let the Reign Reign

I tried my way and see what I wrought
Broken and lost, seeking what was naught
Knowing inside that I was my own aught
Remembering then what Hope had always sought

Choices made and choices ahead
Hoping and praying—yes, even me
But who would listen to this claim I made?
Who would believe such of one like me?

Rain falling from my eyes with no way to see
Weeping for a future that could not possibly be
Hoping there would be Hope for even me
I was Agony and Torment for all to see

But deep inside there was a beat
A cadence that sounded no retreat
A glimmering hope that it could be for even me
This story I know about the King and a Tree

Let the Reign fall like Heaven's rain
Let the Reign reign in me
Let the Reign fall like Heaven's rain
Let the Reign reign in me

Water my heart with this Heavenly rain
Let it rise and swell inside of me
Soaking my spirit with Love's refrain
Growing a son who was meant to be

I find Him in the chambers of my heart
Ruling from His sapphire throne
There lives the Holy One who said to me
Yes, my son, you are My own

Made new by Love's great Grace
I bow before and lower my face
Not in shame or pitiful disgrace
I bow in thanks for entry to this place

A place where one such as even I
Can know the glory of His perfect essence
Not in a far off abstract place or time
But here and now before His presence

Let the Reign fall like Heaven's rain
Let the Reign reign in me
Let the Reign fall like Heaven's rain
Let the Reign reign in me

Now a son I must learn to reign
My life to be lived on a different plane
This the call of each new breath
To be Heaven's reign destroying death

I know what I was and I know who I am
Life's journey a grueling trail of desert sand
Yet there was Hope for even me
Now your Hope is waiting, don't you see?

Life and Death are yours to choose
Each choice a chance to start anew
Which door to take, which path to walk?
The way crooked or the way made taught

Choose well, my worthy friend
Trust your heart and let it mend
Step through the door where Peace is found
Where Love, Mercy and Grace abound

Let the Reign fall like Heaven's rain
Let the Reign reign in me
Let the Reign fall like Heaven's rain
Let the Reign reign in me

Glory Is His Name

Glory is His name
Kingdoms here bow in desperate shame
Theirs a glory without flame
As the trumpet sounds His mighty name

Kingdoms come and kingdoms go
Save the only one I know
All others are charred like humbled stone
While Glory's alabaster shines as snow

Ox, Lion, Eagle and Man on their way go
As man scurries to and fro
Searching, looking, trying to know
Yet unwilling through the door to go

There is a time to which all are called
A time to stand, a time to fall
Now I hear the bugle's call
And stand ready to give my all

Glory is His name
Kingdoms here bow in desperate shame
Theirs a glory without flame
As the trumpet sounds His mighty name

Journey

Before You I fall on my face
Wanting only to know Your holy grace
My life an empty vessel, Father
Fill me with Your Living Water

I seek Your presence
To be awed and amazed
To know Your beauty
To soak in Your peace

Not to say that I have seen and know
But to know that I am seen and chosen
To marvel that I am redeemed
To wonder at Your love supreme

Let me bask in Your chamber for just a while
Let me feel the peace of Your gentle smile
Let me see Your heart's love and kindness
Let me know the safety of the righteous

Prepare me, Father, as a father does
With Correction, Truth, Wisdom, and Love
A hand on my arm to guide and still
Your thoughts, my thoughts; my way, Your will

Then send me, Yah
To places I have not seen
To love people I have not known
To be for them those You sent to me

To Live the Life

I never catch up; I am exhausted each day
But I have faith it will not always be this way
For the time is coming when I shall be free of this pace
A day when I shall bow and glory in His grace

That does not mean I plan to leave, for leaving is not a need
Ah, but to lose myself in Him, that is the deed
For that I long with all my heart
To live the life He desired of me at the start

Walking with the Spirits day by day
Fear and Counsel now on point
Might and Wisdom speaking low at my side
Whilst the Spirit of the Lord hovers over
Knowledge and Understanding search wide

As I walk this path to the narrow gate
Living for the One who sees from inside
I am humbled at His presence and honored to host
My Lord, My God, the King of Kings
The One I love the most

For who am I that He should choose me?
Who am I to claim the glory of His Tree?
And who am I to climb on His knee,
To know this unmerited glee?

I am me and I am you, and I stand free

The Beginning and the End

Something new this way comes
Shadows of Light moving now
Subtle signs and quite whispers
And simple Peace begins to stir

The wind gathers and gale forms
Who knows what this storm
For the Son shines and darkness hides
As sons in white begin their ride

The battle is joined and Faith presses in
Courage and strength the order of the day
Press hard, oh sons of the Most High
For to ourselves we must die

Listen to the trumpet sound
Fall not but rally round
The Eagle soars with talons bared
The Lion roars with fangs flared

Down the flaming chariots of Heaven come
With wrath and fire to charge the field
Evil screams with heart pierced
Dark's forces fall without hope

Sacrifices mount and Glory is served
The gathering beat of Victory heard
For on the wind now peals of Joy
As Heaven smiles and all is won

Ruthie, My Love

She is beautiful
Strong and so tender
Like a petal graced by the sun

Drops of water
Sparkle her lips
Diamonds each to be kissed

She is pink as the morning rose
Deep purple from her royal robe flows
Her heart red with passion knows

While I in my daze
Wonder where came this
She saunters by

And all is bliss

When I Think of You

When I think of you, I fall in love
Each glimpse each image a lingering touch
Your heart on mine a flame
A fire that cannot be tamed

The darkness is gone
Love lives and breathes
A new world full of new truths
Rediscovered refined and made pure

What once was now is
The lost found and claimed
A heart that beats and feels
Food for the soul, love's refrain

Peace settles and soothes
While strife and anguish weep
Hope and hearts soar
As Heaven's tears fall like rain

In the Early Morn

In the early morn when the dew is damp
I find respite in the Word under the lamp
Soft light falling as silent rain
Piercing the darkness of night and pain

It is here I come to hone my faithful Sword
It is here I come to meet my precious Lord
For it is He who gives me strength for the day
It is He who shows me the narrow way

These quiet moments are perfect and still
Like waters soothed before the mill
There they will churn and roil
A sign of the day ahead and its endless toil

But in this moment, in this time
I find my rest in Truth sublime
For the Word is honest and sure
Its peace and power perfectly pure

How Great This Love

How great this Love
That could look down on me
Through the darkness of my sin
And remember what was meant to be

How great this Heart
That knowing could love me still
That caring could weep Mercy
Whose power would turn my will

How great these Eyes
Whose vision sees through all of time
Into the hearts of those deceived
Knows their pain and draws the line

How great this Touch
That reaches out to find
Who will reach in kind
To surrender heart and mind

How great this Voice
That speaks to me in the dark
Calling me to the Light
A new course to embark

How great this Grace
That comes with gentle touch
Guiding me into the Light
Where Darkness sees this Love is too much

How great this blood
That covers all
No sin so great
As to defeat its call

How great His Name
In which I have such Peace
Knowing the Destroyer
Lays broken at His feet

How great this Hope
Eternal in my breast
A new day dawned
Full of Truth and Rest

How great this Love
That can love even me
Darkness's demons are gone
The Lamb stands in victory

Because She Loves Him

She loves me, and this is truly known
With each tender sigh my heart groans
Yet her heartbeat is not mine to own
She loves another in ways I have never known

How she loves Him I can but admire
Her grace and strength through the fire
He loves her too, this much is clear
I see it in the trail of each joyful tear

I listen to her plea and hear her heart
Passion beating against cruel assault
Yet like a river's never-ending start
His love flows without fade or halt

The odds seem long and the chances small
When measured against the heady wall
Still the grace of her love stopped the fall
A vision of Love who conquered all

Now I sit in quiet to search and see
Wondering how this can possibly be
Such a strange thing that none can see
This beating inside that is new to me

Love comes in waves as a sea unknown
Breaking gentle with grace never shown
With eyes that see I marvel how it has grown
I love Him now in ways I have never known

What of a Day?

The sun rises, transits, and sets
Time a memory that lingers yet
Its passage marking the day
Its light showing the way

And what of this day, my love
What worth the hours we have lost
What gained in our quest
What revealed for the cost

It has come and gone
No more to be
And here are we
The eternal you and me

Our love has no bound
Our hearts rejoice in perfect sound
Our eyes meet, love and speak
Our lips caress and my soul weeps

For joy like this I have dreamed
And hoped and lost all hope
For joy like this I have prayed
And cried and surrendered all

Hope became real
Love conquered me
Faith proved true
Grace covered you

The sun rises, transits, and sets
Time a memory that lingers yet
Its passage marking the day
Its light showing the way

It has come and gone
No more to be
And here are we
The eternal you and me